3/99

BATTLING
for
MANASSAS

JOAN M. ZENZEN

BATTLING
for
MANASSAS

The
Fifty-Year
Preservation Struggle
at
Manassas National
Battlefield Park

The Pennsylvania State University Press
University Park, Pennsylvania

Publication of this book was aided by a grant from Furthermore,
the publication program of the J. M. Kaplan Fund

Library of Congress Cataloging-in-Publication Data

Zenzen, Joan M.
    Battling for Manassas : the fifty-year preservation struggle at
Manassas National Battlefield Park / Joan M. Zenzen ; foreword by
Edwin Bearss.
        p.   cm.
    Includes bibliographical references and index.
    ISBN 0-271-01721-X (alk. paper)
    1. Manassas National Battlefield Park (Va.)   2. Virginia—History—
Civil War, 1861–1865—Battlefields—Conservation and restoration.
3. United States—History—Civil War, 1861–1865—Battlefields—
Conservation and restoration.   4. Historic preservation—Virginia—
Prince William County.   I. Title.
    E472.183.Z46   1998
    363.6'9'097552732—dc21   96-53534
                                                                   CIP

*Battling for Manassas is based on an official report of the same name issued by the
National Park Service in 1995, which as a U.S. government work is in the public
domain. The book has been revised and expanded for publication so that it now
contains photographs, maps, and some additions and revisions to the text that were
not part of the original report.

It is the policy of The Pennsylvania State University Press to use acid-free paper for
the first printing of all clothbound books. Publications on uncoated stock satisfy
the minimum requirements of American National Standard for Information
Sciences—Permanence of Paper for Printed Library Materials, ANSI Z39.48-1992.

CONTENTS

MAPS AND ILLUSTRATIONS

FOREWORD

My first experience with Manassas National Battlefield Park was in late 1941, a short sixteen months after the park was established. I had recently turned eighteen, and with Adolf Hitler's armies deep into the Soviet Union, I was touring the country as a hitchhiker, certain that I would soon be in the military. I had gotten a ride from several young men in a Ford roadster just east of New Market in Virginia's Shenandoah Valley. The driver stopped briefly at the Stone House, which at that time was a roadside store, before proceeding to the nation's capital. A Civil War enthusiast since the seventh grade—when living with my family on a ranch in Montana, I had named one of our cattle Bull Run—I reflected on the historical events that had occurred eighty years earlier.

I visited the battlefield park again in the winter of 1949–50, while I was employed by the Naval Hydrographic Office at Suitland, Maryland, during an automobile tour of Civil War battle sites and parks in the Washington, D.C., area. But it was not until the 1950s, at the beginning of a forty year career with the National Park Service, that I came to know the Manassas park. During those two score years I experienced the park from three perspectives. The first was between 1955 and 1958 when I was a park historian at Vicksburg National Military Park and then between 1958 and 1966 when I was regional research historian assigned to the Southeast Regional Office in Richmond, Virginia. Although stationed at the Vicksburg Park, I had regionwide responsibilities insofar as Civil War–related research was concerned.

My first visit to Manassas as a public historian was in conjunction with a regional workshop for rangers and interpreters held in Richmond in October 1956, when I made a side trip to Manassas. At the workshop I met the Manassas park historian and several of his predecessors. During the informal evening sessions I gained valuable insights into the Manassas park, its place in the community, and its current superintendent, Francis Wilshin, and his predecessors, Joseph Mills Hanson and Jim Myers. Hanson commanded awe, Myers respect, but the jury was still out on Wilshin, who was a veteran historian but a newcomer to the superintendent ranks. In those happy days, the park was, like most National Park Service areas, an island in the community, and there were no concerns about burgeoning suburbia.

In November 1958, with the Civil War centennial approaching and the National Park Service in the midst of its Mission 66 program to update the parks' infrastructure, I was assigned to the Southeast Region as regional research historian in response to a request by Maj. Gen. Ulysses S. Grant III, chairman of the National Civil War Centennial Commission. Grant asked the NPS to give priority to completing the programmed Mission 66 development at the Civil War battlefield parks by the one-hundredth anniversary of the battle commemorated. Most of the Service's Civil War parks, including Manassas, were then in the Southeast Region. The centennial for the Manassas park would be 21 July 1961.

Superintendent Wilshin had focused his energies on a major reenactment of the first battle of Manassas, and planning for Mission 66 development either lagged or was postponed in favor of the reenactment. Key managers in the Southeast Regional Office and in Washington did not appreciate how the superintendent allocated the park's resources.

The reenactment took place, after many vexing problems were mastered, as scheduled. The day was hot, dusty, and humid, with large crowds and traffic jams. Insofar as senior management was concerned, the reenactment was of no permanent benefit to the park, the Park Service, or the nation. Because of these views and the damage done to the landscape, the Service made an important policy decision: there would be no more reenactments on national park lands.

The second phase of my experience with Manassas National Battlefield Park began in April 1966 when I came to Washington as a NPS staff historian in the History Division, specializing in the Civil War and nineteenth- and twentieth-century political history. In this position I experienced the park from a closer perspective. I came to know the park, its superintendents, its interpretive personnel, and certain of its problems and needs.

In the late 1950s and the 1960s, the park and its staff and friends became mired in controversy—both on the local level and in the Washington area—because of external threats to the park's preservation and its interpretive mission. The "third" and "fourth" battles of Manassas ensued. Third Manassas was fought over the location of Interstate 66. Initial plans by the Bureau of Public Roads and the Virginia Department of Highways called for locating the four-lane limited access highway through the core of the park on a route adjacent to and parallel to Route 29. Superintendent

Wilshin rallied important political allies and public opinion, and the highway, when constructed, passed to the south of the park, but in doing so it obliterated the pre–Civil War crossroads community of New Market, on the Ball's Ford Road, a mile south of the park's visitor center

The fourth battle was precipitated when military veterans concerned with the need to expand Arlington National Cemetery lobbied William L. Scott, then the U.S. congressman who represented the district in which the park was located. Representative Scott's proposal created an annex for Arlington National Cemetery on lands included in and adjacent to the Manassas battlefield park. After an acrimonious battle, in which Scott used his political muscle to have Wilshin reassigned, the cemetery proposal was tabled in favor of establishing a new national cemetery at Quantico, Virginia.

A more dangerous threat to the park surfaced in 1973 when the Marriott Corporation acquired a nearby 513-acre tract. Marriott planned to build a Great America theme park on this land, to open in time for the nation's bicentennial in 1976. The Marriott proposal was supported by the Prince William County Board of Supervisors, who sought to increase the country's tax base. Senior NPS management, however, took a neutral stance. This, which can be called the "fifth" battle of Manassas, led to legislation signed into law by President Jimmy Carter on 13 October 1980, expanding the park's boundaries. The new boundaries included the Brawner tract within the park, but not the Marriott property. The legislation represented a compromise: the NPS had to forego inclusion of the Marriott tract to secure the county's support for the expansion legislation.

On 1 November 1981 I became the Park Service's chief historian. This signaled the beginning of the most important phase of my involvement with the park. From then until my retirement in September 1995, and particularly during the nearly thirteen years that I was chief historian, Manassas National Battlefield Park was at center stage in the national debate between those determined to protect the park and the public lands that had been consecrated in blood and those who favored development, property rights, and unplanned suburban sprawl.

The sixth of the increasingly bitter struggles over who "owned" the battlefield park concerned the proposed construction of an expanded facility for stabling horses used for ranger patrols. This led to a bitter internecine fight that divided the park staff, then reached and convulsed the National Capital Region office and the Washington office of the National Park Service, and finally pitted senior Department of the Interior officials against National Park Service Director William Mott and his staff. Before the debate was played out, the press, the Congress, and the vice president's office became involved.

The "seventh" battle of Manassas involved a proposal by the Virginia Department of Transportation to add turning lanes at the Route 29–Route 234 intersection. Although this plan would address the severe traffic congestion, it would critically impact a key interpretive area. Director Mott refused to consent to the construction of the turning lanes, and the problem was addressed without significantly altering the landscape.

In late January 1988, the "eighth" battle of Manassas erupted with the announcement that Hazel/Peterson Companies, which had acquired the Marriott tract, had been granted a zoning variance by Prince William County to construct the William Center, a 1.2-million-square-foot regional shopping mall. For the next ten months, Manassas National Battlefield Park, the value of the nation's Civil War heritage, property rights, open space, and national versus local interests held center stage as the public, the media, the NPS, and Congress debated the issues. In the end, on 10 November 1988, President Ronald Reagan signed into law a bill instituting a legislative taking of the William Center tract by the United States, with the compensation to the owners to be determined by the courts. When the court set the price, it exceeded $130,000,000.

A "ninth" battle of Manassas was only five years in the future. In autumn 1993, Michael Eisner, chief executive officer of the Walt Disney Company, announced plans to construct and open a theme park—Disney's America—on land the corporation had optioned northwest of the I–66/Route 15 Haymarket interchange, three and one-half miles west of Manassas battlefield park. This aroused a firestorm among open space advocates, many historians and preservationists, and no-growthers, and it attracted national media coverage. County and state officials gave the project their enthusiastic endorsement. Battle lines were drawn, and in June 1994 Sen. Dale Bumpers convened a congressional hearing on Disney's America. The hearing lasted most of the day and was held before a standing-room-only audience. The decision of the senators was that this was a local issue. Disney and the NPS returned to discussions about how to mitigate the impact of increased traffic in the area of the park. But in late September 1994, concerned about the strength of the opposition and damage to its public image, Disney withdrew its proposal.

The late-twentieth-century battles over Manassas—particularly the William Center and Disney struggles, involving as they did critical land-use, preservation, and planning issues—played out before a nationwide audience and involved Congress. The publicity and resultant rancor caught the NPS, local governments and planners, Congress, and the public unprepared.

Could these battles have been avoided and what do they hold for the future? This is the story that Joan Zenzen documents in a perceptive and balanced account. In researching the story Dr. Zenzen has assiduously combed the paper trail, and, unlike others who have written on the William Center issue, she interviewed major players on both sides of the debate, including Senator Bumpers, John T. ("Til") Hazel, Kathleen Seefeldt, Jerry Russell, and Annie Synder.

While the struggle over who owns Manassas National Battlefield Park and who controls public policy relating to it in the years since 1980 will command most attention, Dr. Zenzen does not ignore the people, long gone, who dreamed the dream. Her description of the park's establishment, its development, the personalities involved, and earlier battles for its protection and interpretation are insightful and invaluable.

Joan Zenzen "tells it like it is" and lets the chips fall where they may. *Battling for Manassas* will command a wide audience. It is must reading for all public officials, developers, land-use planners, preservationists, and land rights activists who in the future will find themselves arrayed on opposite sides of emotional issues, particularly those significant to the fate of the nation's battlefields consecrated as they are in blood.

Edwin C. Bearss
Historian Emeritus, National Park Service

ACKNOWLEDGMENTS

This history of the preservation struggles at the Manassas National Battlefield Park has benefited from the assistance of numerous people. In the National Park Service, Park Historian Edmund Raus opened the door to the battlefield park's historical records, shared valuable information about recent events, and gave helpful suggestions on the manuscript. Ray Brown, the park's cultural resources manager, read drafts of the manuscript with a critical eye, while James Burgess, the park's museum curator, provided helpful materials about the park's history. Jeff Reinbold produced the map of the William Center addition. Bureau Historian Barry Mackintosh gave access to the National Park Service History Division files and answered numerous questions about the history of the agency. National Capital Regional Historian Gary Scott directed me to important land use files and maps. Mackintosh, Scott, and former Chief Historian Edwin C. Bearss contributed their comments on manuscript drafts. Tom DuRant, NPS photo curator, tracked down negatives and furnished many of the illustrations. David Nathanson, archivist for the NPS History Collection, located the Francis Wilshin oral history transcript. Director of Strategic Planning Heather Huyck, who had served as a congressional staffer for Rep. Bruce Vento's subcommittee on national parks during the William Center controversy, read the Manassas mall chapter and provided helpful insights. Chief Historian Dwight Pitcaithley secured National Park Service funding to support the research and writing of the original administrative history and encouraged me to write for a broad audience.

Individuals at non–Park Service repositories aided in the research for this history, including Jimmy Rush at the National Archives, Scott Harris at the Manassas Museum, Don Wilson at the Bull Run Library's Virginiana Room, and Joseph Sheehan at the Philadelphia branch of the National Archives. Anne D. Snyder allowed free access to her extensive document collection on the battlefield park. Bruce Craig, formerly of the National Parks and Conservation Association, furnished his files on the William Center controversy and the park's horse program. Each of the people I interviewed provided invaluable information that enhanced the documentary record and made the events at the Manassas National Battlefield Park come alive.

I owe a special debt of gratitude to my former coworkers at History Associates Incorporated for their many contributions. Jacelee DeWaard served at my side throughout this project, valiantly tracking down sources, conducting primary and secondary research, locating photographs and maps, making the footnotes conform to *The Chicago Manual of Style,* and adding her own humor and insights to the project. Bob Bauman reviewed the Howard W. Smith papers at the University of Virginia. Maryanne Glover addressed interviewees' changes to the oral history transcripts and ensured that early drafts of the manuscript read cleanly and consistently. Gail Mathews and Darlene Wilt produced drafts of the manuscript, turning the text into a professional document. Ruth Dudgeon and Rodney Carlisle contributed their expert editorial skills to drafts of each of the chapters. Phil Cantelon provided me with the initial push to pursue this project and displayed continued support throughout its duration.

Peter J. Potter, my editor at Penn State Press, eased the task of transforming the original manuscript into a book and sought out additional funding. I want to thank Joan K. Davidson of the J. M. Kaplan Fund, whose Furthermore grant program provided critical funding, making it possible for me to conduct more oral history interviews and follow new research avenues. I also thank James M. McPherson and an anonymous reviewer for their helpful comments on the draft manuscript.

Lastly, I acknowledge the encouragement and patience of my husband, Stuart Weinstein, who has shown boundless enthusiasm for my work on this history. To my daughter Sarah, whose birth coincided with the decision by Penn State Press to publish this history, I thank you for the good luck you have brought me and your father. I dedicate this book to my mother Donna Zenzen and my late grandmother Alberta Root, both of whom taught me the beauty of the national parks and history.

ists, believed that Disney's theme park would unleash urban sprawl that would choke the battlefield park and leave the remaining open spaces clogged with traffic. National Park Service officials saw a double-edged sword with Disney: a willing negotiator interested in aiding the federal government in its quest to reduce congestion in the battlefield park and a magnetic company that would draw new development and new problems to the surrounding landscape. Disney retreated in the face of sustained protests that threatened the company's cherished public image. The national park waits for the next development proposal.

The controversies surrounding the William Center and Disney's America were the most recent in a long line of "third battles" of Manassas. This history examines the resulting national debates over a federal highway, national cemetery, two theme parks, and land acquisition and boundary expansions for the battlefield park. What should be emphasized is that each of these battles was national in scope. The battlefield park at Manassas is exceptional in this regard. Its location near the nation's capital ensures that even minor disputes reported in local newspapers gain the ear of congressional members. The transformation of its surrounding countryside from rural outpost to suburban center guarantees that development pressures will continue to spawn concern and controversy over the welfare of the park. The battlefield park has inspired a dedicated group of individuals who are not afraid to act on perceived threats to the park. Other sites within the national park system might have encountered similar threats, but few have attracted the same level of national attention.

This national attention has given Americans the opportunity to debate the intricacies of historic preservation and decide what course to support for the future. By telling the stories of the individual preservation struggles at Manassas National Battlefield Park, this book serves two purposes: first, it explains the legacies of park managers, developers, local and state governing boards, and citizens who determined how not one, but by example all national park sites have been protected. Second, this book examines the complexity of the idea of historic preservation as it has been practiced in one national park. Historic preservation has often been defined by its sometimes conflicting roles of protecting a resource and using the resource to educate the public about its significance. The example at Manassas National Battlefield Park makes clear that a wide range of potential and acceptable uses of parkland exists and that standards of acceptability have changed over time.

My central argument in this book is that historic preservation works, but that it requires vigilance and commitment on the part of all Americans.

INTRODUCTION

Historic Preservation and Use

Headlines reading "Storm over Manassas," "Battling over Manassas," "Where Men Fought and Fell," and "Hallowed Ground" could have been published in the aftermath of the two Civil War battles fought in 1861 and 1862 along Bull Run near the rail center at Manassas Junction. These titles recall the great losses suffered by both Federals and Confederates as they confronted each other in the first major land engagement of the war and later, in the contest that paved the way for Confederate General Robert Lee's first invasion of the North. Victory for either side would be hard won and the lessons long remembered.[1]

But these headlines actually refer to a more contemporary battle over Manassas. In January 1988, the Hazel/Peterson Companies aroused nation-wide concern for the integrity of the Manassas National Battlefield Park when it announced its intention to add a 1.2-million-square-foot regional shopping mall to an originally proposed office and residential park. The commercial complex would have stood on the historic land where General Lee had established his headquarters during the Second Battle of Manassas. Mall opponents ultimately won this battle in the fall of 1988 when the U.S. Congress employed a rarely used procedure called a "legislative taking" to acquire the contested land, but the fight had been difficult and the cost high, as much as $134 million to buy the 550 acres of land from the Virginia development firm, its president John T. ("Til") Hazel, and the other parties who had begun developing the land.[2]

The controversy over William Center, Hazel/Peterson's name for the disputed tract of land, was quickly followed in 1993 by another national debate centered around the Walt Disney Company and its proposed historic theme park. Disney's America, with its accompanying hotels, campgrounds, residential subdivisions, and commercial complexes, would have been located just 3.5 miles from the Manassas National Battlefield Park. Supporters in state and county government welcomed the expected tax benefits and new jobs that Disney promised. Opponents, who included residents in surrounding counties and a national coalition of historians and preservationists

People directly assigned the task of preserving park areas must cast a wide net and actively recruit support from as many sectors of the surrounding population as possible. By building a foundation of support early, many crises as experienced at Manassas battlefield park might be forestalled or minimized. Preservationists will find in this book an understanding of the complexity of the historic preservation concept, which they can then use as a blueprint for combating future preservation battles. Civil War enthusiasts will find a compendium of lessons learned that can be applied to other historic grounds threatened by development or neglect. Policy makers will use this book to understand the motivations of different groups involved in preservation and development issues and so will gain insights on the best approaches of dealing with these diverse interests. Historians of national parks will use this book to augment scholarship on battlefield parks and other historic sites, an area often bypassed in favor of the superlative western national parks. Developers and local planning commissions will find that historic preservation is a serious force in the United States, one that can work to their benefit if they are willing to be partners with preservationists.

The overall status of Civil War battlefield preservation in the United States makes clear the urgency of historic preservation at the close of the twentieth century. The Manassas battlefield park is one of thirty-one existing units in the national park system containing Civil War battlefields. According to the Civil War Sites Advisory Commission, established by public law in November 1990 to assess the status of all Civil War battlefields, only eight of these thirty-one sites are substantially complete in the area preserved through ownership or scenic easement. The remaining twenty-three parks contain only a fraction of the core historic area of each battlefield, leaving the unprotected land open to development. The advisory commission also found that a total of 384 conflicts represented principal battles during the Civil War and thus some protection of the site was justified. Only 58 of these 384 sites of principal conflict fell under National Park Service jurisdiction. The federal government's preservation of the most significant lands associated with the First and Second Battles of Manassas is truly remarkable.[3]

Why Preserve Battlefields?

In September 1861, less than two months after the South won the First Battle of Manassas,[4] Confederates placed a historic marker on the battlefield at Henry Hill in honor of Col. Francis S. Bartow of the Eighth Georgia Infantry. This privately held landscape already evoked powerful memories that compelled individuals to distinguish it from the surrounding farmlands and memorialize Bartow and the other soldiers who had fought and died there. By the 1890s the federal government responded to increasing nationalistic interest expressed by Americans in both northern and southern states to set aside former battlegrounds by creating the Chickamauga and Chattanooga, Shiloh, Gettysburg, and Vicksburg National Military Parks and the Antietam National Battlefield site. Manassas would have to wait until 1940 for its own federal park designation, but in the meantime, a host of reasons for preserving these lands evolved.[5]

One overwhelming reason harkens back to the motivation of Confederate soldiers to establish a marker following First Manassas to commemorate and memorialize the past. Recognizing that many of these battlegrounds were located in rural areas and, with time, might become so overgrown as to vanish from sight, Americans sought to provide permanent identification with enduring monuments, accurately marking the locations where significant stages of the battles occurred. Memorials now scatter the horizon in such parks as Vicksburg and Gettysburg, testaments to nineteenth-century sentiments about the importance of honoring those who died while fighting for their ideals.[6]

With the passage of time after the Civil War, these battlefield parks began to inspire patriotic fervor and a reconciliation of the past while they continued to memorialize. With the abolition of slavery and the restoration of the Union at the close of the Civil War, Americans began to exhibit a nationalistic allegiance that significantly departed from pre-1860s sectionalist attitudes. Establishing further military parks commemorating not just the Civil War but also the American Revolution and other significant wars helped Americans memorialize the roots of their democratic nation. This emerging nationalism also helped salve the emotional and psychological wounds between the sides, symbolically represented in the 1887 Gettysburg veterans reunion when Southerners and Northerners grasped each other's hands on the very battlefield where they had fought against one another.[7]

Military reasons also underlay the federal government's decision to establish Civil War parks. Professional tacticians at the turn of the century, realizing the value of studying troop movements in what they considered the first modern war, documented, mapped, and marked the significant campaigns. These battlegrounds then served as open fields for practicing past tactics and testing new ones. The battlefields of Manassas hosted military maneuvers in 1904 and 1939. Military historians and other enthusiasts have also used the valuable resource of the battlefield landscapes for uncovering additional information on the historic conditions of the battles.[8]

With the closing of the twentieth century, Americans have discovered a host of new reasons for lobbying their congressional representatives to designate further battlefields as national parks. One involves the need for a tangible link to the past that makes these wars real and not just facts to memorize from the history books. By standing on the same ground where Brig. Gen. Thomas J. Jackson repulsed Union troops at First Manassas and received his immortal nom de guerre "Stonewall," individuals gain an invaluable opportunity to link past and present. Cultural values are passed, and lessons are learned. From this experience, many Americans have come to view the battlegrounds as "sacred ground," hallowed by the sacrifices of the soldiers who gave their lives in support of their ideals.[9]

Social reasons serve as significant factors in raising support for battlefield parks among diverse groups. Although the abolition of slavery has always been an acknowledged result of the Civil War, the battlefield parks had largely downplayed its significance. Changing trends in historical interpretation, marked most clearly by the rise of social history in the 1960s and the concerns raised by African Americans and others, led to greater attention to interpretive activities at the parks, taking into account a multiplicity of voices. At the same time, the contributions of individual soldiers—the young, unknown men—have received more notice as history has increasingly adopted a "bottom-up" rather than a "top-down" perspective. Women, who either remained at home and supported their families while the men fought or who were caught in the battles themselves, have also received a voice. Residents of local communities today have the opportunity to address the emotional sides of their past by having battlefield parks established. Each of these social groups benefits from preservation and examination of battlefields.[10]

The media have also served as an important factor in increasing interest in the Civil War. The federal government held special ceremonies commemorating the one hundredth anniversary of the war during the 1960s and encouraged private companies to incorporate Civil War sites in their advertising. The popular television miniseries *Roots* and the accompanying book by Alex Haley sparked interest in tracing family ancestries. This genealogical pursuit often led individuals to follow the paths of their relatives on Civil War battlefields. Most recently, Ken Burns's documentary *The Civil War* for the Public Broadcasting Service reenergized people in learning more about the individual battles.[11]

Finally, environmental and economic reasons make battlefield parks attractive to today's society. Vast expanses of open green space, especially if located near urban centers, provide much-needed room to hike and explore. A piece of the historic countryside is saved, acting as a reminder of what rural America looked like in earlier centuries. As the Disney's America controversy highlighted, these remaining patches of open land must be preserved before urban sprawl overtakes them. The benefits of preservation spread to the local communities, which profit monetarily from increased tourism and associated businesses that accompany park designation.[12] The story of Manassas and its battlefields illuminates the difficult road historic preservation has taken and often won in its fight to save America's historic landscape for posterity.

Chapter 1

EARLY PRESERVATION EFFORTS

Nearly eighty years elapsed from the first attempt to memorialize the Manassas battlefields in 1861 with the Bartow monument to the 1940 establishment of the Manassas National Battlefield Park. Many factors contributed to this delay. Preservation of battlefields became a popular idea at the turn of the century, and Manassas competed with several other battlefields for designation as a national military park. With the increased numbers of possible parks, Congress had to consider the costs involved and therefore displayed reluctance in automatically approving a proposal. Since this legislative body made the final decision to establish a military park, sites having the vigorous support of individual members of Congress had a better chance for success. In the case of Manassas, local residents, Civil War veterans, and a few local Virginia representatives campaigned for its protection. Additional congressional support was weak, possibly because Manassas represented two stunning Confederate victories. This sectionalism translated into political votes, with largely Democratic-supporting Confederate veterans at odds with Republican presidential administrations and a Republican House in the first decade of the twentieth century. The power-wielding North found it easier to support preservation of Gettysburg and Vicksburg, for example, because these battles were turning points that helped to determine the war's outcome—the preservation of the Union.

While obstacles clearly existed in creating Manassas National Battlefield Park, citizens and their representatives supported the protection of former battlegrounds as a way to reestablish national unity and preserve a sense of the past. As a response to the expansive nationalism in the United States during the 1890s, popular opinion swung toward preserving former battlefields. Chickamauga and Chattanooga, Shiloh, Gettysburg, Vicksburg, and Antietam became the original battlefield parks and, in the process, created a unified system. They provided criteria for the future inclusion of other historic areas, including examination of campaign strategy, losses suffered, armies involved, and overall significance of the battle to the welfare of the nation. As Congress expanded its consideration for battlefield parks to the Revolutionary War and other non–Civil War military encounters, it continued to debate the possibility of setting aside the Manassas landscape.[1]

Examination of some of the early steps taken toward preservation of the Manassas battlefields helps establish why this site was significant to Americans following the Civil War. This information, in turn, lays a foundation for understanding the mission of the eventual national park, since ideas about its preservation shaped its administration. Early preservation attempts varied from individuals making regular pilgrimages to the battlefields to Congress reviewing legislative proposals. A summary of the most important events relating to preservation from the 1890s to the 1920s helps to highlight the reasons why the Manassas battlefields warranted protection by the federal government.

Manassas Monuments

Only six weeks following the First Battle of Manassas, soldiers from Col. Francis S. Bartow's brigade placed a marble column on Henry Hill to honor his memory. This monument was the first of a number of memorials that individuals and governments placed on the Manassas battlefields. Two widely recognized and well-visited monuments soon followed. Under orders from the U.S. Army at the conclusion of the Civil War, Lt. James M. McCallum of the Sixteenth Massachusetts Battery oversaw scores of troops from the Fifth Pennsylvania Heavy Artillery. They constructed a twenty-foot-high, obelisk-shaped memorial ornamented with five 200-pound shells on Henry Hill and a complementary sixteen-foot monument at Groveton, which had seen heavy action during Second Manassas, decorated with relic shot and shell found on the battlefield. Both monuments display the inscription "In memory of the patriots who fell." Consecrated on 11 June 1865 in a well-attended ceremony performed by chaplains from Kentucky and Illinois, these monuments came to represent the commitment that the U.S. government had toward preserving the memory of events at Manassas.[2]

Other markers graced the area encompassed by the First and Second

Fig. 1. One of the enduring monuments dedicated to the "memory of the patriots who fell" at Manassas reminds park visitors of the two Civil War battles fought here. (National Archives photo)

Battles of Manassas. The Bull Run Chapter of the United Daughters of the Confederacy erected a Confederate monument in 1904 in the Groveton cemetery, which had been established in 1867 by women of the local community for the purpose of reinterring Confederate remains. The Groveton Confederate cemetery represented just one of many such soldiers' cemeteries established in the aftermath of the Civil War battles. They became one of the earliest efforts to commemorate the soldiers and permanently mark the general locations of the battlefields. Following Abraham Lincoln's famous address at the newly established Gettysburg cemetery in November 1863, these burial grounds gained prominence, and Americans began erecting formal cemeteries with monuments at other battlefields. The marker at the Groveton cemetery echoed this effort.[3]

In 1906 the state of New York added three impressive granite monuments to commemorate the Fifth New York Volunteers, the Tenth New York

Volunteers, and the Fourteenth Brooklyn (84th New York), each of which had experienced significant losses during Second Manassas. The state legislature made the authorization, established commissions with representatives from each regiment to oversee each design, purchased 5.8 acres of land in Manassas, and funded the work. Henry Vollmer created the memorials and John Tillet erected fences and gates to protect them.[4]

These New York monuments, as they have since been called, represent the actions taken by a host of states at the turn of the century to erect markers memorializing the Civil War fallen. These physical reminders helped keep the bravery and sacrifices of the soldiers alive while also forging ties between the war-torn North and South. Memorials to the New York volunteers stood near those for Confederate dead. One did not overshadow the other. The unveiling ceremonies for the New York monuments tried to foster this sense of unity. Col. Edmund Berkeley, wartime commander of the Eighth Virginia Volunteers, shared the podium with his onetime Union opponents. Both saw the value of preserving the past through the monuments and the eventual establishment of a battlefield park.[5]

Erection of durable markers on the battlefields represented overtly public statements about the Civil War and its memory. Private actions involved the regular pilgrimage of Northerners and Southerners to the site. Some people came to remember relatives who had fought and died at Manassas. Others sought to understand the military maneuvers by examining the actual landscape. The local chapter of the United Daughters of the Confederacy held annual commemorations for each battle, which were well attended. Mr. Hugh Fauntleroy Henry, who lived on Henry Hill, welcomed visitors and provided tours of the battlefield. He had amassed a considerable collection of artifacts from the war, and he allowed the curious to view them. His house in effect became a museum and favorite stopping place for tourists. A 1918 visitor register for the Henry House shows people from thirty-one states, ranging from California to Maine, Alabama to New Mexico. Indicating the popularity of this place, in 1900 Henry published a souvenir booklet for the two Manassas battles.[6]

George Carr Round

George Carr Round, a Union veteran who had settled in the small Manassas community following the Civil War, recognized that people needed to visit

Fig. 2. Caught in heavy fighting during both battles of Manassas, the Henry House was rebuilt twice and later served as an informal museum of artifacts collected from the war. (National Park Service photo)

this battle-scarred landscape to come to terms with the past and move forward with their lives. He wanted to provide the same opportunity to later generations of Americans, making federal preservation of the battlefields necessary. Round made protection of the Manassas battlegrounds his personal goal. He was not alone in wanting to save battlefields and other historic sites. Other equally dedicated individuals campaigned to establish a national military park and erect a peace monument at Appomattox, Virginia, and to acquire land related to the Civil War at Wilson's Creek, Missouri.[7]

Round's background played an important role in shaping his commitment to these lands. Born in the Wyoming Valley of eastern Pennsylvania in 1839 and raised in upstate New York, Round enlisted in the Union Army while still in college. Eventually assigned to the Army Signal Corps, he sent the last message in the Eastern theater for the war from the dome of the North Carolina state capitol in Raleigh, proclaiming in colored rockets, "Peace on earth, good will to men." This signal foreshadowed Round's post–Civil War efforts to bring the North and South together in a respectful fellowship. In 1868 Round earned a law degree and also worked for a law firm in New York before deciding to move to North Carolina where he had relatives. Passing through the Manassas area on his way south, he decided instead to settle at this quiet railroad junction, where he opened a law office and engaged in the real estate business.[8]

Round established himself in the civic affairs of the town by supporting public education, which he saw as "the hope of a true reunion" between the former Confederates and Federals. He obtained funding to open the first free public school in Virginia in 1869 and later became the area's first Superintendent of Public Schools. He also prompted an appropriation for the construction of the first state high school in Manassas and started Prince William County's first public library. He saw his efforts toward a complete public school system as helping in the "true reconstruction" of the "great republic" which George Washington had founded and Abraham Lincoln had preserved.[9]

Round further promoted the emotional reunification of the North and South by organizing the Manassas National Jubilee of Peace, held on 21 July 1911 in observance of the fiftieth anniversary of the first battle. As remembered by one longtime resident of the area who witnessed the event when he was seven years old, 350 Confederates and 125 Federals "marched" up to each other, shook hands, and then joined in "laughter and smiles and backslapping." Round considered this display of camaraderie "absolutely unprecedented."[10]

A diverse range of individuals and organizations displayed their support for the Peace Jubilee. Virginia Governor William Hodges Mann delivered the introductory speech, and President William Howard Taft, who was joined on the trip from Washington by an entourage of members of Congress, provided the keynote address to an estimated crowd of ten thousand people. The Southern Railway offered discounts for round-trip travel on its lines for the commemoration, perhaps explaining the larger numbers of Confederates in attendance. Local residents covered the town with bunting, and the United Daughters of the Confederacy took responsibility for the picnic that followed the ceremonies. Several companies of the Virginia state militia and troops from the United States cavalry participated in exercises on the battlefield.[11]

For Round, the outpouring of generosity and goodwill during the Peace Jubilee demonstrated that the "hatred, resentments, misunderstandings and injustices" which had precipitated the Civil War were "buried, forgotten and forever settled." Two years later, he received a resounding endorsement for his efforts when fifty-five thousand veterans joined hands at Gettysburg, marking a national recovery from the many wounds of the Civil War.[12]

Early Legislative Attempts

Round directed his energies toward persuading the federal government to legally acquire the battlefield. He began his legislative attempts with a petition to Congress on 1 December 1901. Rep. John F. Rixey of Culpeper County, Virginia, introduced H.R. 277 the following day, and Round testified before Subcommittee No. 2 of the House Committee on Military Affairs on 2 April 1902.[13]

At the same 1902 hearings, Brig. Gen. George Breckenridge Davis, a distinguished career officer of the U.S. Army, offered a strategy for battlefield preservation, later known as the "Antietam Plan." Davis believed that the federal government need acquire only small tracts of land and place historical plaques at key positions, keeping the remainder of the battlefield in the same agricultural condition it had been in at the time of the war. He based this recommendation on survey work he had done in the early 1890s at Antietam and on his experience as chairman of the Commission for Publication of *The War of the Rebellion: A Compilation of the Official Records of the Union and Confederate Armies,* a massive historical source for which he also conducted surveys at various battlefields. At Antietam, General Davis had the government purchase only narrow lanes along several battle lines, leaving the rest as privately owned farmland, resulting in significant cost savings while memorializing the historic events.[14]

The Antietam Plan provided an attractive alternative to the significant land acquisition and maintenance costs the House Military Affairs Committee had been considering. In addition to H.R. 277, at least eighteen other bills as of April 1902 proposed the establishment of military parks at such locations as Valley Forge and Brandywine, Pennsylvania. The federal government had already spent more than $2 million in acquiring, developing, and maintaining the five original battlefield parks, and the prospect of adding more than a dozen more sites gave pause to the committee members. Although never formally adopted, the Antietam Plan remained a major influence in the federal government's battlefield preservation program until well after 1933 when the National Park Service began administering the national military parks.[15]

Early Manassas legislative proposals serve as specific examples of the influence of the Antietam Plan on battlefield preservation. H.R. 277, which never made it out of the subcommittee, emphasized the protection of the 1865 monuments through limited land acquisition rather than recommending the establishment of a large battlefield park. The bill, which had an overall appropriation of $25,000, allowed the secretary of war to purchase at a reasonable price for the United States a "sufficient" amount of land surrounding the monuments to permit visitation. The bill also provided for the construction of "suitable roadways and approaches" between the sold property and public highways to improve accessibility.[16]

When testifying in support of H.R. 277 and subsequent Manassas bills, Round adopted General Davis's suggestions and argued for acquisition of the "historic positions where the monuments are located," as opposed to a larger parklike area that might be "laid out with walks and driveways and flowers." Significantly, Round's conception of the battlefield park focused on its importance as a historic area rather than an inviting public park filled with diversions to please a range of visitors. Round believed that, most importantly, the battlefields must remain preserved in the condition they had been in between 1861 and 1865, meaning as farmland, and that steel towers—another Davis recommendation—should be built to facilitate viewing the entire scene where First Manassas had occurred. He envisioned the purchase of a total of two hundred acres, including Henry Hill, about twenty-five acres of the Dogan Farm where the Groveton monument stood, and a few isolated strips of land around Maj. Gen. John Pope's headquarters and the unfinished railroad cut. At Henry Hill, Round thought a former soldier should reside at and care for the property, or, if the federal government established a national park at Fredericksburg, this commission could administer the Manassas reservation.[17]

Despite Round's claim that H.R. 277 was the first proposal for purchasing lands at Manassas, an earlier bill introduced by Rep. Peter J. Otey of Lynchburg, Virginia, proposed the establishment of a "national battle park" in recognition of the "world-renowned" conflict along the Bull Run. Introduced on 1 February 1900, H.R. 7837 would have preserved for "historical and professional study" the battleground where soldiers had fought at First Manassas. The bill did not delineate the amount of land to be acquired or create a mechanism for administering the proposed park, and Congress failed to act.[18]

Support of Veterans Organizations

Congressional concern over the multitude and diversity of battlefield preservation bills submitted in the first decades of the century prevented further action on H.R. 277 and the many subsequent Manassas proposals that Congressman Rixey and others submitted. The Antietam Plan may have provided the federal government with an economically attractive solution to establishing parks, but Congress also saw the need for a national historic preservation policy to determine which areas most deserved park status. Toward this goal, Congress debated, but never resolved, the value of a National Military Park Commission that would identify, survey, investigate, and acquire lands for parks. As the possibility of a national commission persisted through the 1920s, Congress delayed action on specific park proposals, including Manassas, resulting in only five battlefield bills becoming law between 1900 and 1925.[19]

While Congress remained stalled on the Manassas bills, George Carr Round garnered support for the battlefield park from the Grand Army of the Republic (GAR), the largest of the Civil War veterans groups, which met in annual reunions called encampments. Capt. C. A. E. Spamer, impressed by a tour of the battlefield he took in 1901, wrote a personal recommendation to the Cleveland national encampment to call attention to the idea of establishing a park at Manassas. The encampment failed to address the subject due to the furor resulting from the assassination of President William McKinley.[20]

With interest aroused within the Grand Army of the Republic, Round pursued the idea of a Manassas park. In 1903 he attended the San Francisco national encampment as a delegate-at-large from the Department of the Potomac and secured the endorsement of the committee on resolutions of H.R. 1964, which Congressman Rixey introduced that year. During the same convention, the Manassas Picket Post of Union Veterans presented a memorial to the encampment, asking for such action by the organization to carry on the "pious and patriotic" goals that had inspired the erection of the Manassas monuments. Despite the favorable support of the committee, Round failed to get the full endorsement of the encampment due to resistance by the Department of Pennsylvania. The following year, the Department of Maryland reintroduced the resolution at the Boston encampment, but action did not reach beyond the committee.[21]

Grand Army of the Republic support for the Manassas park proposal gained a new infusion of energy when the Society of the Army of the Potomac met in Manassas in May 1905. Some of the Pennsylvania delegates who had opposed the 1903 proposition attended this convention, and Round took the opportunity to educate them on the resolution's significance. He succeeded in converting at least one of the opponents, Brig. Gen. Lewis Wagner, who later worked with Round to provide the phrasing for one of the subsequent Manassas bills.

In 1906 Round finally succeeded in gaining the formal support of the Grand Army. The 1905 Denver encampment established the Bull Run Battlefield Monument Committee and authorized it to consider the original proposition. This committee, composed of three Grand Army members, reported favorably the following year at the Minneapolis encampment. At this convention, the Grand Army resolved that the United States should acquire the land where the 1865 monuments stood and provide for roadways to these areas. The resolution also suggested that the federal government administer Manassas through the proposed park at Fredericksburg. E. W. Whitaker, one of the Bull Run Battlefield Monument Committee members, testified in 1912 before the House Military Affairs Committee and provided Congress with the Grand Army's resolution.[22]

Promise of Action

Round waited an entire decade from his first appearance before Congress until April 1912 when the full House Committee on Military Affairs conducted a hearing on H.R. 1330, the ninth incarnation of H.R. 277. Submitted by Rep. Charles C. Carlin of Alexandria, Virginia, Rixey's successor, H.R. 1330 provided for the secretary of war to purchase sufficient lands around the 1865 monuments and to build roadways from the property to public highways. The bill recognized that United States troops had erected the Henry Hill and Groveton monuments following the conclusion of the

Civil War, and that the federal government had never obtained legal title to this land. H.R. 1330 also acknowledged the interest of veterans organizations in further memorializing the Manassas landscape and provided for the establishment of a commission to consider the perpetual care of additional monuments erected by these groups.[23]

Discussion in the 1912 hearing embodied many of the central issues that battlefield preservationists encountered in trying to obtain park designations, namely, justification of national significance and demonstration of reasonable cost. Round addressed the first concern by gathering a diverse group of supporters who testified to the patriotic reasons for having Manassas formally acknowledged and preserved by the federal government. But, as Thomas H. Lion of Manassas recognized, Congress also placed importance on "practic[ing] economy" when deciding how best to display national pride. Committee member Lynden Evans (D-Ill.) agreed with Lion and admitted that "patriotism is a valuable sentiment" that should be kept "alive in the hearts of the people," but he also wondered what exactly Round's group wanted done and how much it would cost. Questions then proceeded to uncover what parcels of land the government should buy at what price and where access roads should be placed for what distance.[24]

Land costs consumed the remainder of the hearing, though committee members agreed in the end that the proposal deserved further investigation. At the heart of the discussion, Congress wanted to know at what price the Henry heirs would sell their land. Committee members understood that the historical associations of the 128-acre farm justified some increase in price over comparable lands in less historically significant areas, but they questioned the reasonableness of paying more than $100 per acre, the amount paid for the New York monument land. Acting as a legal representative for the Henry family, Round defended the $20,000 amount the Henry heirs requested, which equaled about $156 per acre, by reminding Congress that the family had cared for the Henry Hill monument long after the federal government had abandoned it. In Round's mind, the historic value of the land justified an amount ten times over the $50 per acre other farms might receive.[25]

Attainment of battlefield park status appeared closer when Congress passed and the president signed into law the Manassas bill on 3 March 1913. Under the provisions of P.L. 412, the War Department appointed a board of three officers who surveyed the site, interviewed the land owners, and attempted to obtain a reasonable purchase price for the 128-acre Henry Farm and the identified 145 acres of the Dogan Farm. Still representing the

Henry family, Round continued to justify in correspondence to the board $20,000 as a reasonable price for the historically significant land. The Dogan family agreed to sell their 145 acres, which included the Groveton monument and a section of the unfinished railroad where fighting in the second battle ensued, for $80 an acre.[26]

Success seemed imminent when the War Department submitted its report in December 1913 recommending that the federal government repair and preserve the two 1865 monuments and purchase the lands on which they stood. By obtaining these two tracts, the board noted that "ample means" would then be provided for the protection of the monuments and for allowing visitor access to the "principal points" of historic interest associated with the two battles of Manassas. In its opinion, acquisition of additional lands for memorial purposes was not warranted. However, Congress failed to act on the board's recommendation as international events turned its attention away from commemoration of past wars to the demands of World War I.[27]

George Carr Round, who died in 1918, did not see the Manassas battlefields he had fought so long to preserve attain park status. A year before his death, he made one more public plea, in a *Manassas Journal* pamphlet titled "Is the United States Too Poor to Own Its Own Monuments?" Driven by the knowledge that he and his fellow remaining Civil War veterans were quickly passing away, he pleaded that Congress replace this "National Disgrace" with a park. He argued that while the United States expended "billions for preparedness in the future," the nation should devote a few thousand dollars to preserve the Manassas monuments as "lessons for posterity." The Manassas battlefields traversed a few more curves along the national park route before the federal government satisfied Round's pleas.[28]

Chapter 2

ESTABLISHING A PARK

George Carr Round's vision for the Manassas battlefields laid the foundation for preserving this Civil War site. Further contributions came from the Sons of Confederate Veterans (SCV) and the Franklin D. Roosevelt administration. In 1921 the SCV established a Confederate park at the Henry farm, the location of heavy fighting during First Manassas. Fourteen years later, the Roosevelt administration incorporated the Confederate park into a New Deal recreational demonstration area, which included a sizable amount of land associated with both battles. Only after the federal government obtained control of these lands did Manassas National Battlefield Park come into existence on 10 May 1940.

Preservation of the Manassas battlefields during the interwar period was symptomatic of a larger movement in the United States that embraced tradition and history. Collecting Americana, from books and manuscripts to furniture and folk art, became an obsession for some of America's wealthiest citizens. These vast collections, valuable for their insights into past ways of life, eventually became the foundations for many important museums, including the Winterthur Museum (housing the Henry Francis du Pont collection of furniture and decorative arts) and the Shelburne Museum with its folk art. This collecting boom soon spilled over into the preservation of buildings and even sections of towns. Henry Ford relocated historic buildings to his Greenfield Village near Detroit, while John D. Rockefeller Jr. bankrolled the massive restoration of Colonial Williamsburg.[1]

Participation by middle-class Americans in this love affair with history took several forms. They drove their newly affordable automobiles, another contribution by Henry Ford, on the growing national system of highways and explored many out-of-the-way historic sites. States and organizations assisted these travelers' history bent by erecting roadside plaques describing significant events or directing tourists to notable stops along the way. Best-seller lists for the 1920s and 1930s revealed America's penchant for history books and biographies, especially for the Revolutionary and Civil War eras. Local associations flourished with activity, celebrating occasions of both regional and national significance. People also celebrated their family histories by delving into genealogical research. Many New Deal agencies supported the chronicling of American history, whether in Farm Service Association photographs of the dust bowlers or in Works Progress Administration murals and theatrical productions. Each stage along the way to national park status for the Manassas battlefields reflects this feverish interest in history and provides specific examples of how Americans thought lands should be preserved and interpreted.

Confederate Achievement

E. W. R. Ewing, the historian-in-chief of the Sons of Confederate Veterans, took up the cause that Round had initiated and rallied support from the various Confederate organizations to establish a Confederate park at Henry Hill. In 1920 he called a mass meeting of the Washington Camp of the SCV, along with members of the public and representatives from several southern states. Around the same time, Mrs. Westwood Hutchinson, president of the Manassas chapter of the United Daughters of the Confederacy (UDC), obtained an option for the purchase of the Henry farm, totaling 130 acres, for $25,000. With this option in hand, Ewing and his supporters wrote a charter that the Virginia State Corporation Commission granted under its nonstock laws in May 1921. The resulting corporation provided a vehicle for accepting contributions and raising funds toward the acquisition of land and maintenance and development of the park.[2]

Controlled by a board of three directors, for which Ewing served as president, the Manassas Battlefield Corporation promoted memorial, educational, and historical activities. Its mission was to seek cooperation and fairness between North and South. The corporation, however, also wanted to give voice to the South's "distinct, wonderful, equally thrilling, all-important story." In the opinion of the corporate directors, recent historical treatments of the Civil War had depicted their "Confederate ancestors as enemies of [their] country," arguing that the perpetuation of slavery, not states' rights, had prompted the Southern states to secede. In response, the corporation saw the Confederate park as a way to "offer the full truth," in the hopes that the "'truth shall make' our children free."[3]

Education was a primary focus of the Confederate park, and planned developments reflected this mission. The Henry House, which the Henry family had turned into an informal museum prior to the establishment of the Confederate park, continued to serve as a museum for war relics. To facilitate the educational benefits of this collection, the corporation began seeking donations to build a larger, fireproof museum at the park. To assist visitors as they toured the battlefield, a caretaker living on the grounds provided directions and answered some questions. The corporation hoped to have a full-time guide on the premises at some future date. Eventually, the corporate directors also planned to publish "an impartial and full history" of the Manassas battles and of the Civil War and its causes. These educational efforts served the stated mission of giving more sympathetic treatment to the South's understanding of the history of the Civil War than had so far existed.[4]

Paired with education, the corporate directors intended the Manassas Battlefield Confederate Park to serve as the "supreme battlefield memorial" to all Confederate soldiers. Ewing lobbied individual state legislatures to appropriate money for the erection of memorials and markers to recall Southern, as well as Northern, strategies and displays of courage in the battles. The Virginia State Highway Commission had already placed markers along Lee Highway, providing directions to the Confederate park. A landscape architect, detailed from the U.S. government, had begun landscaping the acquired lands. Ultimately, the corporate directors wanted to create "the most beautiful memorial Park in all the land." The resident caretaker maintained the grounds until further financial assistance could pay for more extensive changes.[5]

To show their support for the educational and memorial mission of the Confederate park, a range of interests became involved during the first years of the park's creation. In 1923 the Virginia state legislature authorized payment of $10,000 toward purchase of the Henry farm, under the condition that the Manassas Battlefield Corporation provide the remaining $15,000. Representatives from the United Daughters of the Confederacy, the Southern Confederated Memorial Association, the Confederate Veterans, the Sons of Confederate Veterans, and each southern state served on the corporation's audit board and thus directly contributed to the organization and planning for the park. Officials, ranging from the governor of Maryland to a past commander of the Grand Army of the Republic, expressed their enthusiasm for the Confederate park, while individuals throughout the South sent contributions.[6]

Despite the early optimism, the Manassas Battlefield Confederate Park had difficulty meeting its financial obligations, which slowed its momentum. Although the corporation had received $10,000 in individual contributions and another $10,000 from Virginia during its first fund-raising efforts, the last $5,000 remained elusive. Under the threat of losing the battlefield lands, the SCV renewed its support and convinced each of its divisions to donate between $500 and $1,000 toward the final payment, made in June 1927. The battlefield corporation also needed finances to cover litigation costs when, in 1924, the board of directors fought off an attempt by a subgroup within the organization to acquire the lands. Maintenance of the property continued to tax the remaining limited resources, leaving the corporation without the funds to accomplish its primary goals: erecting memorials on the battlefields, building a fireproof museum to house its collection of artifacts, and writing a history of the Manassas battles.[7]

The financial condition of the Confederate park continued to worsen into the 1930s, prompting the corporation to consider alternatives to its administration of the Manassas battlefields. Ewing, the park's chief proponent, had died in late 1927, leaving a vacuum that few could fill with the same enthusiasm and dedication. Financially, by 1935 the corporation had spent more than $50,000 toward the park, and yet it encountered difficulties in raising the $30 required each month to pay the caretaker's salary. Recognizing this situation, Edmond Wiles, the chairman of the Manassas Battlefield Committee, which the SCV formed to erect markers and other memorials at the park, began corresponding with the National Park Service in 1933. Wiles asked NPS Director Horace Albright for aid in building a museum at Manassas, to which Albright responded that Congress had not authorized the Park Service to assist the private organization. Recognizing the opportunity presented, Albright instead asked Wiles if the Manassas Battlefield Committee would be "disposed to turn over to the Government" the battlefield for designation as a national monument. Wiles thought Albright's idea possible, in light of the current financial difficulties and past discussions held on this topic at SCV conventions. Following one more detour through the New Deal's recreational demonstration area program, these first communications eventually led to incorporation of the Henry Hill tract into the Manassas National Battlefield Park.[8]

A New Deal for Manassas

Reflecting a renewed interest in commemorating the actions of American soldiers in World War I and previous conflicts, Congress reconsidered the idea of establishing battlefield parks at Manassas and elsewhere between the end of World War I and the onset of the Great Depression. By 1926 the Manassas battlefields competed in the House Military Affairs Committee with twenty-eight other bills that proposed creating national military parks. Rejecting the idea of a military park commission study, Congress turned instead to a 1925 memorandum, written by Lt. Col. C. A. Bach of the Army War College and approved by the secretary of war, which provided a comprehensive battlefield classification system. Congress passed and in June 1926 President Calvin Coolidge signed legislation authorizing the War Department to survey identified battlefields using Bach's classification system, the first time the federal government had authorized a broad historic sites study.[9]

Bach's classification scheme relied on past congressional legislation and thus incorporated the ideas presented by such influential individuals as Brig. Gen. George B. Davis, originator of the Antietam Plan. Bach ranked various battlegrounds based on his determination of what level of commemorative action would appropriately memorialize the events that took place at each site, ranging from national military parks to the placement of historic markers. Class 1 battlefields, according to Bach's organization, represented battles of "exceptional" political and military significance with "far-reaching" effects that justified designation as national military parks. Bach identified Yorktown and Saratoga, from the American Revolution, as the only sites that met this criterion and were not yet incorporated into parks. Bach subdivided Class 2 battlefields, which overall warranted designation as national monuments, into two groups. Class 2a, in which Bach placed Manassas, justified marking of the battle lines of the engaged forces with markers but not necessarily memorials, while Class 2b battles required only a tablet or monument to indicate the location of the battleground. Bach's scheme reconfirmed the historic significance of the Manassas battlefields.[10]

Under the congressionally sanctioned War Department surveys conducted between 1926 and 1932, Manassas received attention but still failed to reach national park status. In 1928 district engineers performed a preliminary field investigation of the two battlefields at Manassas and noted that $2,600 would be needed to complete a detailed survey. Congress finally authorized this sum in 1931, but because of worsening national economic conditions, the War Department excluded Manassas in its fiscal year 1933 budget estimates as a cost savings measure. Fourteen other areas became federal parks between 1926 and 1933, including Virginia's Petersburg National Military Park (1926) and Fredericksburg and Spotsylvania County Battlefields Memorial National Military Park (1927), but Manassas remained without the coveted designation, perhaps again due to its connection to two stunning Confederate victories.[11]

Support for the Manassas surveys, and thus a park, evaporated in Congress in the late 1920s, and it was not until the Roosevelt administration that the idea of a national battlefield park was revived. First, in 1933 President Roosevelt reorganized the National Park Service and transferred the previously established military parks to the agency. Although not included in the transfer, Manassas did inspire Roosevelt to pursue this step. In early April 1933 Horace Albright had the fortunate opportunity of riding in a touring car along Lee Highway from Shenandoah National Park to Washington with the president. Referring to the lands where initial fighting had occurred during the Second Battle of Manassas, Director Albright suggested that the Park Service obtain administrative control over the War Department's historic parks and monuments. Roosevelt readily agreed and urged Albright to "do something about this tomorrow," resulting soon afterwards in the transfer.[12]

Second, Roosevelt's New Deal recreational demonstration projects provided the funding and human resources for acquiring land, planning development, and ultimately preparing Manassas for transfer to the Park Service. Originated in 1933 under the authority of the National Industrial Recovery Act, recreational demonstration projects served a long-identified need for providing more recreational facilities to lower-income families. In 1935 Roosevelt incorporated the recreational projects into the newly established Resettlement Administration, which served to demonstrate the proper use of land by buying inferior and unprofitable farmland and using it for other, more beneficial purposes.[13]

From the start, the National Park Service supervised the planning for the forty-six recreational demonstration project areas located in twenty-five states. Using funding available from other New Deal programs, including the Public Works Administration, the Civilian Conservation Corps, the Emergency Relief Administration, and the Works Progress Administration, the Park Service converted old farms and woodland into recreation areas with cabins, picnic areas, and trails. On reclaimed lands, the government built playgrounds for low-income urban populations. Farm families struggling on submarginal lands were transferred to more productive lands. In each case, the recreational demonstration program served the larger mission of the Resettlement Administration to better the lives of both rural and urban dwellers.[14]

By 1935 the Roosevelt administration had designated 1,476 acres of the Manassas battlefields as the Bull Run Recreational Demonstration Area. Howard W. Smith, recently elected representative for northern Virginia, assisted the government in identifying tracts for the project area and obtaining competitive prices for the land. Smith considered the Manassas battlefield park one of his pet projects. He justified the program to Conrad Wirth, then assistant director of the Park Service, pointing to three beneficial aspects: preservation of a significant historic site, provision of recreational facilities for area residents, and availability of submarginal land that could be put to more productive use as a military park. Interestingly, Smith had opposed some of the New Deal programs that had made the recreational demonstration project possible, such as the $4.8 billion work relief program contained in the emergency relief appropriation bill of 1935. However, Smith recognized the value of the Bull Run Recreational Demonstration Area to his voting public and remained a longtime advocate of the battlefield park.[15]

The reasons why the Roosevelt administration included Manassas in the recreational demonstration program are complex. Certainly the many unsuccessful attempts to obtain park status through Congress may have convinced some enterprising and farsighted individuals, including Smith, to use the vehicle of the recreational demonstration areas, which bypassed the legislative branch almost entirely. Albright had gone on motoring trips through the historic and scenic areas of Virginia with both President Roosevelt and Secretary of the Interior Harold L. Ickes, providing the historic preservation-minded Albright with ample opportunity to plant the idea. The battlefields' proximity to Washington also presented an exemplary chance to display the virtues of the recreational demonstration program to a sometimes critical Congress. For a combination of reasons, the National Park Service embraced the Manassas project.[16]

Bull Run Recreational Demonstration Area

Initial plans for the Bull Run Recreational Demonstration Area departed significantly from the previous legislative attempts to preserve the Manassas battlefields. Instead of modestly acquiring a few hundred acres of land that had important historic associations, as favored by the Antietam Plan and by George Carr Round, the Bull Run project proposed a maximum area of almost 10,000 acres to provide for a "complete visualization" of the two battles. Even the smaller "primary purchase area" of 1,600 acres represented a sizable increase over Round's recommendations, and Park Service planning documents repeatedly prioritized holdings with the view of obtaining the larger park. The National Park Service wanted Bull Run to become a point of historic interest of the same caliber as Gettysburg, a project that would require restoration of the battlefields, development of adequate facilities to accommodate the expected thousands of visitors, and marking of the historic areas in the park.[17]

The National Park Service justified its planning for Manassas using a three-pronged approach emphasizing the historical, recreational, and work relief advantages. By tying historic preservation and use together, the Park Service met both the requirements of the Resettlement Administration and its own vision of the value and importance of battlefield parks. Historic preservation served as the guiding force for locating the park and designing its overall layout. The Park Service wanted to include the most historic areas associated with the two battles of Manassas. The story of these battles would be told in conjunction with other important Virginia campaigns during the Civil War. Park Service historians envisioned a linked national battlefield system, in which visitors could trace the movement of soldiers from one Virginia battlefield to the next and emerge from the experience with an overall understanding of the Civil War.[18]

To fulfill this historic preservation mission at Manassas, the Park Service pursued several development projects. Landscape work completed by the Works Progress Administration followed the advice of historians, who researched the war records and reconstructed the appearance of the land at the time of the battles. Among other areas, workers cleared the rounded crest of Bald Hill, which had been free of trees during 1862 and had proved of tactical significance to the events of Second Manassas. Some landscape work was dictated by the poor condition of the soil. The Park Service recommended keeping gullies and erosion areas protected with vegetation until suitable grass cover secured the soil. Workers saved historical relics unearthed during clearing operations for an eventual park museum. Laborers also opened and improved formerly overgrown roads and braced the falling Chinn House until a set of plans could be drawn for its possible restoration.[19]

Other development projects supporting the historic preservation mission of the demonstration area involved interpretation. Joseph Mills Hanson, a trained historian who later served as the park's second superintendent, provided historical research support. With guidance from Branch Spalding, the coordinating superintendent at Fredericksburg who directly supervised all recreational demonstration work at Manassas, Hanson conducted research on the Manassas battles. He retraced the routes different forces had taken over the battlefields and sought out period maps. This research aided workers in clearing fields to resemble their historical appearance. Hanson's understanding of the battles also proved useful for writing texts for more than sixty markers, which were placed at strategic areas on the battlefields.[20]

Recreation, the second of the three-pronged approach at the Manassas battlefields, aimed to serve the Washington, D.C., regional population, which in the "not distant future" was expected to house almost a million people in need of space and an outlet for outdoor activities. Representative Smith predicted in a letter to Assistant Director Wirth that the Bull Run demonstration area, located about thirty miles from the district line, "would be visited daily by thousands of people from Washington who lack any large park area of this character . . . for an afternoon's recreation." The Park Service's final project report for the demonstration area echoed this sentiment: "When the Battlefield with its many springs and streams and its 5,000 acres of woodland is properly developed, not as a cemetery, but as a pleasure ground," it will attract more visitation than Gettysburg. Suggestions for recreational developments ranged from picnic areas to athletic fields, camp sites to bridle paths. With access assured through paved roads and proper management, the possibilities seemed boundless.[21]

Ideas about serving the recreational needs of the nation's capital reflected an underlying mission for the recreational demonstration areas.

The Park Service argued that the Manassas area, "teeming with history and romance," could serve to inspire future generations if the "deeds of heroism" were properly memorialized. Here, history and recreation went hand-in-hand to aid in the furtherance of the democratic nation. These lofty goals for a national park site were not unusual. Interior Secretary Ickes had designated 1934 as National Park Year to promote travel to America's natural and historic areas and to provide a needed respite from the worries of the Depression. Many people spent all of their energy trying to find work, food to feed their families, and a warm, dry place to sleep. Projects like the one at Manassas offered hope through rejuvenation. Taking a break from these worries by going out into the country refreshed the mind and renewed the spirit. This reenergized electorate, the Roosevelt administration predicted, would return to their plights with sustaining hope. Better times would be that much closer when everyone joined together, renewed in purpose.[22]

When considering the underlying goals of the Bull Run Recreational Demonstration Area, it becomes evident that the Park Service did not favor one particular type of recreation over others. In addition, what the Service considered "recreation" in the 1930s varies from present understandings of the term. Taking a leisurely drive and following a battlefield tour qualified as a form of recreation. Today, this activity seems more focused on history than recreation. Hiking along Bull Run and enjoying the rural countryside or picnicking in the shade of a hillside and exploring the historic events of the Manassas battles, although certainly an educational experience, was also considered recreation. What these activities had in common was the opportunity to leave the city, walk or drive in open spaces, and immerse oneself in enjoyable diversions. The end result, the Roosevelt administration hoped, was a refreshed American public able to take on the challenges of the economic hard times.

In addition to history and recreation, the recreational demonstration area served the third important function of using unemployed local labor to assist the Park Service in implementing its development plans. Viewed as an ideal work relief program, this project employed residents of Prince William and adjoining counties to clear grounds and restore the landscape using proper natural resource conservation techniques. Stabilization of historic structures and control of erosion were largely done by relief workers. The "demonstrated" concept was that the "ennobling inspiration" and valuable instruction gained from the preservation and development of the battlefields would be heightened by the fact that local laborers in need of work immediately benefited from the establishment of the park.[23]

Although recreation and work relief continued to be important factors, history remained the driving force for the recreational demonstration area. Historian Hanson's research into the two battles of Manassas enabled him to identify the most significant properties for inclusion in the Bull Run project area, those lands which had sustained the heaviest fighting. The National Park Service used Hanson's research to determine the core area for the battlefield park. Acting Director Arthur E. Demaray noted in summer 1937 that the Park Service would acquire only the most important sites, including the Henry House, the Chinn House, the Stone Bridge, the Stone House, the Van Pelt House, and Sudley Mill. Adjacent land that had been under cultivation at the time of the battles, in Demaray's estimation, could remain in private ownership "unless developments occur thereon which would be incompatible" with the battlefield park's mission. By November of the same year, Hanson reported that more than 1,400 acres had been secured from such families as the Robinsons and Dogans for inclusion in the park. The Park Service, however, still needed to find a way to acquire the crucial Henry Hill tract.[24]

Due to his close supervision of the historical research and development projects at Bull Run, Coordinating Superintendent Spalding took on the delicate issue of securing the Manassas Battlefield Confederate Park for the federal government. When members of the Sons of Confederate Veterans learned in July 1935 of the proposed transfer, significant opposition, led by Col. Walter L. Hopkins, rallied to keep the park privately owned. Primarily, Hopkins believed that the Manassas Battlefield Corporation's board of directors had exceeded its authority in making the offer without first consulting the general organization, but he also held some reservations about having the federal government take control of a park that southern money and dedication had created. Spalding feared that the opposition did not have confidence in the National Park Service's ability to administer the land, but this issue proved less significant.[25]

Relying on his detailed knowledge of the Manassas project and other Park Service efforts in the South, Spalding addressed the concerns expressed by Hopkins and his followers. As Hopkins later admitted to Arno Cammerer, the director of the NPS, Spalding's scholarly understanding of the issues, his courteous and diplomatic manner, and his long-term dedication soothed the rumpled sensibilities of the membership. Based on first-

through woods, down into ravines, plunging into streams, up again onto rising meadows, eager, excited, thrilled with hot desire to bear our share in routing the enemy." For Lusk, the continually changing environment reflected his boundless energy in defeating the Southern cause. Confederate soldier Charles Minor Blackford described his view of Henry Hill in quiet terms, suggesting a more ambivalent mood. Blackford wrote to his wife Susan: "we were thrown into line about sunrise on the brow of a hill which overlooked Bull Run, with quite a wide valley (two hundred yards at least), below us. On the other side the bluff rose quite steeply, but on top of it there was an open field." Not elaborated, snippets of description provide clues to the lay of the land and its importance in the experiences of the men fighting. The National Park Service, in turn, strove to capture for its visitors these and other Civil War experiences that the land held.[3]

Stonewall Jackson Statue and the Administration-Museum Building

The National Park Service retained the basic administrative structure established under the New Deal's recreational demonstration area program when Manassas became a unit of the national park system in 1940. Branch Spalding continued to serve as coordinating superintendent from the Fredericksburg and Spotsylvania County Battlefields Memorial National Military Park, where he remained closely involved in making park decisions. Regional direction came from Region 1 headquarters in Richmond. For managing routine activities at Manassas, the Park Service appointed Raleigh C. Taylor as the first superintendent. Taylor supervised relief workers employed by the Bull Run project, who remained until June 1941 to complete various special improvements.[4]

In spite of a tenure shortened by his taking military furlough in early spring 1942, Taylor saw the long-awaited transformation of the battlefields from privately owned lands to a national park site with the appropriate visitor services. This change in ownership led to the development of the historically rich Henry Hill area, with the Park Service focused on educating Americans about the battlefields. Two early and significant projects proceeded with the nudging, or outright contributions, of outside organizations. First, in 1938 the state of Virginia appropriated $25,000 for the erection of an equestrian statue commemorating Stonewall Jackson's unassailable line on Henry Hill. Second, as a result of negotiations with the Sons of Confederate Veterans for the Henry Hill tract, the Park Service promised to build a museum at Manassas. These two landmarks, located on Henry Hill, focused attention on the First Battle of Manassas and proclaimed the existence of the national park.[5]

Initial thoughts for a Jackson statue emerged from the seventy-fifth anniversary reenactment of the first battle, held 21 July 1936. Sponsored by the National Park Service, a local community organization, and the Manassas-Prince William County Chamber of Commerce, the event brought 2,000 Army and Marine Corps troops onto the field that had witnessed the climax of operations in 1861. During these festivities, Coordinating Superintendent Spalding suggested erecting a "suitable monument" for Jackson to replace the poorly lettered sign that marked the historic site. No action was taken until 1938 when the Virginia legislature appropriated funds and the Sons of Confederate Veterans included a provision for its construction in its deed of conveyance with the federal government.[6]

Virginia state agencies selected the sculptor and design, and the Park Service advised on the placement of the statue. Originally, the Virginia Museum of Fine Arts, acting for the Virginia Conservation Commission, intended to cooperate with the National Fine Arts Commission in artistic review of the submissions, but controversy resulted concerning the ultimate jurisdiction and final authority of the two agencies. The state agency held its ground and chose Italian-born Joseph Pollia. Trained at the school associated with the Boston Museum of Fine Arts, Pollia had sculpted several monuments to American history, including a Spanish-American memorial on San Juan Hill in Cuba and a statue of Union General Philip Henry Sheridan.[7]

Pollia faced scrutiny as he translated his proposal into a finished model. A furor, dubbed the "third" battle of Manassas, arose when veterans and members of Confederate organizations criticized Pollia's rendition of Jackson, who looked more like Union General Ulysses S. Grant in their estimation, and Jackson's mount Sorrel, which appeared as a common plow horse instead of a prize mount. Pollia addressed the concerns and won praise from a local paper for "patience, for fortitude, for gallantry" displayed under such a barrage.[8]

As time for the dedication ceremonies approached, representatives from

Fig. 3. Towering over Henry Hill, the imposing figure of Thomas J. Jackson astride his mount Sorrel commemorates the point during the First Battle of Manassas when this Confederate commander stood "like a stone wall" against Union fighting and inspired his troops to victory. (National Park Service photo)

the Virginia agencies and the National Park Service met at Manassas to determine a location for the statue and for the museum-administration building. The delegation agreed to place the monument on the same commanding ridge where Jackson was then believed to have stood while directing his brigade's tactical maneuvers, with the statue facing toward the Union position near the Henry House. The Park Service and state agents selected the companion elevation for the site of the museum building, orienting the building so that visitors would have a clear view of the Jackson statue from the museum's observation terrace.[9]

Unveiling ceremonies on 31 August 1940 tied the bronze statue and the recently established national battlefield park to the events surrounding World War II. Mounted atop an eight-foot base of black granite etched with Brig. Gen. Barnard Bee's immortal phrase, "There Stands Jackson Like a Stone Wall," the stalwart Jackson in the saddle projected the same strength and determination that Americans needed in the current perilous affairs. Dr. Douglas Southall Freeman, a Richmond editor and authority on Confederate leaders, reminded the more than 1,500 attendees of Jackson's use of discipline and vigorous training, which would serve current military commanders well.[10]

Whereas the Stonewall Jackson statue aided visitors in visualizing a key moment during the First Battle of Manassas, the administration-museum building represented the core of educational activities at the park. In preparing for its construction, the National Park Service decided that locating the building on a historic spot provided the greatest opportunity for educating visitors. This would also fulfill the requirements of the deed of conveyance. For late-twentieth-century viewers, the eventual placement of the building on Henry Hill may seem incongruous with the mandate to preserve the battlefield, but at the time, the amount of expected development on the battlefield seemed small in comparison to the benefits reaped in visitor contact and education.[11]

Size, design, and location served as the three important planning features of the museum-administration building. Carl P. Russell, who guided National Park Service interpretive efforts at Yosemite and other sites, used the combination of these three factors to lay out his vision of the building. During master planning for the Bull Run Recreational Demonstration Area project, he argued strenuously that adequate space be provided for administrative duties and for exhibits and lectures. Since the Park Service expected to launch tours from the museum, Russell wanted the building "strategically located in the historical area," such as on a site overlooking the battlefield, on a hilltop within the field, or in some "less conspicuous but easily reached" spot.[12]

Spalding, the coordinating superintendent, supported Russell's vision for the museum. Spalding agreed that selecting a site near the Henry House would be ideal, assuming that the building provided sufficient space to support both administrative and educational activities. When considering possible intrusions on the historic scene by the placement of visitor services, Spalding and other Park Service officials fought more over the number and location of picnic areas than the siting of the museum. Historical assistant Joseph Mills Hanson joined Spalding in this appraisal. Hanson wrote in the 1939 museum prospectus that the proposed alteration of the historic terrain for the museum was "necessary here," though mitigative steps in locating the building away from the center of Henry Hill would reduce the sense of encroachment.[13]

Discussions about the placement of the museum needed to incorporate the conditions placed on the Henry Hill tract in the 1938 deed of conveyance. In this document, the Manassas Battlefield Confederate Park, Inc., in accordance with the wishes of the Sons of Confederate Veterans, required that the Park Service erect a museum and suitable historical markers and monuments "upon the historical spots" of the conveyed land to the memory of both the Southern and Northern soldiers. Historic markers and monuments had to display the "strictest accuracy and fairness" and not detract from the "glory due the Confederate heroes." In addition, the Confederate organization required that a historic marker be erected "near the 'Henry House' or at or near the main entrance to this property" which recognized the donation of land made by the Sons of Confederate Veterans. Underlying all of these requirements was the goal to make the battlefield park a real memorial to the soldiers, and these conditions defined the location and intent of the park museum.[14]

Architectural plans proceeded from the initial discussions of the space requirements and location for the visitor building. For the exterior, planners envisioned a fairly simple design evoking the antebellum period using stone instead of brick. Space allocation included first-floor visitor contact and exhibit areas, administrative offices, and a library; second-story storage and work rooms; and basement storage and heating plant facilities. Some discussion ensued concerning adding an observation platform on the second floor, which would allow visitors a "full panoramic view" of the First Manassas battlefield. While the Park Service believed a battlefield over-

Fig. 4. The museum-administration building has served as the principal contact station between National Park Service personnel and park visitors since its construction in 1942, providing exhibits describing key events of the two Manassas battles. (National Park Service photo)

look was "a most vital part" of the interpretive program, the location of the museum building itself offered a more promising alternative than adding a balcony that would radically change the character of the proposed building.[15]

Construction of the administration-museum building began in June 1941. Southeastern Construction Company of Charlotte, North Carolina, won the contract to build the two-story main building in native brownstone with a classically inspired portico. A single-story museum wing of cinderblock construction with stucco extended perpendicularly from the east side of the building. The Park Service paid $55,000 for construction of the building, while the New Deal's Emergency Relief Administration provided funds for the road to the museum. In accordance with the 1938 deed of conveyance for the Henry Hill tract, the Park Service placed a plaque inside the museum lobby that recognized the significance of the Sons of Confederate Veterans' land gift to the federal government. In February 1942 Superintendent Taylor and temporary exhibits moved into the new quarters.[16]

Early Interpretive Efforts

To facilitate decisions on the size and shape of the museum building, Hanson prepared a preliminary museum development plan in 1939. This outline, written before the national battlefield park had been officially designated, embodies the original design work for the proposed 10,000-acre Bull Run Recreational Demonstration Area project. Although not implemented, the museum plan still warrants careful examination because it reflects ideas of what the museum and the national park should provide visitors.

The interpretive focus rested on the two battles fought within the intended park boundaries. Devices for explaining strategies employed by the Union and Confederate armies, the tactical movements used by individual commanders, and the resulting losses sustained and victories won by the opposing sides were key to the museum's interpretive program. Placing a context around these central points was also important, so that visitors understood the Manassas battles within the overall Civil War experience.[17]

Additional factors, such as expected visitation, overall park interpretive program, and coordination with other area museums, influenced the particular subjects and level of detail for the display cases and panels. Hanson noted that the park's location along a main highway in a populous region close to the nation's capital would attract motorists who might stop on their way to other destinations. These casual visitors, whom Hanson considered the largest proportion of park users, demanded a "compact, simple, colorful digest" of the battle stories, which they could read and understand within two hours, the projected average stay for this group. For the smaller numbers of visitors with special interests in Civil War campaigns or in relatives who may have fought at Manassas, Hanson envisioned more individual contact with Park Service representatives.[18]

Interpretation at the Manassas National Battlefield Park museum com-

plemented information services planned throughout the park and at neighboring national parks. The land itself where the North and South had
battled provided an important educational tool that distinguished the park
from any other resource or museum, and the Park Service intended to have
a number of programs centering on the land. Using historical markers, visitors could take a self-guided battlefield tour. Projected to total fifteen to
twenty miles with large portions over one-way dirt roads in the park, the
route would cover both battles and fortifications located near Centreville.
Historians assigned to five planned contact stations located at strategic
points around the park would direct travelers and answer questions. Groups
making special requests could take guided tours. The Park Service also expected to coordinate museum displays at Fredericksburg and other parks
so that visitors could draw parallels and not see duplicated information.[19]

In consideration of these factors, Hanson suggested building a museum
that would hold about thirty separate exhibits grouped together in four
main subject areas: the geographical setting of the battles, First Manassas,
Second Manassas, and the war in northern Virginia. Displays of weapons or
uniforms would carefully connect the items to the larger interpretive story
and so avoid the appearance of being merely relic cases. Maps, including
animated and relief, along with panels and a diorama would enliven the
presentation and encapsulate an array of complex information. A room
with a projector and lecture space would allow for group presentations.[20]

With its heavy concentration on troop movements, the museum plan devoted little attention to the social and economic aspects of the Manassas
battles. Hanson proposed two exhibits describing small prosperous plantations in northern Virginia before and after the war, showing the absence of
men, destruction of crops, and the commandeering of livestock. Hanson did
not address other questions about the effects of the battles on the slave populations and white women and children living on the plantations, subjects
that gained increased public attention as a result of social movements in
the 1960s. The National Park Service expected to attract white visitors interested in the battles themselves and thus directed its story to this audience.[21]

Causes of the Civil War also did not find expression in the museum plan.
While contemporary historiography had addressed issues such as the polarization of North and South over slavery, states' rights, economic considerations, and international relations, the Park Service chose to focus on military maneuvers. In this way, the federal government did not antagonize its
northern and southern visitors by discussing contentious issues.[22]

Visitor Services During World War II

When the administration-museum building opened in 1942, the Park Service set up temporary display areas that reflected the intent of Hanson's 1939 prospectus but on a smaller scale. Four large dust-proof and fluorescent-lit exhibit cases displayed relics collected from the nearby fields. Troop position and combat maps described both Manassas battles, while numerous photographs and engravings of wartime scenes provided visitors with a sense of the historical setting. Park personnel expected to incorporate relevant parts of the temporary displays into the ultimate museum plan, which did not materialize until after World War II.[23]

World War II interrupted both general administrative activities and interpretive programs at the Manassas National Battlefield Park. In April 1942 Hanson replaced Taylor, who had joined the U.S. Army, first as acting superintendent and later as custodian. Originally from South Dakota, Hanson had served in the American Expeditionary Forces in Europe during World War I and later wrote a history of the American combat divisions for the *Stars and Stripes*. Hanson also published histories on South Dakota and the conflicts between whites and the Plains Indians of the mid-1860s, and he had a personal interest in the Civil War since his grandfather had served as an officer in the Union army. He joined the National Park Service as a historian in the mid-1930s, where he applied his historical research and writing experience to Manassas under the recreational demonstration area program. As superintendent, he continued to devise interpretive activities based on his extensive knowledge of the Manassas battles.[24]

Gas rationing and other wartime restrictions contributed to a sharp drop in park visitation by civilians. In May 1942 Hanson remarked that visitation had dropped noticeably as a result of the war. The numbers remained low throughout the early 1940s and did not rebound until after V-J Day. Visitation between September 1944 and 1945 more than doubled when the war ended. This dramatic increase in travel to Manassas reflected a larger trend; national park sites became the vacation destination of millions of Americans in the post–World War II years.[25]

The composition of visitors also changed dramatically with the start of the war as officers from local military camps replaced tourists and local families. During the 1943 fiscal year, more than 10,000 military personnel in comparison to an estimated 2,300 civilians visited the park. The graduating classes from the Marine Corps base at Quantico and the Army base at

Fort Belvoir, both located within thirty miles of Manassas, composed the greatest number of visitors. The Virginia Protective Force and the Virginia Reserve Militia also made regular stops at the park.

Military personnel used their park visits for several purposes. The Virginia Protective Force and Reserves conducted overnight bivouacs and infantry maneuvers, while the classes from Quantico and Fort Belvoir worked on tactical problems and carried out minor maneuvers. Hanson provided each group with guided tours of the museum and lectures on the two Civil War battles. In June 1943 the 11th Battalion of the Virginia Protective Force conducted a program of intensive infantry training at Manassas without motorized transportation, which included cross-country marching and patrol along with outpost and combat exercises. The battalion then held a review on Chinn Ridge.[26]

As had been the case with Taylor, Hanson served as the sole contact person at the park. He greeted visitors at the museum and directed them on routes to explore the battlefields. Because he could not go out and walk the land with each visitor, he devised interpretive aids for use out on the field. He replaced the illegible self-guided tour markers that Taylor had erected in 1940 with new signs in the Henry Hill area to explain the important historical and tactical points of First Manassas. Each marker consisted of a case that held a small guide map of the field, a list of all the markers, directions for the tour, and descriptive text for the particular locale. Many of the cases also contained a reproduction of a pertinent drawing or photograph from the Civil War. Hanson prepared all the texts and accompanying materials; park laborer Douglas Leonard built the wooden cases with glass tops. By June 1945 Hanson placed another case near the museum's observation terrace containing five maps showing the topography of the battlefields and troop movements for First and Second Manassas. These maps, sketched by Hanson and painted on masonite by his wife in 1939, had served as visual aids for lectures.[27]

For Second Manassas, Hanson tried to provide specialized interpretive services for knowledgeable visitors interested in the finer details of the campaigns. In March 1945 he completed a troop position map that overlaid a property map, showing the relation of the Civil War battles to the current park boundary lines. He then had two electroplates done to show the first, intermediate, and final positions of the Union and Confederate armies during the decisive last day of the second battle. Hanson also considered erecting markers in the area between Sudley Church and Groveton, which was the scene of the greater part of Second Manassas, but concluded that this idea was impracticable, probably recognizing his own limitations in time and the fact that the Park Service did not own any of the nearby land.[28]

Hanson remained sensitive to the historical significance of the Manassas battles to twentieth-century Americans. In recognition of the losses suffered during World War II, he posted comparative statistics on these casualties and those of the Union and Confederate armies in Second Manassas. Visitors showed a "surprising amount of interest" in these displays. He also compared the "moral expediency" of preserving Manassas with the World War II battlefields. The Civil War battlefield park landscape supplied the same "spiritual dividends" for park visitors to take home as the World War II battlefields did for soldiers who later returned to them. These connections between past and present made places like Manassas National Battlefield Park important and helped later visitors understand their heritage.[29]

Chapter 4

PARK ADDITIONS

The construction boom that northern Virginia and the town of Manassas experienced beginning in the late 1940s demonstrated that historically significant lands excluded from the initial park boundaries were threatened. Park superintendents responded by identifying the most important areas and canvassing a variety of agencies to obtain these lands. Their efforts led to the passage of boundary legislation, which added 1,400 acres to the existing park.

The superintendents focused on lands that had been listed as high-priority acquisitions for the battlefield park; they did not involve themselves in developments on nearby lands that failed to meet this test of historic significance. Lacking funds for obtaining historic lands, the Park Service sought assistance from any friendly source. In many ways, the NPS displayed creativity and diligence by asking for help from states, private individuals, organizations, and even the developers themselves. Park Service representatives found many friends of preservation, reflective of an interest in the post–World War II era to capture and retell the past. The Service's ability to communicate effectively with all parties resulted in the successful expansion of the battlefield park. And, while adding to the park's boundaries, the early superintendents also made sure that visitors had a proper orientation about the landscape's historic significance.[1]

New York Monuments

A high-priority area for acquisition included the site of the New York monuments. Raleigh C. Taylor contacted the state of New York, which owned the monuments and the land they rested on, and owners of some of the surrounding lands to suggest that the National Park Service obtain ownership. As had been the case for the Bull Run monuments at Henry Hill and Groveton, by 1940 the New York monuments had fallen into a state of disrepair. Taylor stressed that the Park Service would provide the expertise and commitment to address their threatened condition.[2]

Hanson continued the boundary expansion effort by staying in touch with the landowners and the state of New York. He served as a conduit for the National Park Service to relay its interest in acquiring the monuments and lands and remained apprised of any potentially disruptive actions taken by the owners. An increasingly pressing concern was the fear that present owners would allow residential developments on these historically significant lands. Hanson noted that in 1944 a Confederate earthwork near Centreville, Virginia, was destroyed during commercial development, and he wondered if a similar fate awaited tracts closer to the park.[3]

Soon after the end of World War II, Hanson's fears became reality when John T. Hottel, who had recently bought the lands adjacent to the New York monuments, initiated plans to sell suburban home lots. By 1947 three parties had purchased a total of thirty-seven acres and had begun building houses. In response to Hanson's urgings to secure the remaining land before further disruptions of the historic scene occurred, the underfunded National Park Service advised him to research the record and valuation data for the lands under consideration. Not content with such limited action, Hanson had the land appraised. He then proceeded to negotiate a six-month option with Hottel to sell a portion of the land to the Park Service for $14,000. This option ran out before the Park Service obtained the necessary funding to act, and the Hottel tract remained in private hands when Hanson retired from the National Park Service on 31 December 1947.[4]

Lacking the funding to buy the Hottel property, the Park Service shifted its attention to the state of New York. In 1949 Assistant Director Conrad Wirth informed James Evans, director of the New York state parks, of gates rusting, monuments falling apart, and the constant threat of vandalism. United States Senator Irving McNeil Ives from New York confirmed from firsthand knowledge the "unprotected" and "uncared for" status of the monuments. He urged the state to take action in reverence of the many New Yorkers who had died on that land during Second Manassas.[5]

Prompted by these appeals, the New York state legislature passed and on 10 April 1950 the governor signed into law an act authorizing donation of the three monuments to the federal government for inclusion in the Manassas National Battlefield Park. Although pleased with this step, the Park Service had to delay transfer of the parcels, which were not contiguous with the park's boundary, until sufficient lands were acquired to protect them properly. The state agreed to this request and sent Evans to Virginia to determine the next best course of action.[6]

Evans, "quite distressed" by the "deplorable" condition of the monuments, agreed that the state should acquire lands around the monuments and transfer them to the federal government. The governor of New York shared this concern, wondering "how the hell" the monuments had reached such a state of disrepair. To determine the value of the lands, James B. Myers, a specialist in the military history of the Civil War who replaced Hanson as the battlefield park's third superintendent, provided the New York state legislature in September 1950 with a report on a series of land appraisals. Despite heavy support from the governor, tight budget constraints in 1951 kept the New York Assembly Ways and Means Committee from approving the required funds, and the issue waited another year.[7]

Evans, his department of state parks, and the New York state land office continued to seek ways to address the abandoned New York monuments. They found $1,500 in the budget to hire a contractor in fall 1951 to clean up the small plots of land and repair the monuments and their surrounding gates and fences. In February 1952 the New York state legislature reconsidered the issue and appropriated $49,470 for acquiring approximately 160 acres. The Park Service obtained the funds in early August.[8]

As the Park Service began negotiating options to buy these lands, it discovered that the trickle of development that had begun in the late 1940s had swelled. Wirth, now director, informed Evans in May 1952 that four acres originally earmarked for inclusion in the battlefield park had since been purchased and a motel planned for the site. Wirth also noted that local publicity on the New York appropriation had sparked a "certain restlessness" among landowners, making the Park Service anxious to finalize the process.[9]

Further evidence of increased building became visible. Nearby armed service installations prompted "enormous housing programs" around the town of Manassas, while a steady flow of house seekers drew attention to the lands the Park Service hoped to acquire. As demand rose, prices increased accordingly. By early 1953 the Park Service needed the full $49,470 to buy four tracts, and it estimated that another $60,000 to $70,000 would be needed to purchase the remaining properties identified under the state appropriation. Without further funding available from the state, the Park

Service waited until Department of the Interior land acquisition funds came available in subsequent years.[10]

Historic Houses

As Hanson and Myers addressed land acquisition issues around the New York monuments, they also worked to incorporate the Dogan House and the Stone House into the Manassas National Battlefield Park. Rated second only to the Henry Hill area for purchase in the Bull Run Recreational Demonstration Area's 1937 report on proposed boundaries and areas, the modest one-story Dogan House, constructed of hand-hewn logs covered with weatherboarding, was mute witness to the most bitter fighting during the Second Battle of Manassas. Built before the Civil War, its original structure offered a more direct link to the war than the Henry House, all of which had been rebuilt following the battles.[11]

Recognizing the shortage of funds in the Park Service for acquiring the Dogan House, Hanson displayed ingenuity by working directly with the owners and local area businesses to preserve the building and eventually annex it to the park. He contacted the park committee of the Prince William County Chamber of Commerce and proposed the idea of the chamber buying the house and donating it to the federal government. A local engineer and architect assessed the extent of damage to the house, which suffered from a badly perforated roof that allowed water to enter and decay the interior of the building. Hanson also talked with William H. Dogan, the current owner of the house, and found Dogan congenial to the idea of selling the property for a nominal fee, with the stipulation that the house would go to the battlefield park. Dogan appreciated the historical significance of the structure enough to disregard the lot's high potential commercial value, since it sat at the crossroads of State Highway 622 and Lee Highway. In September 1947 the chamber of commerce purchased the Dogan House, and the retiring Hanson urged the Park Service to continue his work in securing its donation.[12]

The Park Service did not have the funding for repairs, and Superintendent Myers feared criticism from the local community if the federal government allowed the structure to disintegrate. Therefore, the federal government delayed acceptance of the Dogan House from the Prince William

Fig. 5. At the urging of Park Superintendent Joseph Mills Hanson, the Prince William County Chamber of Commerce purchased and completed a rough stabilization of the Dogan House, which had sustained bitter fighting during the Second Battle of Manassas, before donating it to the park in 1948. (National Park Service photo)

County Chamber of Commerce to encourage this organization to complete the necessary repairs to the structure. The chamber of commerce completed a rough stabilization of the Dogan House by fall 1948, installing an asphalt covered paper roof and repairing the walls and foundation. Official transfer of the property was completed just five days before a special 27 August program commemorating the Second Battle of Manassas.[13]

Hanson also laid the groundwork for the acquisition of the Stone House. A solidly constructed two-and-a-half-story structure of reddish brown native stone with a gabled roof, the Stone House has remained a conspicuous landmark at the crossroads of State Highway 234 and Lee Highway. Frequently represented on Civil War–era maps of the battlefield areas, it served as a military field hospital during both Manassas battles. Although considered a key property for its interpretive significance, the Park Service had not placed a high priority on its acquisition because its owner, George H. Ayres, had been friendly toward the park. Upon Ayres's death in May 1947, Hanson determined that Ayres's heirs would need to sell the property for financial reasons, jeopardizing preservation of the building.[14]

Hanson turned to the Virginia General Assembly for support, urging it to appropriate funds for the park's acquisition of the Stone House. Just before his retirement from the Park Service, Hanson and two members of the Prince William County Chamber of Commerce "laid the wires" with the county's two state representatives for obtaining $15,000 from the state. With this backing and the support of the chamber, the self-appointed committee, with Hanson as its spokesperson, went to Richmond to lobby the governor. Feeling ambitious, they proposed a state appropriation of $25,000, which the governor viewed favorably. They were equally successful in presenting their case before the full appropriations committee. In March the assembly agreed to the lesser amount of $17,000, the result of bartering for other projects but still above what Hanson had originally sought.[15]

Supporters of the Stone House acquisition continued to look for funds. Hanson tried to obtain $5,500 in private donations from the local community, but this effort failed. Instead, the Park Service sought authorization to spend Interior Department funds on Manassas. When first considering this idea in 1947, Acting Director Hillory Tolson expressed the opinion that the Park Service could not use the Interior funds because the park had been created under authority of the Historic Sites Act and its legislation did not provide for the eventual inclusion of other properties. Associate Director Arthur Demaray disagreed with Tolson's assessment, noting that the Stone House property had been included in the proposed boundaries of the Bull Run Recreational Demonstration Area. In addition, the Bull Run project was listed in a series of presidentially approved land utilization projects conducted by the Resettlement Administration and later the National Park Service. In light of these circumstances, Demaray felt justified in using Department of the Interior funding, which came available in 1949.[16]

Complications arose when the Park Service obtained three appraisals in 1948, the highest of which valued the property at $35,695, or $14,000 below an October 1947 appraisal requested by the owners. Mrs. Ayres agreed to average these two values and signed an option in June 1948 to sell the property to the United States for $42,597. Since the asking price was more than 5 percent higher than the Park Service appraisal, the secretary of the interior had to approve the purchase, which he did in August. On 17 June 1949, with the $17,000 provided by the state of Virginia and the balance from

Fig. 6. An appropriation from the Commonwealth of Virginia aided the Park Service in its 1949 acquisition of the Stone House, which was later renovated to display its use as a Civil War hospital following both Manassas battles. (National Park Service photo)

the Department of Interior, the Stone House and associated sixty-six acres transferred to the battlefield park.[17]

The following year, the Park Service initiated an extensive renovation and modernization program at the Stone House. Contracted out for $6,500, the project involved reroofing the structure and installing new electrical and plumbing systems. When this work was completed, the Park Service used the building as a residence for park employees.[18]

The Chinn House, already located inside the park's boundaries, was not so successfully restored. In the first year of the national battlefield park's existence, the relief workers who remained under the recreational demonstration area program had removed the Chinn House's weatherboarding as the initial step in its rehabilitation. With the disbandment of this group of workers in June 1941 and the United States' entry into World War II six months later, Park Service protection of this structure became negligible. Lack of personnel and funding precluded any full-scale restoration effort, so the Service covered the building with tar paper. Exposure to the elements destroyed the tar paper and left the underlying structure exposed. High winds eventually ripped off a portion of the tin roof.[19]

Benign neglect of the Chinn House aroused concern among local residents and forced the Park Service to address the house's deteriorated condition. By 1948 people in the community had shown their active support for historic preservation in the case of the Dogan House and looked to the Park Service to follow suit in protecting resources already under its care. National Park Service historian Francis Wilshin, who was stationed at Fredericksburg and later became superintendent at Manassas, recognized this concern and advised park superintendent Myers that demolition of the building, an idea then under consideration, would "have an adverse effect" on Manassas residents. Still, the Park Service failed to act until early 1950 when inspection revealed that the building constituted a serious safety hazard. By then restoration was no longer an option, so the Service removed the wood framing and left the two chimneys. Within days, severe winds destroyed the east chimney. Knowing that the west chimney would not withstand continued exposure to the elements, the Park Service leveled the structure and capped the chimneys at their foundations.[20]

The Chinn House has since been viewed as the single greatest preservation loss on the Manassas battlefields. Before the acquisition of the Dogan and Stone houses, it had been the only original wartime structure standing within the park's boundaries. An imposing building with architecturally distinctive chimneys, it had featured prominently in both battles and had served twice as a field hospital. Longtime neighbors of the park remember the historic house. Some occasionally point to its fate as an example of the Park Service's failure to meet its mandate. Its story serves as a reminder of the risks involved when park management fails to act forthrightly in preserving its resources.[21]

Permanent Museum Exhibits

Concurrent with attempts to acquire the historic Dogan and Stone houses, Hanson revised his 1939 museum plan in preparation for erecting permanent displays. Work on museum exhibits had stalled during World War II, but by summer 1946, the National Park Service had allocated almost $15,000 for designing and assembling the interpretive sections of the museum. Francis Wilshin, a staff historian at Fredericksburg, assisted Hanson with this effort. The exhibits that eventually graced the museum tied directly to the battlefields themselves, explaining for visitors how such structures as the Stonewall Jackson statue and Henry House are connected to the Civil War events.[22]

Hanson and Wilshin drew on their considerable expertise in their museum prospectus. They divided the task so that Hanson wrote about the historical events surrounding the Civil War battles and the current park interpretive program, especially the self-guided tours and how to improve them. Wilshin drafted the voluminous section—totaling almost 150 pages—on the park museum itself and discussed the different exhibits that he and Hanson envisioned. Wilshin also provided an extensive bibliography to serve as a reference for checking the historical accuracy of any details that might surface as the Park Service developed the displays.[23]

The museum exhibits that Hanson and Wilshin proposed in 1947 reflected in many ways the preliminary museum development plan that Hanson had written in 1939 for the Bull Run Recreational Demonstration Area. Both plans outlined the significant campaigns of First and Second Manassas, noting the important commanders involved and the decisive battle tactics they employed. In both plans Hanson suggested using a large relief map to indicate the changing terrain and how it influenced the movements of troops. Both plans also called for relic cases to show such items as the types of weapons used and the confusing array of uniforms worn by both sides. Neither plan ventured far in subject from the Civil War battles themselves, allowing visitors to draw their own conclusions about the long-term results of the war.[24]

In keeping with the 1939 plan, Hanson and Wilshin geared their exhibits to casual visitors who stopped at the Manassas National Battlefield Park while touring the metropolitan Washington area. These visitors needed a quick digest of the battles to supplement sometimes sketchy knowledge of the Civil War and to appreciate the significance of the Manassas encounters in the larger context of American history. As Wilshin remembered later, he used illustrations, artifacts, and contemporary newspaper accounts in the museum exhibits so that visitors got a feel for the story. A proposed diorama in the museum would show the moment during the First Battle of Manassas when Stonewall Jackson obtained his famous nom de guerre and would

Fig. 7. The 1949 museum displays, including the diorama illustrating the moment when Brig. Gen. Thomas J. Jackson received his famous nom de guerre, gave park visitors important background information that they then used to explore the battlefield. (National Park Service photo)

connect the statue to the actual events and make them real. Armed with this background information, visitors could better appreciate the tour of Henry Hill and other sections of the park.[25]

Park Service personnel introduced some significant modifications to Hanson's and Wilshin's museum plan that incorporated newer technologies and methods. These changes included an electric perspective map of the theater of war in northern Virginia and moving the proposed diorama to a less prominent position in the museum. Hanson questioned the use of the electric map because the benefits of its novelty would be contradicted by its expense, limited point of view, and complicated nature. Relief maps allowed greater freedom for speakers to describe tactics, in his opinion. Hanson wanted the diorama to remain situated in a central location of the main museum room, next to the relief map, to provide viewers with an understanding of the geography of the area. Other details, such as the use of a large display area to compare the magnitude of the Civil War with World Wars I and II, seemed to Hanson to use too much of the museum space for a concept that could be visualized relatively simply.[26]

Hanson and Wilshin checked the historical accuracy of the exhibits as museum laboratory personnel at Ford's Theater and Fort Hunt translated their ideas into tangible displays. The two historians conducted field studies to determine the orientation point for the diorama, and they expressed concern when the first artist's conceptions failed to include the proper numbers of troops or an accurate rendering of the terrain. Their interpretation of the source material did not serve as final authority, though. Ronald Lee, as chief of the History Division, differed with Wilshin on the level of artillery fire and position of troops for the diorama, and Lee's interpretation took precedence. Following Hanson's retirement, Wilshin continued to provide historical assistance, checking the accuracy of wall text and suggesting items for inclusion in the cases.[27]

Construction of the wall cases for the exhibits began in January 1949, and the museum opened to the public on Memorial Day weekend. Thanks to good publicity in the Sunday editions of the Washington and Baltimore papers and excellent weather, Superintendent Myers found the park "inundated" with visitors who left "highly complimentary" comments in the guest register. Local officials, impressed with the exhibits, instructed the Prince William County schools to have all students above third grade tour the park museum before school closed for the summer. The first bus load of high school students arrived on 31 May.[28]

Instead of crowding floor space with exhibits, the Park Service used wall cases containing explanatory text, illustrations, and artifacts. This arrangement allowed visitors the opportunity to view panels of interest to them, gain important background information, and then explore the battlefields. The first room off the administration building lobby focused on the overall causes of the Civil War and key events during First Manassas, while the smaller second room contained the electric perspective map and room for a projector and lecturing space. Colorful panels compared the textbook tactics commanders had been trained to use and the troop movements during the First Battle of Manassas. Portraits of significant actors in the battles, including Robert E. Lee and Stonewall Jackson, and personal memorabilia of Generals James B. Ricketts and Fitz John Porter provided a human side to the history. Guns, swords, and uniforms gave evidence of the implements

Fig. 8. Superintendent Joseph Mills Hanson and Park Service historian Francis Wilshin incorporated portraits of significant actors in the battles and the weapons they had used into the 1949 museum displays to give park visitors an understanding of the human side of the Civil War. (National Park Service photo)

soldiers used in the battles. The electric map and the diorama, the latter much reduced in size from Hanson's and Wilshin's original plan, placed the exhibit artifacts in the larger setting of the northern Virginia terrain.[29]

1954 Boundary Legislation

Interpretive activities at the museum could succeed only if the park itself remained a viable entity containing the most historically significant properties. As the Park Service sought protection for more lands through

Fig. 9. Park historians manipulated the light switches of the electric map to illustrate troop movements in the Northern Virginia Theater of the Civil War for school groups and other park visitors. (National Park Service photo)

acquisition, it saw the need to define the extent of the battlefield park's boundaries.

Initial discussions concerning Manassas boundary legislation proceeded from early attempts to purchase the Stone House. As Acting Director Tolson and Associate Director Demaray debated the legality of applying Interior Department funds to the Stone House acquisition, the larger concern of defining the ultimate park boundaries emerged. Demaray justified use of 1949 Interior funds for purchasing the Stone House, but he encouraged the idea of getting an act of Congress to identify further land acquisitions and fix the boundaries. Otherwise, an order of the secretary of the interior amending the original park legislation might be necessary for each addition of property. As a result, the Park Service turned to Congress for help in defining the Manassas National Battlefield Park's boundaries.[30]

Limited success in acquiring the lands around the New York monuments added greater urgency to the idea of congressional action. The Park Service used the attention generated from the spread of residential and commercial developments near the monuments and the concurrent increase in property values to urge Interior and the Bureau of the Budget to approve a proposed bill defining the park's boundaries. Further prompting came from Al Gregory, a United Press correspondent noted to have considerable interest in the Civil War, who alerted President Harry S. Truman of the need for more land at Manassas. In response to these circumstances, Interior concurred with H.R. 3297, the second of eventually five bills that defined the Manassas National Battlefield Park's boundaries.[31]

Key aspects of the Manassas boundary extension bills that elicited concern and resulted in revision or clarification included the amount of acreage to be added and the funding mechanism for purchasing the lands. House bills 5911, 3297, and 3041 allowed the addition of up to 2,500 acres while H.R. 5529, which became the final approved legislation, reduced this sum to 1,400 acres. H.R. 5911 and 3297 specified that the secretary of the interior acquire the lands by donation, purchase, or condemnation, but the final bill contained the changed phrasing to procure "in such manner" as considered in the public interest. Congress also sought assurances from the Department of the Interior that the bill would not necessitate a special appropriation of funds. Instead, the Park Service expected to acquire the lands through donations, land exchanges, or purchase using regular land acquisitions funds. The Bureau of the Budget signaled its concurrence with the boundary extension bill in February 1954. Approval of H.R. 5529 came on 17 April 1957.[32]

Public Law 338 set the boundaries for the Manassas National Battlefield Park. While the southern boundary remained fixed along the Henry Hill property, Congress extended the southwestern boundary to include the New York monuments area. The act extended the western and northwestern boundaries from the New York monuments to the Sudley Church property, following State Highway 622. The Sudley Church property remained the northern limits of the park, but the law allowed for up to 250 additional acres adjacent to the north and west boundaries, so long as the total acreage added to the park under P.L. 338 did not exceed 1,400 acres. These proposed boundaries rounded out the park and provided a mechanism for connecting scattered tracts.[33]

With the boundary legislation in hand, the Park Service continued its efforts to acquire the remaining lands around the New York monuments. Using 1954 and 1955 Department of the Interior funds, the Park Service spent $32,000 to purchase properties from Joseph Patterson and Willis Early. John Hottel had originally subdivided and sold these lots to Patterson and Early as housing tracts in 1947. In 1953 Hottel had sold a portion of his property, totaling twenty-three acres and including areas adjacent to each of the three New York monuments, for just under $12,000 to the Park Service. In November 1955 Hottel sold another five acres to the federal government, which centered on the 14th Brooklyn monument site, for $7,000. This five-acre tract commanded the significantly higher price due to its location in a commercially attractive area at the intersection of State Highway 622 and Lee Highway.[34]

The New York monuments remained under state ownership well after the acquisition of the final critical tracts. In March 1953 Secretary of the Interior Douglas McKay expressed interest in having the state of New York transfer the New York monuments to the federal government, noting the Park Service's success in obtaining funding and making substantial progress in purchasing identified lots. But final action waited until May 1957 when the state deeded the three parcels of land containing the monuments. The Park Service accepted these monuments in June 1958.[35]

Chapter 5

REENACTING THE PAST

Francis Wilshin loved to tell the story of the First Battle of Manassas. During his tenure as superintendent of the Manassas National Battlefield Park, from 1955 to 1969, he had many opportunities, big and small, to enthrall listeners with his dramatic and accurate renditions. He could quote from soldiers' letters archived in the park's library and articulate complicated events so that visitors became converts to the cause of preservation.[1]

Wilshin's devotion to the history of the Civil War stemmed from his familial connection to this event. One of his grandfathers had served in General J. E. B. Stuart's cavalry; the other had been a blockade runner. A native Virginian, Wilshin pursued his interest in Civil War and United States history, receiving a bachelor's degree from the College of William and Mary and a master's degree from Columbia University. He taught history briefly at Staunton Military Academy before joining the National Park Service in 1934 as a park historian at the Vicksburg National Military Park in Mississippi and then at the Saratoga National Historical Park in New York. Later, assigned to the Fredericksburg and Spotsylvania County Battlefields Memorial National Military Park in the 1940s, Wilshin delved into the history of First and Second Manassas and assisted Hanson with the Manassas National Battlefield Park museum displays. Through this experience, Wilshin developed an intense love in telling the story of First Manassas, to the benefit and detriment of the battlefield park.[2]

Planning for Interpretation

Wilshin's vision for educating visitors about the Manassas battles derived in part from ideas suggested by his predecessor, James Myers, who remained as superintendent until September 1955. Myers focused on expanded interpretive activities both in the administration-museum building and on the battlefields of First and Second Manassas. Having seen firsthand the phenomenal increase in park visitation following World War II—from 8,200 visitors in 1947 to more than 66,000 in 1951—without a concomitant increase in personnel, Myers devised additional ways to reach the public.[3]

In the museum, Myers pushed for two additional electric maps with an accompanying taped talk to handle the increase in the number of school groups visiting the park. The number of students touring the park had increased from fewer than fifty in 1948 to two thousand in 1951. The existing electric map of the northern Virginia theater provided a good overall picture of the events leading to the two Manassas battles, but the map failed to show the tactical details of the battles themselves due to the map's spatial limitations. To tell the Manassas story, a trained park employee, usually the superintendent, had to manipulate the switches and narrate. An audio program linked to more maps would offer greater opportunities to educate school groups and other visitors without taxing the park's limited personnel.[4]

Beyond the museum, Myers recognized that visitors needed more markers to explore the battlefield terrain on their own. The Henry Hill walking tour contained seven stops, while a separate six-stop driving tour directed visitors to the Stone House, the Sudley Church, the Stone Bridge, and the site of the Chinn House. Many spots on the driving tour did not include historical markings or had markers erected by state agencies. Recognizing the popularity of the Henry Hill tour, Myers recommended adding four stops to it and eventually integrating both the walking and driving tours into one comprehensive course.[5]

Second Manassas remained almost entirely unmarked and undeveloped. The Dogan House had the only narrative marker devoted to the second battle, thanks to a $100 donation by a visitor. A few markers on the First Manassas driving tour provided references to the second battle, but for the most part interpretive efforts for the 1862 battle remained hampered by the fact that the federal government did not own key areas, such as the Deep Cut-Groveton monument area.[6]

Until funding became available to acquire lands associated with the Second Battle of Manassas, Myers focused on developing text for a series of historical markers that would be put in place after acquisition of the lands. With guidance from the regional and Washington offices of the Park Service and assistance from NPS historian Frank B. Sarles, Myers identified nine locations for the proposed self-guided auto tour and composed the historical narratives for the markers. Areas specific to Second Manassas included Buck Hill, Groveton, and sites along the unfinished railroad.[7]

Myers's efforts to expand interpretive activities in the museum and on the self-guided tours could go only so far in accommodating the staggering increases in visitation. Assistance from a permanent historical aide, who joined the park staff in 1948, and a seasonal ranger-historian, who helped for at least two summers in the early 1950s, gave Myers more flexibility than the two previous superintendents. But on Saturdays, Myers remained the sole park employee on duty.[8]

Myers's efforts served as an immediate stopgap to the demands of surging visitation. All national park sites had become overburdened with eager tourists, and long-term planning, including interpretation and preservation, received insufficient focus. To address this worsening situation, the National Park Service adopted the Mission 66 program. This ten-year parks improvement program, slated to end on the Park Service's fiftieth anniversary in 1966, provided funding and direction for each park. At Manassas, Myers's interpretive planning became a foundation for the park's Mission 66 prospectus, which was implemented by Wilshin as the new superintendent.

Mission 66 Planning

Wilshin identified land acquisition and interpretation as the two focal points for Manassas National Battlefield Park under the Mission 66 program. The federal government owned scattered tracts mainly associated with First Manassas. By acquiring the intervening lands, the Park Service hoped to create a cohesive park with readily apparent boundaries. This approach would buffer the parklands from future outside developments. The Park Service also recognized that key tracts related to Second Manassas were needed to tell the story of this battle.

Wilshin knew that a successful interpretive program relied on incorporating these lands. First, visitors could explore more areas and obtain a fuller understanding of the significant activities associated with each battle. Second, the Park Service planned to build an internal road system linking the different sections. Visitors would then have leisurely and safe access to the chief points of historical interest without having to fight outside traffic traveling through the park. Third, the Park Service would incorporate the new lands into an improved system of trail-side markers and exhibits, as Myers had suggested.[9]

Land acquisition plans under Mission 66 focused on those tracts designated for inclusion in the 1954 boundary expansion legislation. Much of the property north of Lee Highway remained privately owned and had priority attention during Mission 66. Wilshin also pushed for two properties not identified in the 1954 legislation, namely, Battery Heights, a key artillery position of the battle of Second Manassas, and the Stone Bridge, a significant landmark in both battles. According to the 1954 legislation, the Park Service could pursue acquisition of these lands so long as the total amount did not add more than 1,400 acres to the existing park.[10]

With the addition of these areas, Wilshin could focus his attention on interpretive improvements in both the museum and around the park. For the museum-administration building, now called the visitor center, Wilshin proposed adding a wing for group presentations and orientation purposes. He also saw the need for expanding the parking lot to accommodate increased numbers of visitors and for installing the two electric maps that Myers had previously suggested. To provide greater museum exhibit space, he suggested finishing the second floor of the visitor center. Park Service officials could not justify the second-floor exhibit space, but they did approve construction of the wing and again considered building the electric maps.[11]

Within the park, Wilshin recommended a system of hard-surfaced roads with adequate parking areas to make the different historic areas of the park more accessible. Directional markers would lead visitors to these sites, and permanent narrative markers would describe the significance of each point. To augment the number of visitor contact places, Wilshin proposed rehabilitating and opening the Stone House for exhibit as a field hospital. He also suggested stabilizing the Dogan House and stationing interpretive personnel there. Ronald Lee, chief of the NPS Division of Interpretation, agreed with most of Wilshin's proposals, except staffing the Dogan House. Its proximity to the visitor center and the Stone House precluded adding another contact station there.[12]

Mindful of the value of providing the public with tangible indications of troop positions for both battles, Wilshin proposed mounting cannon and markers. He suggested that the park's library collection be bolstered to assist in the extensive research needed to establish the exact positions of key batteries. Wilshin initiated a search for cannon and quickly achieved success, obtaining seven cannon from the Chickamauga-Chattanooga and Petersburg National Military Parks in 1956. The Eastern National Park and Monument Association also provided period guns and two carriages, which were used to mark the location of James Ricketts's and Charles Griffin's Federal batteries during First Manassas.[13]

Wilshin's suggestions for Mission 66 at the Manassas battlefield park did not depart significantly from proposals offered by previous park superintendents. Myers wanted to augment the tour marker system, especially for Second Manassas. Hanson had conducted initial research on troop positions and had tried to replace temporary markers with permanent ones. Hanson had also proposed constructing a separate assembly space in the museum-administration building in his initial 1939 museum plans. In the 1930s the National Park Service had intended to build a system of roads and contact stations to assist viewers in touring the proposed 10,000-acre Bull Run Recreational Demonstration Area. Wilshin had the good fortune to serve as superintendent when enhanced funding levels made these dreams a possibility, and he incorporated them into his Mission 66 planning.[14]

Wilshin laid out an ambitious program for the battlefield park that relied on adequate funding and proper management to succeed. His anticipated land acquisition program alone would have required several hundred thousand dollars. When he pursued this funding in conferences with the regional office, he quickly learned that land money remained limited and that Manassas would have to compete with a host of other park areas for what was available. Funding levels also influenced how many narrative markers, museum displays, roads, and other interpretive aids could be built.[15]

To achieve all these Mission 66 plans, the park needed leadership capable of finding the necessary resources and guiding each of the projects to completion. Wilshin eventually overcame the funding limitations for land acquisition, and he oversaw an expansion of the visitor center with a new auditorium wing. Despite these successes, Wilshin failed to complete other significant Mission 66 projects for the park, most notably the renovation of the museum displays. His devotion to certain aspects of the Manassas battlefield story and his commitment to acting both as superintendent and

historian at the park determined which Mission 66 projects had his full
attention.

Threatening the "Very Heart" of the Park

Before Wilshin had the opportunity to delve into any of the Mission 66 projects, he had to contend with the Virginia state highway department, which
proposed to route a new interstate along Lee Highway through the middle
of the park. Wilshin recognized immediately the terrific impact the proposed interstate would have on the battlefield park. He first heard of the
state's intentions in spring 1957 when the Virginia Department of Highways
announced that a new interstate highway would run east-west from Washington, D.C., to the Shenandoah Valley, following Lee Highway in Prince
William County. Needing further information to evaluate the road's impact
on the park, Wilshin requested, and obtained, from the state highway officials a map superimposing their plans on the layout of the battlefield park.
In early March, state officials presented their proposal to a packed house in
the park's museum building.[16]

At the 12 March meeting, Wilshin, Region 1 Director Elbert Cox, and
retired superintendent Hanson learned that the new interstate would require widening Lee Highway to at least three hundred feet for the combination of the east-west lanes, median strip, side strips, and service roads.
Engineers also expected to place an interchange at Route 234, where the
Stone House stood. The resulting cloverleaf would necessitate the development of additional land at that intersection.[17]

Listening to the state's plans, Wilshin and the other National Park Service attendees knew that the interstate would do "irreparable damage to
the very heart" of the battlefield park. The widened road would make a
"major intrusion" on Henry Hill and destroy some of the historic areas near
the Stone Bridge. The Stone House frontage and the high ground where
the New York monument honoring the 14th Brooklyn Regiment stood
would be jeopardized. And how could the Park Service preserve the overall
battlefield appearance and complete its plans under Mission 66 with this
modern intrusion? Wilshin, Cox, and Hanson expressed these misgivings at
the 12 March hearing, and later Cox and Director Wirth filed formal statements asking the state to reconsider its plans.[18]

Wilshin knew that the Park Service's arguments alone would not sway the highway department. Despite the concerns raised by the NPS, state officials held firm to their proposal, "like a horse with a bit in his teeth," noting the plan's economic advantages. Fearing the worst, Wilshin resolved to act aggressively. With permission from interpretive chief Lee, Wilshin addressed the Civil War Round Table of Washington, D.C., which coincidentally met the evening of the state highway hearing. Round Tables represented local clubs of Civil War enthusiasts. Acclaimed Civil War historian Bruce Catton was the scheduled speaker, and three hundred members were in attendance. In a booming voice that echoed over the microphone system, Wilshin painted a somber picture of Manassas National Battlefield Park once the interstate had "carve[d] it up." Henry Hill would be "mutilated beyond recognition," and the monument land that the state of New York had recently donated to the National Park Service would be "completely despoil[ed]." He urged his fellow members to take a stand, like the Greeks at Thermopylae, against this threat.[19]

The response was immediate and effective. That night the D.C. Round Table adopted a resolution that protested the proposed "desecration" of Manassas National Battlefield Park and petitioned the state highway department to select an alternative route for the interstate. The D.C. Round Table sent its resolution to some eighty other Round Tables, with a total membership of about ten thousand, and various other patriotic organizations, alerting them to the danger. Round Table members and others flooded Congress and the Virginia state highway office with letters objecting to the proposed route. In a typical response, the Robert E. Lee Camp No. 726 of the Sons of Confederate Veterans of Alexandria, Virginia, lodged a complaint against any highway that would interfere with or destroy the monuments and memorials erected on the hallowed ground at Manassas.[20]

Building on this support, Wilshin adopted a publicity strategy that became his standard tactic for future battles to protect the park. He appeared before a host of civic and patriotic organizations, including the Manassas Chapter of the United Daughters of the Confederacy, the Warrenton Rotary Club, and the Manassas Historical Association. Even before the 12 March state highway meeting, he had spoken to the Manassas Chamber of Commerce, the Lions Club, and the Kiwanis Club. He obtained support from the mayor, members of the Manassas town council, and the Prince William Board of County Supervisors. Newspapers in Manassas, Washington, and Richmond printed articles and editorials informing readers of the situation. Local radio and television stations aired stories. The plight of the

Manassas battlefield park gained national attention when Chet Huntley and David Brinkley presented the story on the 24 March airing of *Outlook*.[21]

Wilshin enlisted help from everyone he met, and fortuitously he gained a lifelong ally in Anne (Annie) Delp Snyder. Snyder and her husband Waldon Peter (Pete) had bought a 180-acre cattle farm next to Manassas battlefield park following World War II. Originally from Pittsburgh, she had thought of the Civil War only as a "name in the history book" until she had a personal tour of the Manassas battlefield with Wilshin. As she later recalled, Wilshin made you feel as if you were there, seeing the soldiers and hearing their thoughts as they engaged in battle. Nothing was left to the imagination in his presentation, and Snyder walked away so awed and overwhelmed that she became an instant convert to the importance of the battlefield park.[22]

Snyder's conversion coincided with the interstate highway controversy, and Wilshin recruited her for his letter-writing campaign. It was the first campaign of many that she would embrace in connection with the Manassas battlefields. Snyder was accustomed to challenges. During World War II she had dropped out of law school and joined the first class of women to graduate from the Marine Officers Candidate School to "free a Marine to fight." She worked as a recruiter in New Orleans, convincing men that having their daughters, sisters, and wives in the Marines was not "selling [them] into prostitution." She gained sophisticated public relations skills that she honed in her future Manassas battles. She credits Wilshin with sparking her preservationist sympathies and teaching her many of the methods for accomplishing her goals.[23]

Wilshin's strategy in the interstate highway crisis proved pivotal. Inundated with letters from Civil War Round Tables as far away as England, the state highway commission quickly agreed to consider alternative routes. With continued pressure from Wilshin and his supporters, the state eventually adopted a southern route. This decision proved a happy solution to the issue because it saved the park from destruction and provided room for future highway expansion without harming the park.[24]

Surprisingly, the chairman of the Prince William Board of County Supervisors resurrected the idea of using Lee Highway for the interstate in early 1958. As Wilshin later recalled, the chairman wanted to protect two farms held by his friend William Wheeler, which would be affected by the southern routing of the interstate. In response, Director Wirth, Wilshin, and other NPS representatives together with Virginia state highway and Prince William County officials presented their case to Rep. Howard Smith, who had expressed support for widening Lee Highway. Smith had long been interested in the battlefield park, having assisted the Park Service in acquiring lands during the Bull Run Recreational Demonstration Area period and drafting the first boundary expansion bill in 1949. Wirth argued strenuously against the highway change, saying that he could "never live with it" or the idea of letting down the Round Tables and other groups who had come to the park's defense. Using troop position maps to show that the proposed area included the sites of some of the heaviest fighting in both Manassas battles, the Park Service convinced Smith to stay with the southern route.[25]

More Lands for the Park

With the battle over the routing of the interstate highway won, Wilshin still had to contend with the larger issue of land. A housing boom hit the town of Manassas in 1958, and land values steadily increased by 15 to 20 percent each year during the remainder of Wilshin's superintendency. The prospect of direct access to Washington made the area near the battlefield attractive to developers. Wilshin knew that lands designated for inclusion in the park might become prohibitively expensive if the Park Service did not act quickly. Tracts might end up part of housing developments or shopping centers, their historic landscapes buried under concrete and asphalt.[26]

Wilshin understood the value of these lands to the battlefield park, and he shared this knowledge with anyone who would listen. His modus operandi was to depict on maps troop movements during each Manassas battle, explaining that the Park Service established the relative significance of given tracts based on the official records of the war. Land acquisition plans developed from this information. Finally, as the park's interpretive program took shape, Wilshin incorporated information on battle movements and historic lands in museum displays and historical markers. In this way, Wilshin showed that the park's land acquisition program followed a thoughtful approach based on the history of the battles and alleviated fears that the Park Service wanted the lands for other purposes, such as park housing.[27]

Wilshin used every means available to him to acquire historic lands. He learned in 1957 that the owners of the Stone House Inn planned to sell their property at public auction. The inn's land adjoined the Stone House tract, which the park had purchased in 1949, and consisted of a restaurant, warehouse, and three cottages. By virtue of its proximity to the site of heavy fighting during the Civil War, the Stone House Inn was an important tract long considered for inclusion in the battlefield park. Wilshin prodded the regional and Washington offices to find the necessary $35,000 to buy the inn. National Park Service interpretive chief Ronald Lee scraped up the money, and the Stone House Inn transferred to the federal government in 1958.[28]

The experience of purchasing the Stone House Inn with miscellaneous NPS funds indicated to Wilshin that he needed a large, secure financial base to accomplish his Mission 66 land acquisition objectives. The interstate highway controversy taught him the importance of gaining allies and publicizing his efforts. He applied these lessons to the park's land program. Wilshin often gave personal tours of the battlefield, especially for congressional and other political representatives. By making contacts, Wilshin hoped to attain his goals for the park. His efforts were richly rewarded in 1958.[29]

Sen. John Stennis (D-Miss.) arrived unannounced at Manassas National Battlefield Park one day in April 1958 and accepted Wilshin's offer of a guided tour of the battlefield. Wilshin took Senator Stennis to the Stonewall Jackson statue. While looking north across Lee Highway, Stennis asked what lands the federal government actually owned. Wilshin replied that the park included "a solid block of land" south of the highway running from the Stone Bridge almost a mile and a quarter to Groveton. But, pointing to Matthews Hill behind the Stone House where Mississippi troops had fought with Confederates Barnard E. Bee, Nathan G. Evans, and Francis S. Bartow the morning of 21 July 1861, Wilshin stated, "Sir, we don't own that land." Stennis struck his fist into his hand and exclaimed, "That's not right!"

Wilshin then escorted Stennis to the high ground west of Deep Cut. He related the story of how Confederate Stephen D. Lee's artillery permitted Robert E. Lee's army to sweep the field, thus turning the tide of Second Manassas. With perfect timing, Wilshin ended with the reprise, "Sir, we don't own that land." And, Stennis returned, "That's not right!" Back in Wilshin's office, Stennis asked what lands had the highest priority, and Wilshin responded with two key areas of Second Manassas, Battery Heights and Deep Cut. Stennis wrote them down, and by the end of August he had coaxed the Senate to pass a Supplementary Appropriation Bill providing $100,000 for land acquisition at Manassas.[30]

Stennis remained committed to getting more lands at Manassas, partly

Fig. 10. Superintendent from 1955 to 1969, Francis Wilshin enthralled listeners with his retellings of the First Battle of Manassas, often gaining allies in the process who later proved crucial in opposing adverse development projects or in providing money to acquire more lands for the battlefield park. (National Park Service photo)

because some of his relatives had fought there. He and Wilshin kept up a correspondence, and the senator provided the park with some letters from his family collection relating to the battles. In 1959 Stennis returned to the funding issue and convinced Congress to appropriate $450,000 toward land acquisition at Gettysburg and Manassas.[31]

The Manassas battlefield park eventually obtained the entire sum because Congress had stipulated that the money could not be obligated until the secretary of the interior confirmed that local governments had adopted adequate zoning regulations to assure against future commercial developments in the park areas. Gettysburg did not have any zoning laws, but the Prince William Board of County Supervisors had already zoned the area surrounding Manassas battlefield park as agricultural-forestry, which was in line with the congressional requirement. The board of supervisors disapproved the proposal supporting further land acquisition for the park, but the Manassas town council had passed a resolution in April 1959 expressing its support for further land acquisition. With the proper zoning in place, the total obligation of $450,000 went to Manassas.[32]

With $550,000 available, the Park Service embarked on an extensive land purchase program at Manassas. Most of the land acquired lay north of Lee Highway, the area Wilshin had pointed out to Senator Stennis. The Stone House and the Dogan House, which had been the lone park properties on the north side of the highway, now had the protective embrace of national parkland around them. Tracts immediately along Bull Run remained privately owned, but most of the land along Route 234 to Sudley Church came into the park.[33]

Wilshin explored the possibility of using land exchanges to acquire other significant tracts, including the Stone Bridge. The Stone Bridge had served as the left anchor of the Confederate line at First Manassas and had been an avenue of Union advance and the principal avenue of Union retreat during Second Manassas. The Commonwealth of Virginia held title to the bridge and about three acres of land around it. The Park Service offered to exchange its temporary leases on roadway relocations near Sudley Church and the south boundary of the park for the Stone Bridge and its land. Virginia agreed to the proposal, but with a stipulation. The federal government had to obtain an agreement from the United Daughters of the Confederacy to transfer to the Park Service a monument the organization had erected on the bridge.[34]

Wilshin faced a delicate situation when he approached Isabel Hutchison, the president of the UDC chapter in Manassas, about the Confederate monument on the Stone Bridge. He wanted the bridge, but the monument represented an intrusion on the historic scene. So he had to convince Miss Hutchison, a devoted Confederate, to agree to the transfer and demolition of her organization's memorial. He had already established friendly relations with her chapter by assisting in First Manassas anniversary ceremonies, so he built on that relationship. He showed her Civil War–era photographs of the bridge to indicate its original appearance and explained its significance to the battles. He then argued that transfer of the bridge and removal of the monument would "further the cause of her dear Confederacy" by restoring the historic appearance of the Stone Bridge. Miss Hutchison and her chapter agreed to Wilshin's proposal, and the Stone Bridge came into the park in 1961.[35]

The Park Service sometimes acquired lands under less friendly circumstances. The federal government, anxious to consolidate its holdings in Manassas now that it had the money and the impetus provided by Mission 66, resorted to a process known as a declaration of taking to condemn property that landowners refused to sell. Government officials also used this procedure if a property owner threatened the historic features of property that had been designated for inclusion in a park. In response to a refusal to sell land associated with Battery Heights, the Park Service chose to use a declaration of taking against the Steele family, who owned one tract of this historic scene, and Luther Tinsley and Virginia Huffman, who owned one of the other tracts.[36]

As one longtime neighbor of the park remembers, Arthur and Rosalie Steele had built a nice house on their property in anticipation of retiring there. They had no children, and they intended to will their tract to the Park Service, but they wanted to spend their last years on their land. The Park Service did not want to accept this condition and proceeded with a declaration of taking. The United States District Court ruled on the price for the settlement, based on an assessment of the land, and the Park Service accepted the land in October 1960. The rest of Battery Heights transferred to the Manassas National Battlefield Park in 1962.[37]

Land condemnation antagonized relations between the battlefield park and its neighbors. People like the Steeles, who had either grown up on these lands or spent most of their adult lives there, wanted to decide for themselves when to leave, not be removed forcibly by the government. In the case of the Steele property, the Park Service exacerbated the situation by turning the Steeles' retirement home into park housing. Further conflicts occurred because land acquisition plans remained confidential to avoid driving up prices. But landowners never knew for sure if their property, which may have been within the designated park boundaries, was on the list for immediate acquisition. This situation increased tension and drove rumors of massive land buying by the government.[38]

Wilshin tried to alleviate residents' fears. He met with them and explained why certain tracts merited inclusion in the park, and he stressed that the Park Service intended to limit its purchases to ground essential to park interpretation. These efforts settled some of the wilder rumors, but the park continued to have opponents within the local community because of its land acquisition dealings, lasting for decades.[39]

Planning the Reenactment

In late 1958 Wilshin and fellow Civil War enthusiasts in the local community conceived the idea of staging a reenactment to mark the one hundredth anniversary of the First Battle of Manassas. This reenactment was only one of many programs around the country sponsored by the national Civil War Centennial Commission and various state organizations to commemorate the events of 1861–65. President Dwight D. Eisenhower and Congress encouraged these tributes, but local communities and private organizations did most of the work for the centennial. Companies like Sinclair Oil Company tied their product promotions to specific commemorations and helped inform Americans about the centennial.[40]

National interest helped keep Wilshin and other supporters committed to the idea of a reenactment. In early 1960 they established a nonprofit agency dedicated to producing the reenactment. First Manassas Corporation, Incorporated, gained early support when the governor of Virginia, the Virginia Civil War Centennial Commission, and the counties of Prince William and Fairfax contributed $50,000. Adding further impetus to their plans, organizers hired Maj. Gen. James C. Fry (Ret.) to serve in a full-time capacity as executive director of the corporation.[41]

Planning for the reenactment accelerated once the First Manassas Corporation became a reality. Wilshin completed an advance plan for the event in February 1960, in which he proposed staging the intense artillery fight on Henry Hill during which Jackson acquired his nom de guerre. Wilshin provided cost estimates and ideas on where to find the needed cannons and individuals for the event. Two months later, the First Manassas Corporation released a more formal prospectus to generate interest in the reenactment and, it was hoped, drum up further financial support. By the end of summer, the corporation had obligated considerable sums of money and had arranged for national and international advertising.[42]

National Park Service involvement in the reenactment developed gradually. Wilshin remained active in the First Manassas Corporation as a director, and his participation gave the appearance, at least, of Park Service support for the corporation's activities. As the First Manassas Corporation made further commitments toward staging the reenactment, Park Service personnel slowly realized that the battlefield park and its caretaker, the federal government, had unofficially blessed the event. This relationship was formally acknowledged in May 1961 when the National Park Service entered into a cooperative agreement with the corporation.[43]

Under the agreement's terms, the First Manassas Corporation would provide the facilities and services necessary "to produce and present the historical pageant" of First Manassas. These conveniences included adequate seating and sanitary facilities for the expected crowds. The agreement required that parking and shuttlebus services be provided to accommodate the expected crowds. The Park Service also stipulated that the corporation make refreshments available to visitors. In return, the National Park Service agreed to provide the land for the event at no cost, with the condition that the historical character of the park be preserved. Park Service personnel would also provide technical advice.[44]

Long before the cooperative agreement was signed, Wilshin helped cement the Park Service's commitment to the reenactment. As superintendent, he made the reenactment an integral component of the park's Mission 66 program despite the fact that he had not included the reenactment in his original development planning for the park. In many ways, this decision complemented the Mission 66 goals he had set for the park. The 22 July 1961 date was a closer and more historically relevant deadline than the fiftieth National Park Service anniversary in 1966. Wilshin accelerated land acquisition and other Mission 66 projects so that they might be done in time for the reenactment.

Some Mission 66 plans, such as historic structure improvements, gained heightened attention. The Dogan House and the Stone House were valuable stage props, with the Dogan House serving as a small rural home caught in the crossfire and the Stone House representing a building forced into use as a field hospital. Exterior restoration of the Dogan House, completed between June and November 1960, involved straightening and leveling the building, replacing rotted timbers, and rebuilding the stone foundation walls. Interior work, completed in May 1961, included replacing plaster, trim, and floorboards. Planned Stone House restoration work involved repair of the foundation and masonry walls and replacement of the roof.[45]

While land acquisition and historic structure renovations proceeded on schedule, delays plagued other aspects of the park's Mission 66 program. The planned revisions to the museum displays in the visitor center and the field hospital exhibit in the Stone House were not completed until well after 1961, despite their relevance to the reenactment. The Stone House exhibit as outlined in the Mission 66 plan would explain the conditions soldiers faced when injured. The museum displays would be upgraded to provide more background information about the battles. Wilshin was interested in these interpretive displays, as evidenced by his extensive research on the Stone House and his involvement with Park Service exhibit planning teams. However, he came to rely on the reenactment for fulfilling significant interpretive plans.[46]

Instead of completing museum displays, Wilshin hoped to enhance the park's interpretive program through reenactment activities. Spectators would gain greater understanding of battlefield conditions by witnessing a historically accurate staging. Filming the event would allow later visitors to share this experience. Wilshin intended to show the resulting movie regularly in the park's visitor center. Another interpretive aid that Wilshin hoped would materialize was construction of an impressive facility to house a Civil War hall of fame at the battlefield park. As proposed by the First Manassas Corporation, this large marble building would house a library, flag hall, large rotunda, and administrative functions. Park Service Director Wirth lent his support to the hall of fame idea; however, because of funding and organizational problems associated with the reenactment, neither the film nor the hall of fame advanced beyond the planning stages.[47]

Producing the reenactment proved more difficult than Wilshin and the First Manassas Corporation had anticipated. The enterprise encountered serious financial difficulties. Individual donations and sponsorships by interested organizations augmented the $50,000 provided by the state of Virginia and local counties, and a professional fund raiser was hired to help secure financing. But these efforts did not produce the $200,000 estimated for the event, and the First Manassas Corporation came to rely on expected revenues from the actual event to cover its costs.[48]

Organizational problems compounded the financial worries. Major General Fry continued to direct the operation, but the expected full-time twelve-member staff never materialized. Instead, planning devolved to committees, which worked on a part-time, voluntary basis. Committee members often failed to coordinate their activities. The lack of overall leadership left the National Park Service committing personnel to the daily planning of the reenactment, a task the Service had assigned to the First Manassas Corporation in its cooperative agreement. Wilshin devoted his energies to the production, and in May 1961, the regional director added J. Leonard Volz as the National Park Service coordinator to assist in the final planning and preparations.[49]

The National Park Service had expected the First Manassas Corporation to address certain details early in the planning, but many crucial tasks remained incomplete as the date of the event neared. As late as 19 June, Volz warned the regional director that the corporation had not addressed the "extremely important matter" of sanitation facilities. Press relations, which

waited until "late in the game," suffered from Major General Fry's "dicta-
torial manner." The Park Service's regional publications officer had to step
in ten days before the reenactment and run interference by providing adequate parking, phone access, and press boxes because Major General Fry
had refused to make special accommodations for the press, except for *Life
Magazine* and *National Geographic*, which had made prior arrangements.[50]

Some Park Service personnel believed that the administrative difficulties
resulted in part from Wilshin's participation in the planning of the reenactment. Wilshin had a personal passion for the First Battle of Manassas, drawn
from his southern background and interest in the Confederate cause. His
enthusiasm for staging a historically correct and awe-inspiring recreation
overrode more practical considerations. For instance, he pursued the idea
of lining both sides of Lee Highway, from Fairfax to the Manassas battlefields, with the flags of the Union at the time of the Civil War. When asked
who would pay for the flags and protect them, Wilshin dismissed the query.
He talked of crowds numbering 200,000, but he could not imagine the lo-
gistical details needed to accommodate so many people. He even remarked
at one point that two latrines on Chinn Ridge would be sufficient.[51]

Reenactment organizers chose to depend on Wilshin's historical understanding of First Manassas and not on his weaker administrative skills. As
technical adviser, Wilshin prepared the script for the reenactment and provided information on the placement of troops and cannons. Volz highly
recommended Wilshin to serve as narrator during the actual production
because he could accurately and dramatically cover any delays in timing. At
times, Wilshin's command of the history put him at odds with the management of the event. He insisted that all reenactors wear authentic uniforms,
down to the style of buttons. In 1961 reenactors had not developed the
sophistication in attire and weapons that they displayed in later decades.
Requiring authenticity would have added large expenses to the already
strapped finances. Instead, Fry and others convinced Wilshin to use inex-
pensive substitutes, like standard gray pants and jackets from Sears Roebuck
and Company.[52]

First Manassas Reenactment

Administrative problems and financial worries melted away under the blaz-
ing sun and 90-degree temperatures when Manassas National Battlefield

Fig. 11. The July 1961 reenactment of the First Battle of Manassas gave spectators a rare opportunity to touch the past by hearing the sound of Civil War–era cannons and experiencing the fear and carnage of battle. National Park Service Director Conrad Wirth later determined that the potential for injury to participants and the historic resource during this restaging justified banning future reenactments on lands administered by his agency. (National Park Service photo)

Park hosted the reenactment of the First Battle during the 21 July weekend. On Friday the First Manassas Corporation staged an open dress rehearsal before an audience of 20,000 visitors and the press. Stories in the morning papers attracted another 55,000 people on Saturday and 45,000 on Sunday. A number arrived in period costumes, reminiscent of the audience that had traveled from as far as Centreville on that July day in 1861 to witness the first "skirmish" of the war.[53]

For Wilshin, the reenactment was a very exciting thing. He long remembered the feeling of being right in the battle, with bombs going off and dirt flying around the charging men. The sight of the battle flags and the sounds of the men yelling gave a real sense of the actual battle experience. Timing of the attacks and counterattacks sometimes varied from the script, but the general effect was so close to the original that viewers experienced the fear, the excitement, the carnage of First Manassas.[54]

The zeal of the reenactors added to the drama. Many belonged to the North-South Skirmish Association, a national organization that represented units of both the North and South and was dedicated to the preservation of the history and spirit of the Civil War. As the skirmishers assembled in mass formations, attacked over open ground, and fired point blank at each other, the audience gained a real sense of battle conditions. The sound of cannons and the crack of a Civil War musket provided a rare opportunity for everyone to touch the past. As Wilshin fondly recalled, some reenactors were so interested in being part of the action that they were unwilling to play dead but got up and reentered the fray.[55]

Spectators and some of the press responded warmly to the show. One viewer noted that the reenactment allowed a greater visualization of history than "cold stone monuments or words on paper" do. The audience was caught up in the reenactment toward the end of the production. At the point late in the battle when Confederate forces pushed Union forces off Henry Hill and into retreat, "sustained rebel yells" erupted from the mostly southern audience. Newspapers took this spontaneous show of support for the South as indicative of a larger involvement in the nation's past. Accounts emphasized the sense of national unity that the reenactment drove home. People had the chance to see the sacrifices Americans had made to defend deeply held beliefs, both for the North and the South.[56]

This enthusiasm from participants and spectators for the reenactment made assessing the value of the event difficult. In his opening remarks for the 22 July presentation, Director Wirth welcomed the reenactment as a way to "visit the inspiring scenes of the past" and gain "strength, imagination, and wisdom" to prepare for the future. Wirth recognized the educational benefits the reenactment and proposed film provided the public, but he also saw the effort, expense, and hazards inherent in the production. The National Park Service had paid a heavy cost in terms of personnel time to supervise the event and in direct outlays, such as $10,000 for sanitary facilities. The potential for serious injuries or damage to the battlefield remained a concern. Some resource damage to the historic lands included Chinn Ridge, where heavy usage by camping reenactors necessitated reseeding. Well-defined wagon wheel tracks from the show cut into other parts of the battlefield and required attention.[57]

Another significant concern involved the overall appearance of the reenactment and how this event influenced opinions about the Park Service.

While the spectators and some of the press gave favorable reviews, other newspaper reporters slammed the reenactment as a "farce" which allowed "overgrown boys" to get a "thrill" from hearing guns go off. An editorial cartoon in the *Washington Star* showed the endless traffic, with cars banged up against each other and people fuming in the heat, instead of the more historically significant aspects of the event. Even Park Service personnel admitted to the commercialism of the production, especially the "Coney Island" atmosphere behind the spectator stands. After coordinating the final aspects of the reenactment, Volz concluded that the show appeared to be more a celebration than a commemoration of a tragic historical event, a result that the organizers of the overall Civil War Centennial had feared, leading them to advise against planning reenactments. Volz and others realized that although the National Park Service was not blamed for the less dignified aspects of the Manassas reenactment, the agency might not receive the same treatment in the future.[58]

Based on these concerns, Director Wirth established a National Park Service policy not to authorize any future reenactments on parklands. A previous commitment to hold a reenactment at Antietam in September 1962 would be honored, but further productions would not be sanctioned by the Park Service. Wirth encouraged demonstrations of musket firing and troop drills, flag presentations, and parades in period costumes as suitable replacements for reenactments. The Park Service saw the value of "some sort of pageantry" to help visitors visualize the past through a "dignified and impressive commemoration." At Manassas National Battlefield Park, newly enlarged and enhanced through Mission 66 improvements, these quieter commemorations marked subsequent anniversaries of the two historic battles.[59]

Chapter 6

CHANGING OF THE GUARD

Change characterized Manassas National Battlefield Park in the late 1960s and early 1970s. Changes to the surrounding countryside necessitated revising past management decisions. Suburban development with its ancillary shopping centers mushroomed around the town of Manassas as the new interstate reached completion. With more and more families moving into the area and building on the once open land, the green spaces at the battlefield park became a precious recreational outlet. As a longtime resident of the area sympathetic to the needs of his neighbors and friends, Superintendent Francis Wilshin allowed a range of activities at the park, from kite flying to fox hunting. These seemingly harmless recreational uses eventually overwhelmed historic interests at the park.

Other changes followed. Park administration, which had once been the eminent domain of the superintendent, was now accountable to outside political forces, including local and national interests. Individuals, with Wilshin as one painful example, who failed to make this adjustment often found their jobs on the line. At the same time, the Park Service began expecting superintendents at historical parks to devote their energies to park management, leaving the historical work to the professional staff. In the past, superintendents had contributed considerably to a park's interpretive efforts, often because they were the only staff members with the proper expertise. Increased funding under Mission 66 and the accompanying growth in the number of Park Service positions allowed for a greater division of responsibilities. These changes prepared the battlefield park for the phenomenal growth in park visitation and the loss of insularity.

Change at the Manassas battlefield park happened concurrently with larger changes in the nation. The United States in the 1960s and 1970s underwent heart-wrenching transformations in its social institutions and the development of its physical space. African Americans sparked the Civil Rights movement by opposing segregationist practices in the South. These efforts inspired other minority groups to question their underclass status and demand change. Concerns over the degradation of the natural environment launched a series of protective actions by the federal government and an avalanche of private watchdog organizations. Expanding cities ringed by suburban developments ate up land and released dangerous levels of pollution. Although the Manassas National Battlefield Park heard only distant echoes of the Civil Rights struggle, the park sat squarely in the middle of conflicts over land use. Changes in visitation numbers, which had begun in the 1950s, put heavy demands on the park's outdated interpretive displays, leading to significant improvements at the end of Wilshin's superintendency.

Enhancing the Museum Exhibits

The exhibits at Manassas remained essentially unchanged for the twenty years following the installation of the first permanent displays in 1948. Mission 66 planning included updating these exhibits, and the Park Service's History Exhibits Planning Team designed a new museum plan in 1960. Although Superintendent Wilshin approved the plan, he did not guide it to completion. At the time of his dismissal in 1969, the museum plan required revision to incorporate additional artifacts acquired during the 1960s, such as a twenty-six-star American battle flag carried during the battle of Second Manassas and a fife found on the battlefield.[1]

Wilshin's concentration on the 1961 reenactment left him little time to devote to the installation of new displays based on the 1960 museum plan, although these exhibits would have complemented the reenactment. The plan provided added contextual details about the two battles and set the Manassas confrontations in the larger framework of the Civil War. Significantly, the proposed museum plan would have augmented discussion of the Second Battle of Manassas by highlighting that two battles had been fought here. Existing displays placed so much emphasis on First Manassas that visitors sometimes missed the fact that a second battle occurred a year later. Several displays for the second battle were planned, including a diorama of the fighting at Deep Cut and a panel explaining the Brawner Farm battle of 28 August when Jackson's Stonewall Brigade clashed with what would be called the Iron Brigade, composed of troops from Wisconsin and Indiana. This confrontation was the first meeting of these two famous commands.[2]

After the reenactment had been staged, Wilshin had the opportunity to install new exhibits and other interpretive aids, but he failed to do so. Funding did not pose an obstacle. The Park Service continued to dedicate Mission 66 funds for this work on an annual basis. Each year, as it became apparent that the money would not be used, the Park Service transferred the funds to interpretative programs at other parks. One factor in the decision to use the Manassas money elsewhere, Wilshin claimed, was that newly established Civil War areas were taking precedence over parks like Manassas with existing museum displays. But, in reality, Manassas funding was simply transferred to other units because it was not being used at Manassas. In fiscal year 1965, unspent Manassas funds went to electrical work at Castillo de San Marcos National Monument, a seventeenth-century Spanish fort in St. Augustine, Florida.[3]

During the mid-1960s, interest in revising the Manassas museum panels increased, although implementation continued to be stalled. The exhibits planning team met with Wilshin and the park historians to discuss ideas about the displays, but the Park Service did not execute these plans. Service memoranda referred to the anticipated museum revisions at Manassas, and Wilshin incorporated planned interpretive changes in the park's 1965 master plan, but the plans did not proceed. Visitors disappointed with exhibits at the park prodded the Park Service to update them. One tourist, a William Hauser, wrote Secretary of the Interior Stewart Udall that the Manassas displays were one of the "shoddiest collections of mementos" he had ever seen. In reply, the Park Service noted that new exhibits were planned for installation in 1964. In fact, it would take another four years.[4]

Wilshin's administrative style accounted for the repeated delays. He alienated Park Service employees both on his staff and at the regional office, ironically because of his devotion to history, especially the telling of the First Battle of Manassas. As former chief historian Edwin C. Bearss remembered later, Wilshin held the title of superintendent but he practiced the role of park historian. He left the everyday management of the park to his administrative assistants, first Joe Vaughn and later Mildred Gay. These individuals capably handled the daily affairs, but long-term planning, for such projects as Mission 66 interpretive programs, suffered.[5]

A long line of park historians passed through Manassas National Battlefield Park because of Wilshin's insistence that he do their job. Bearss described the situation as a swinging door: historians would come to the park full of expectations and would leave in disgust. One such historian, L. Van Loan Naisawald, had far better credentials than Wilshin as a military historian and had practical combat experience as an artillerist during World War II. But, as Naisawald recalled, his ideas for new narrative markers and for lectures failed to materialize. Wilshin would not let go of the historical work, nor could he follow through on projects Naisawald initiated. Naisawald's job as historian eventually degenerated into the role of "ticket-taker, a Howdy Doody role," a problem succeeding historians also encountered.[6]

These battles between park historians and Wilshin required intervention by the southeast regional office, which had direction over the Manassas battlefield park. The regional historian frequently had to travel from Richmond to Manassas and salve the festering wounds resulting from these turf wars. This spent energy left the regional office less inclined to devote added time to interpretive planning at Manassas. Wilshin compounded the problem by not pressing the regional office to follow through on its museum proposal. A stalemate resulted, with the park's interpretive program the principal victim.[7]

Wilshin's filling the role of both superintendent and historian need not have prevented change in park interpretation. Joseph Mills Hanson and James Myers had accomplished significant milestones in park interpretation while serving in both capacities. They ushered in the first permanent exhibits in the museum and augmented the self-guided tours around the park. While Hanson and Myers had fewer visitors during their tenures, they also had much smaller staffs. They had to do the historical research, the initial interpretive planning, and the park management alone. Wilshin, in contrast, had two park historians in addition to an administrative aide. It was not lack of support but Wilshin's single-minded focus on the First Battle of Manassas along with his indecisiveness and poor relations with the park historians and regional office that slowed the progress of change at the park.[8]

With the end of the Civil War Centennial in 1965 and Mission 66 a year later, the National Park Service could devote more concentrated time to individual parks and accomplished what Wilshin had been unable to do. In

1968 the Park Service's museum planning team designed a new exhibit plan for the visitor center. Before Wilshin had the chance to review the final draft of wall labels, and possibly stall the project with further concerns, workers began revamping the museum space. Work progressed steadily, and visitors were enjoying the new exhibits by the end of the year.[9]

In a significant departure from the 1960 plan, the 1968 visitor center plan relied on an improved audiovisual program to explain the principal tactical aspects of First and Second Manassas. This program, which was not completed until 1971, included a taped narrative with appropriate sound effects, projections of strategic maps and pictorial graphics, and a diorama terrain model. The 1960 plan had relied on the exhibits to describe many of the key events during the battles.[10]

With the audiovisual program interpreting individual battles, the 1968 exhibits focused on more general concerns. Filling the first-floor museum space and the downstairs public area, the 1968 displays looked at such themes as the confusing array of uniforms soldiers wore and the weapons they used. This thematic approach avoided concentration on just First or Second Manassas and made good use of the park's extensive and growing artifact collection. One display showcased the different objects that soldiers used while camped at Manassas, including knapsacks, canteens, field glasses, and knives. Illustrations portraying the lay of the land helped explain why Manassas Junction became the battleground for two conflicts. Although the 1960 plan had explained similar ideas, it had relied more heavily on text and less on artifacts to educate visitors. On the other hand, the 1960 plan did have the advantage of being more interpretive in its approach, telling a more finished story about the battles than the 1968 plan, which relied heavily on visitors making their own conclusions about the array of artifacts.[11]

As the National Park Service installed the new museum exhibits in 1968, Wilshin readied the Stone House for its role in the park's interpretation. For more than ten years, Wilshin had intended to turn the Stone House from a park residence to a field hospital exhibit. Although the Stone House did not open until after Wilshin left, he oversaw the research and initial planning for the project. "Like a lonely sentinel brooding over a nation's wounds," as Wilshin described the structure, the Stone House represented a significant historic resource at the park due to its hasty conversion from a tavern to a hospital during both Manassas battles. The proposed Stone House display was viewed by Wilshin as a "giant step forward" in battle interpretation.[12]

Burial Ground for the Nation's Veterans

A new threat to the integrity of the battlefield park appeared just as the new exhibits graced the visitor center and Wilshin prepared the Stone House for its opening. In January 1969 Congressman William L. Scott (R-Va.) introduced H.R. 1357, which proposed establishing an annex to the Arlington National Cemetery within the boundaries of the Manassas National Battlefield Park. Scott, who sat on the House Committee on Veterans' Affairs, reasoned that the undeveloped sections of the battlefield park offered an attractive location for the national cemetery. With Arlington close to full, a new national cemetery near Washington was needed, and Scott thought a location in his home district would address this need.[13]

Debate on the appropriateness of housing a national cemetery at the battlefield park erupted soon after Scott introduced his bill. In 1968 Scott had surveyed his constituents about the idea and had gained overwhelming support for having a portion of the Manassas park designated a national cemetery. H.R. 1357 did not, however, specify how much of the park would be used, and some park neighbors concluded that the historic scene at the park would be jeopardized by the intrusion of the cemetery. Annie Snyder, whom Wilshin had converted to the battlefield cause during the interstate highway controversy, joined forces with Gilbert LeKander, another local resident who also worked as a legislative aide for Congressman Frank Bow (R-Mo), to oppose Scott's proposal. The battle between Scott and the park neighbors who supported preservation stretched into the 1970s and across three park superintendencies.[14]

Although many park neighbors opposed any proposal to use the battlefield park for a national cemetery, National Park Service Director George Hartzog gave conditional support for the idea. In a 10 February 1969 meeting with Scott and Wilshin, Hartzog suggested that the cemetery use lands within the authorized park boundaries but currently privately owned. Hartzog believed that approximately 500 acres along the southern border of Bull Run and lying northeast of the park had only "moderate historical significance" and could be designated a national cemetery without conflicting with the park's interpretive plans. Hartzog convinced Scott to consider this land as opposed to the "most valuable historic portion" of Manassas battlefield, and Scott submitted revised bill H.R. 8818 to Congress on 12 March. This bill proposed acquiring the lands suggested by Hartzog, which lay adjacent to the northeast corner of the park along Bull Run, for the national cemetery.[15]

The Department of the Interior supported Hartzog's proposal. Under Secretary Russell Train told the chairman of the House Committee on Veterans' Affairs that Interior had no objection to establishing the cemetery on the proposed 500 acres because the lands had only moderate historical significance. Train also believed that the cemetery would be more compatible with the park's mission than some "future adverse private development." Interior did want to take part in selecting the specific tracts for the cemetery, and the department also wanted the legislation to make clear that land chosen for the cemetery would no longer be considered within the authorized boundaries of the battlefield park. In this way, Train could object to any proposals that intended to place the cemetery on federally owned park land.[16]

Both Hartzog and Train based their decisions on the idea that the adjacent 500 acres of land had only moderate historical significance. Ed Bearss, at the time a Park Service historian in the Washington office, questioned this interpretation. He noted that the 500 acres had "at least as high a degree of historical significance" for Second Manassas as areas already included in the battlefield park.[17]

When Representative Scott first submitted H.R. 1357, Wilshin considered the proposal "absolutely adverse to the whole concept of park development." He worried that using Manassas for a purpose other than the one for which it had been created would set a dangerous precedent. The integrity of other national park sites would be threatened. In response to these fears, Wilshin acted as he had during the interstate highway crisis. His talks to local community groups and Civil War enthusiasts, informing them of the situation and enlisting their support, helped generate letters to Capitol Hill and the secretary of the interior.[18]

In addition to giving talks to local organizations, Wilshin attended several strategy meetings with the newly formed Friends of the Park, later called the Save the Battlefield Committee. Annie Snyder and fellow opponents to the national cemetery proposal had organized this group. As Wilshin freely admitted to the southeast regional director at the time, he provided the Friends of the Park with specific information on the extent to which the cemetery proposal would adversely effect interpretation and development at the park. Wilshin's information became the basis for numerous letters of protest to Congress.[19]

Wilshin's actions soon drew the attention of Congressman Scott. Scott accused Wilshin of voicing opposition to the cemetery bill when Wilshin attended the first public meeting of the Friends of the Park and a Prince

William Board of County Supervisors' meeting in March 1969. The Department of the Interior defended Wilshin's actions at both of these meetings, indicating that Wilshin had acted as an official observer, answering questions about park development and interpretation plans. But Scott was unconvinced. As Bearss later remembered, when word arrived that Wilshin had publicly denounced Scott in "rather acerbic language" at a Manassas supermarket, Hartzog decided to transfer Wilshin. Wilshin left the Manassas National Battlefield Park in April 1969 and took a Park Service historian position in Washington.[20]

Wilshin believed that he was acting in an appropriate manner when he helped the Friends of the Park develop their strategies to oppose the cemetery. In reply to Scott's first concerns about his actions, Wilshin stated that "any contacts" he had had in talks before various organizations "reflected *solely* the official policy" (his emphasis) of the Department of the Interior and the National Park Service. He believed that both agencies opposed establishing the national cemetery at the battlefield park, and so his efforts to help the opposition seemed correct official actions to him. In reality, the official policy articulated by Park Service and Interior favored establishing the cemetery on less historically significant lands designated for inclusion in the battlefield park but not yet acquired. Wilshin's opposition to the cemetery contradicted this official determination.[21]

Hartzog's decision to remove Wilshin from the park superintendency followed federal agency protocol. Once an agency had established a policy on a particular issue, subordinates had the option of either accepting that decision or resigning. Since Wilshin did not resign, he had a responsibility as an agent of the National Park Service to accept Interior's decision on the national cemetery proposal.[22]

Public debate over the national cemetery proposal continued after Wilshin's removal. On 23 September 1969, when one of the subcommittees of the House Committee on Veterans' Affairs held a hearing on H.R. 8818, almost 150 people submitted letters or gave statements. Opinions varied on the merits and problems associated with the bill. Veterans groups favored establishing the cemetery adjacent to the Manassas National Battlefield Park because it would give appropriate recognition to the sacrifices made by all veterans in serving their country. The Prince William Board of County Supervisors opposed the idea of taking the privately owned 500 acres off the tax rolls and placing them under federal ownership, whether for a cemetery or for the battlefield park. Park neighbors who favored the cemetery argued that the loss in taxes on the land would be more than made up by the increased amount of sales tax generated by cemetery visitors who chose to purchase goods or services in the county.[23]

Although joined in opposition to H.R. 8818 with the Board of County Supervisors, the Save the Battlefield Committee, led by Snyder, considered the historic significance of the battlefield lands and the opportunity for recreational activities more important than any perceived loss in taxes. Snyder argued that the scores of gravestone markers, chapels, military barracks, and supporting maintenance buildings would "destroy the mood and visual aspects" of the park. The somber cemetery would discourage park visitors from hiking and picnicking in the park's inviting green space. Snyder used soil maps to suggest that the land, believed to be underlain by a thick layer of rock, would require dynamiting grave spots and special sanitation measures since the soil did not drain well. Snyder also expressed concerns about the expected future expansion of the cemetery, which would spread to the battlefield park itself.[24]

In light of these concerns, the Save the Battlefield Committee urged Congress to support H.R. 8921, which was introduced by Congressman Bow in March. LeKander, Bow's aide and also a vocal member of the Save the Battlefield Committee, had contributed to this bill's creation because he wanted to provide an alternative location for the cemetery. Both LeKander and Snyder recognized the need for an annex to the almost filled Arlington National Cemetery and did not oppose a location somewhere in Prince William County, so long as it did not destroy historically significant land. Bow's bill proposed placing the cemetery within the boundaries of the United States Marine base at Quantico, Virginia, the Fort Belvoir Military Reservation in Virginia, Andrews Air Force Base, or Fort George G. Meade, the latter two located in Maryland.[25]

Congress failed to pass any of the 1969 cemetery bills, and the issue remained unresolved. In Snyder's opinion, public opposition was a significant factor in defeating Scott's proposal. In response to the Save the Battlefield's successful public relations tactics, people from across the country wrote to Congress and registered their views.[26] These tactics echoed the work done in 1957 to fight the interstate, and the same method would serve equally well in subsequent campaigns. Save the Battlefield Committee members wrote letters to the Civil War Round Tables and other people who had previously expressed support for the park. They encouraged the local papers to run stories, hoping the issue would be picked up by the national press. With the story out, Snyder later said, "people will come to you." And when people came to help fight the cemetery proposal, Snyder and the Save the

Battlefield Committee got them involved stuffing envelopes, circulating pe-titions, and making phone calls. As these people got involved, they became committed and served as allies in future controversies.[27]

Wilshin was one of these committed individuals until his death in 1990. According to Snyder, he designed and colored maps for her to use in her appearances before Congress. Wilshin obtained the names of committee members and researched which regiments from their states fought in what place. He then tutored Snyder on this information, ensuring that each com-mittee member would take an interest in Snyder's presentation.[28]

"Seventeen Gates, Three Logs, and a Load of Gravel"

The change in leadership following Wilshin's fourteen years as superinten-dent involved more than new faces. The National Park Service now empha-sized specialized training for its managers and a clearer demarcation be-tween positions than had been the case earlier. In the historical parks, historians were supposed to focus their attention on doing the research and interpreting the site for visitors. Park superintendents, though they may have history backgrounds, were responsible for daily affairs and planning for long-term improvements. Each position had a function that was flexible but focused on specific tasks and objectives.[29]

Russell W. Berry Jr., who replaced Wilshin, benefited from this new Park Service approach. Berry had joined the NPS in 1966 just as he completed his undergraduate degree in history, specializing in the Civil War, at Old Dominion University in Virginia. Instead of sending new employees di-rectly to a park site, as had been the case with Wilshin, the Service arranged for a three-month orientation program at the Grand Canyon. Here Berry learned about the history and traditions of the Park Service while also gain-ing practical skills in interpretation and protection. He applied this training to his historian position at the Jefferson National Expansion Memorial be-fore heading to the East Coast and Manassas.[30]

When Berry arrived at Manassas in summer 1969, he encountered many reminders of Wilshin's reign. First, Wilshin himself continued to live in the park superintendent's house for the next several months. Berry commuted from Annandale, Virginia. Second, Mildred Gay, who had served as Wil-shin's administrative officer and then acting superintendent until Berry came, expected to continue in her administrative role, in practice if not in title. Gay proposed to take the "burden of administration" so that Berry could be the "dreamer and the keeper of the history and the vision." Berry did not accept Gay's offer. He understood his job as being the park's manager. He wanted the historians to recommend changes to the park's interpretive program without getting involved in the details himself.[31]

Another carryover from Wilshin's superintendency involved visitors' use of the park. When Berry arrived, the "whole park was saturated with recreational use." On the battlefield, it was "solid cars and picnic blankets and frisbees and dogs running." Local hunt clubs had permission from Wilshin to chase foxes throughout the park. These different activities encompassed all areas of the park, including Chinn Ridge and Henry Hill. The Robinson House area served as a softball park in the daytime, while other spots became the "evening social haven" for local area high school students. Without gates to control the level of access to certain areas, the entire park served as a recreational outlet for the local community.[32]

The need for recreational space in Prince William County had risen sharply toward the end of Wilshin's administration of the park. Completion of Interstate 66 to the south of the park in 1966 made the Manassas area a viable bedroom community for Washington. Housing spurts that had begun in the immediate post–World War II period accelerated in the late 1960s, bringing more and more families to the area. In the same period, the Prince William Board of County Supervisors had decided not to join the Northern Virginia Regional Park Authority, which maintained a series of public parks in the area. The Park Authority charged residents of non-participating counties, including Prince William County, for using any of its regional parks. The Bull Run Regional Park, a large recreational area located nearby in Fairfax County, was one park under the authority's jurisdiction.[33]

The Manassas National Battlefield Park provided a free alternative. Wilshin's close connections with local community organizations and park neighbors made it difficult to say no, which exacerbated the growing problem. When Gary Farley of the county's Parks and Recreation Department contacted the Park Service about the recreational opportunities at the Manassas battlefield, Wilshin did not express opposition. Farley wanted assurances that the park would play a "much more active role" in the county's recreational program. Specifically, Farley pointed to the battlefield's many acres of "unused lands." With some funding assistance from the county, Farley thought these areas could be improved with more adequate sanitary facilities and the like. Wilshin assured Farley that the Park Service had development plans for the park that would address some of the county's concerns.[34]

In Berry's mind, "total recreational use" as it developed under Wilshin's administration threatened the park's mission to preserve and protect the Manassas battlefields. Restoring historic use to the park became one of his most significant contributions. He had the chief maintenance worker at the park design gates to blend with the historic scene and had them placed on each of the dirt roads leading into the park. These seventeen gates allowed Berry to control access and reduce unauthorized recreational use. He established horse trails that removed equestrian usage from the most historic parts of the battlefields. Berry moved the picnic area from Chinn Ridge to its current location, a generous piece of land along Route 234 north of Lee Highway. He placed signs on Chinn Ridge stating: "In order to preserve the historic area, recreation is restricted to the picnic area." The zoning of recreational use inside the park represented an essential change in park management, one that the National Park Service in time adopted for other historic park sites.[35]

With historic use reasserted, Berry encouraged park historian George Reaves to develop more interpretive programs. Immediately apparent to Berry and Reaves, both newcomers to the park, was the need to give equal voice to the Second Battle of Manassas. Reaves suggested adding a guided driving tour, and Berry agreed. They walked the park and chose areas based on historical significance, distance, and safety concerns. Then, with "every spare dime that [he] could scrape together," Berry asked the maintenance foreman to put "three logs and a load of gravel" at each spot to establish a widened shoulder for pulling out. The driving tour emerged one stop at a time. At the visitor center on Henry Hill, Berry and Reaves inaugurated guided tours of First Manassas, which three seasonal employees conducted. The Stone House also finally opened with its living history display of the field hospital.[36]

Berry revamped some parts of the visitor center and walking tour by drawing on the mutual needs of the park and other Park Service divisions. He turned to the Harpers Ferry Design Center, which needed a place in the vicinity to try out new technologies in interpretation, to improve the battle map that Wilshin had started at the end of his tenure. The design center also introduced an audio narrative for the Henry Hill walking tour, using the voices of a Northerner and a Southerner talking about the battles they had fought at Manassas as if they were at the reunion fifty years later. With the designs in hand, Berry went to the Job Corps Center for student workers to construct the interpretive displays. The battlefield park provided temporary housing for the Job Corps workers, making the effort mutually beneficial.[37]

Berry oversaw one other lasting change to the visitor center exhibits. He had adopted the practice of keeping the museum open after hours when he was working in the building so that latecomers had the opportunity to tour the museum. One night while Berry was sitting at the information desk reviewing paperwork, a gentleman stopped by and struck up a conversation. The visitor noted that his great grandfather had been killed at Manassas and that he always wondered what the spot on the battlefield looked like. Berry asked for the name and took the visitor to check the official records. Based on the description Berry found, he knew within twenty or thirty feet where the site was. He took the gentleman out to the battlefield, to a place in the midst of the woods near the old railroad embankment, where he determined the man's great grandfather had been mortally wounded. The man was thrilled.

On returning to the museum, the visitor mentioned that he had a few things relating to his great grandfather that he wanted to give to someplace where people cared. On two previous trips to the park, he had not found anyone to answer his query about where his relative had died. Berry had shown that the park was indeed responsive to its visitors, and the gentleman offered to donate his items. The great grandfather's sword, the surgical kit used by his brother to try to save him, and the railroad pass used to bring the body back to Ohio were incorporated in a special exhibit in the park's museum.[38]

Berry continues to share the story of the surgical kit with his seasonal employees at other parks. In his mind, the story encapsulates the Park Service mission of serving people and preserving parks for future generations. And sometimes the park gets something in return from smiling at visitors, saying hello, and offering to lend a hand. This story also serves as a reminder that despite the many changes occurring at national park sites, one constant remained: service to the public.[39]

Chapter 7

GREAT AMERICA IN MANASSAS

"We intend to honor or celebrate the great things that make the United States," proclaimed Marriott official David L. Brown in a congressional oversight hearing in 1973 when he described the Great America theme park his corporation planned to build adjacent to the Manassas National Battlefield Park. Guests would have the opportunity to participate in living history and become involved in things that played a part in the development of the United States. Skeptics feared the entertainment complex would produce a "carnival atmosphere" next to the battlefield. As Congressman John Seiberling pointedly remarked when touring the battlefield, Marriott wanted to replace an "authentic piece" of American history with "something that's fake." Eying the promise of increased tax revenues, more jobs, and a boosted local economy, many Prince William county residents, including a voting majority on the board of county supervisors, embraced Marriott's proposal.[1]

The Marriott theme park proposal confronted the Park Service with questions central to historic preservation in an age of rapid change. These questions would reverberate years later when a shopping mall and a Disney theme park, among other projects, were proposed for the area. What say did the NPS have over the development of lands adjacent to national parks? How could the Park Service protect the lands in its care while also respecting the decisions of local communities? Left unresolved in the 1970s was the question of whether the Marriott tract, known to have historical significance to the Second Battle of Manassas, should be annexed to the national park. As indicated in this and subsequent chapters, Park Service officials consistently addressed land development outside the Manassas battlefield park's boundaries on a case-by-case basis. Little attempt was made to act proactively and set an agenda for the future.

Setting the Stage: Marriott's Proposal

Early in 1973 the Marriott Corporation announced its intention to build a theme park on 80 acres of a 513-acre tract adjacent to the Manassas National Battlefield Park. To coincide with the nation's bicentennial in 1976, Marriott planned to re-create six historic areas that would reflect the idea of "Great America." According to the original proposal, guests could visit different sites important in American history, including a New England seaport, a New Orleans French market, the Southwest, the frontier Yukon, a rural town, and the turn-of-the-century Midwest. In addition to these areas, created through architectural styling and landscaping, there would be amusement park rides, musical productions, and craft displays to entertain guests. Marriott anticipated two million visitors each year during the theme park's May-through-September season.[2]

On the same parcel of land, Marriott later planned to build a specialty shopping center where people could purchase goods made by on-site artisans. A hotel would house visitors. Marriott also wanted to develop an additional area of approximately 185 acres as an industrial park. Light industry and research and development firms would be housed in one- to two-story buildings placed in a landscaped setting.[3]

Before Marriott took shovel to dirt, state and local governments had to assess and consider a variety of things. The catering services and hotel chain needed commitment on zoning permits and support facilities from Prince William County and the Commonwealth of Virginia. The existing agricultural zoning had to be switched to commercial usage, and a special use permit was required for a 350-foot landmark structure planned in the theme park. Additional special variances were needed for an undetermined number of 100-foot structures. Marriott requested that the state build an interchange on Interstate 66, which would allow direct access to the property. Marriott considered the interchange essential to the project and threatened to abandon the site if it were not approved. Other services were also crucial to the Marriott proposal. Prince William County had to ascertain if its existing water and sewer capacities could accommodate the projected increased usage and then construct lines to serve the site. And there were environmental factors to consider, including the effects on water and air quality in the county. Safety features relating to fire protection and crime needed to be addressed. Taking into account all of these requirements, the board of supervisors had to assess the impact of the project on the county's overall financial health.[4]

Effects of the theme park and light industrial area on neighboring Manassas National Battlefield Park also required consideration. Marriott originally chose the site because it met certain selection criteria, none of which were proximity to the battlefield park. After selecting the site but before making a public announcement, Marriott considered the relation between its development and the national park. The corporation concluded, without seeking input from the National Park Service, that the most significant impact would be increased visitation at the battlefield, which Marriott considered a benefit for the national park. Satisfied with its site choice, Marriott began negotiating with the Prince William Board of County Supervisors for zoning and support services. The National Park Service remained unaware of the project until Superintendent Berry and others saw a story describing Marriott's plans "splashed across" the front page of the *Washington Post* in mid-February.[5]

With the publication of that article, battlefield park neighbors and other county residents drew up on opposing sides. A voting majority of the board of county supervisors, known as the "Four Horsemen" and led by Supervisor Ralph Mauller, welcomed the tax income that the projected $35-million development would bring. The sobriquet "Horsemen" alluded to what opponents saw as the potentially Apocalyptic consequences of the Marriott development or perhaps to the supervisors' perceived effort to ride roughshod over opposition. The Four Horsemen saw the Marriott project and the projected tax revenue it would generate as a way to address recent changes. The county had experienced explosive growth, with its population increasing from 50,000 persons in 1960 to more than 111,000 in 1973. Tax revenues were needed to provide these new residents with schools, sanitary processing facilities, and health and safety services. Homeowners could carry only a portion of the burden, so county officials sought other sources. Industry and businesses, drawn to the county by the recent opening of Dulles International Airport and the completion of two major interstate highways, provided an attractive funding resource. The Marriott development represented just the type of income generator that county supervisors, especially the Four Horsemen, were looking for.[6]

Many local residents were also enthusiastic about the Marriott proposal.

C. Mason Gardner, who lived within five miles of the battlefield park and represented thirty members of a pro-Marriott ad hoc committee, argued that Prince William County needed an expanded tax base to ease rising property taxes. In Gardner's mind, Marriott provided a perfect remedy to this situation. After the development was completed, the corporation would pay its share of taxes but not require the additional services—such as schools—that residential construction needed. Gardner pointed to other potential benefits: sales tax revenue would increase, businesses would gain a boost from tourists, and summer employment possibilities for local young people would expand.[7]

Others considered the Marriott proposal a threat. Gilbert LeKander, who had worked with Annie Snyder against the 1969 national cemetery proposal, joined forces with Memory Porter and the Prince William League for the Protection of Natural Resources. The league included some one hundred Prince William County residents who questioned the value of the Marriott development. Snyder, who was recovering from a skiing accident, stayed behind the scenes during the opening salvos of the debate.[8]

Porter, as president of the league, argued that approving development on the Marriott tract would open the door for further commercial rezoning in the surrounding area. Availability of increased capacity public water and sewer lines and the presence of both an entertainment facility and an industrial office complex would encourage other businesses to consider the remaining space. Porter feared that the existing agricultural-residential area would be replaced by gas stations, food outlets, repair shops, shopping centers, and other convenience facilities. She argued that with these added buildings, the county would experience rising traffic, noise and air pollution, and the general degradation of the aesthetic and historic aspects of this section of the county. Porter pointed out that the water quality of nearby streams would inevitably decrease from storm runoff over parking lots and road surfaces. Crime and the incidence of vermin would increase.[9]

Of particular concern to Porter and LeKander was the effect the Marriott development would have on the battlefield park. Porter expressed concern about the visual impact of the projected 350-foot-tall structure and the undetermined number of 100-foot-tall structures. These tall modern edifices would intrude on the historical scene and become constant reminders of the twentieth century as park visitors attempted to step into the past. Porter and her fellow supporters remembered the Gettysburg Tower controversy, in which a corporation won local zoning approval, over adamant preservationist opposition, to build a 307-foot observation tower on private property adjacent to the Gettysburg National Military Park in Pennsylvania. Battle-field park supporters in both Pennsylvania and Virginia were particularly sensitive to high-rise structures as a result of the Gettysburg controversy. Projected visitation at the Marriott theme park brought further questions regarding adequate lodging and camping facilities. Porter argued that ex-isting services would not be able to accommodate the surge of Marriott vis-itors. Instead, the battlefield park's proximity and inviting open fields might encourage large-scale unauthorized camping.[10]

Defining the National Park Service Position

The instant polarization of views, with Porter and her fellow supporters ada-mantly opposing the Marriott proposal and others strongly favoring con-struction of the theme park left the National Park Service with a limited range of options. The agency could join one side, but this would involve complications. First, Superintendent Berry and other NPS officials needed specific and reliable information about the theme park proposal and its relation to the battlefield park. To get the hard facts, Berry approached Marriott when news of the proposal first broke and explained that the Na-tional Park Service would not be an ally, but the agency had not decided to be an opponent. If Marriott refused to sit down and provide the informa-tion the agency needed, Berry explained, "I will have no choice but to op-pose because I will fight the unknown." Marriott agreed to cooperate with the Park Service and began conferences with the agency in March 1973.

During the course of these meetings, the Park Service outlined its four major concerns about the theme park: (1) the location and uses of the 350-foot tower; (2) possible pollution and planned mitigations; (3) access to the theme park and whether Marriott expected significant travel along Lee Highway through the battlefield park; and (4) Marriott-provided picnick-ing and camping facilities to reduce recreational pressures on the battle-field park. Marriott agreed to take these concerns into consideration when finalizing its theme park plans, but the corporation did not provide a de-tailed site plan for the Service to review.[11]

A second factor that influenced the National Park Service's reaction was the increasing fervor of debate. In Berry's mind, supporters and opponents of the Marriott proposal had fallen into the trap of engaging in hysterical rhetoric, a tactic the Park Service wanted to avoid. The four controlling members of the board of county supervisors so fully supported the Marriott plan that they attracted more than the usual amount of attention. A group of residents joined together to publish a newsletter reporting on county board meetings in an attempt to increase public surveillance of the Four Horsemen's activities. Opponents to the theme park also contributed to the rising tone of the controversy by presenting what Marriott vice president David L. Brown called a "parade of horrors" of potential, but not probable, environmental and social effects of the theme park.[12]

Questions about the historical significance of the Marriott tract gave the Park Service further reason to avoid joining either side of the controversy. Former superintendent Francis Wilshin, keeping active in park affairs while living in Fredericksburg, Virginia, provided the Prince William League in March 1973 a historical evaluation of the Marriott property that supported incorporation of this tract into the battlefield park. Wilshin argued that the Marriott tract "profoundly influenced" the Union and Confederate battle strategies at Second Manassas. General Robert E. Lee established the Confederate nerve center and a signal station on Stuart's Hill in the western part of the tract. Under cover of the woods on this property, Lee concealed the major portion of Maj. Gen. James Longstreet's wing of 30,000 men. Knowing Longstreet was on the tract but unaware of his exact position, Union Maj. Gen. John Pope gravely weakened his left by advancing on Maj. Gen. Stonewall Jackson's troops in an unsuccessful and bloody attack at Deep Cut. Seizing on this defeat, Lee ordered Longstreet's troops into action and launched a successful counterstroke. Longstreet emerged from his woodland screen to hurl Pope's weakened left to Chinn Ridge and Henry Hill. A second Confederate victory at Manassas resulted.[13]

Joseph Mills Hanson, the historian who had developed the interpretive narratives for the Bull Run Recreational Demonstration Area and had served as the national park's second superintendent, was well aware of the historical events connected with the land later purchased by Marriott. Hanson had argued in his 1937 report on the park's proposed boundaries that its southwestern edge should extend half a mile west of the apex of Stuart's Hill to include the area where Longstreet's troops had deployed, screened by the topography and the vegetative cover. However, Hanson had placed a low priority on acquiring this land because it had not seen the heavy fighting that other areas experienced. He had ranked land acquisition based first on the intensity of fighting a given tract saw and second on how acquisition would assist in park development, especially the construction of an internal system of park roads. In the first round of obtaining lands, Stuart's Hill had been a low priority.[14]

Stuart's Hill was included in later efforts to expand the battlefield park's boundaries. In the late 1940s and early 1950s, Superintendents Hanson and Myers tried to convince Congress to add Stuart's Hill to a larger battlefield park. Opposition from the Prince William Board of County Supervisors successfully defeated this proposal, and the resulting 1954 law set the designated western park boundary east of Stuart's Hill along Highway 622 and Compton's Lane. In the early 1970s the National Park Service revisited the idea of acquiring the Stuart's Hill tract when Sen. Alan H. Bible and his park subcommittee requested a review of the boundaries of certain national parklands. The National Capital Region's Land Use Coordination office investigated possible changes to the Manassas battlefield park boundaries, including the incorporation of Stuart's Hill, just as the Marriott proposal became public and the debate soared.[15]

The National Park Service avoided taking sides for several reasons. The Service needed hard data on the theme park and its effect on the battlefield park, which the agency sought through discussions with Marriott officials. The Park Service needed to present itself as a responsible party separate from the immediate hysteria, and this required that the agency avoid voicing an opinion until it had received all the information from Marriott. And the Service needed to determine the best course of action toward a piece of property known to have historic significance for the Second Battle of Manassas. In Berry's opinion, this neutral stance kept the agency above the fray and helped the park come out "with more respect for its ability to act calmly in the midst of a firestorm." This neutral stance did not prevent park officials from conducting meetings with the involved parties, which continued throughout the controversy.[16]

The Park Service also insulated itself from potentially damaging political undercurrents. Prince William officials committed the county as early as 16 February to Marriott's theme park and office building complex by voting to sign a letter of intent. This agreement outlined the county's determination to provide the necessary public services, highway access, and special permits for the project. Open opposition to the Marriott proposal by the Park Service would be seen as interference in local governmental affairs. In contrast, had the Park Service endorsed the plan, other charges might surface. In the national arena, the Marriott Corporation and the executive branch had unofficial ties because President Richard Nixon's brother, Donald Nixon,

headed Marriott's theme park division. Such circumstances made it necessary for the Park Service to act dispassionately and reasonably.[17]

The National Park Service and its employees had learned from past experience the difficult lesson that the Service must keep attuned to political forces to protect the agency's overall goals and avoid the pitfalls of
participation in acrimonious public debate. Wilshin's removal from the superintendency during the national cemetery controversy served as a recent
reminder of the costs of taking a firm stand for preservation without considering the political implications. Similar dilemmas had occurred in the for-
mative years of the national park system. When the city of San Francisco
successfully petitioned the United States government in 1913 to dam the
Yosemite's Hetch Hetchy Valley for a reservoir, national park supporters
lost an important battle. The strength of local political support for the dam
and of federal interest for promoting resource use over resource preservation left the keepers of national park lands with a lasting awareness of the
power of politics. Once established in 1916, the National Park Service and
its agents clashed from time to time with local political interests over dams,
roads, and other developments that threatened national park lands. Sometimes the Park Service won, many times compromises ruled, and always the
agency grappled with the delicate balancing act of upholding its mission
while also addressing political exigencies.[18]

Congress Looks at the Marriott Theme Park

Despite its attempts to stay out of the clamorous debate, the National Park
Service continued to garner attention from theme park opponents and
Congress. Opponents wanted to know what information the Park Service
obtained from Marriott and how this data would influence the agency's decision on the proposal. When it became clear that the Park Service had
deferred a decision until Marriott submitted detailed site plans, these opponents went to Congress for action. The Civil War Round Tables of Alexandria, Virginia, and the District of Columbia asked Washington lawyer
Frederick Simpich to appeal on their behalf to the House Subcommittee
on National Parks and Recreation. The Round Tables wanted Congress to
hold hearings to determine whether the amusement park would have a detrimental effect on the Manassas National Battlefield Park. If assurances of
the integrity of the national park could not be obtained, these organiza-

tions wanted the federal government to acquire the 513-acre tract by outright purchase or scenic easements.[19]

The national parks subcommittee needed little prompting from the Round Tables to investigate the Marriott project. One committee member, Ron de Lugo (D-V.I.), lived on the boundary of the Manassas National Battlefield Park and knew how similar developments affected other areas of the country. He wondered how Manassas could be saved from "giant traffic jams" and unauthorized camping if the theme park opened. Another committee member was suspicious about the haste with which the Prince William County officials had pushed the Marriott project. A congressional hearing would bring out the facts for public review. Initial questioning of National Park Service Director Ronald H. Walker at a recent hearing on other matters had further convinced committee members that the issue needed exploration.[20]

Congressional query into the Marriott proposal was limited to the theme park's impact on the national battlefield park. Decisions on the rezoning of the tract from agricultural to commercial use and the special use permit for tall structures remained in local hands. Congress, however, had authority to step into the debate if federal roads or other improvements were involved. If testimony presented at the oversight hearing indicated that the theme park would be detrimental to the battlefield park, Congress also wanted to know what action the National Park Service was taking to protect the park. Legislation had not been proposed in relation to this issue; hence, the congressional hearing was a quest for background information as part of the committee's oversight role.[21]

Supporters and opponents of the Marriott proposal packed the 3 April oversight hearing. David Brown, vice president of the corporation's theme park division, tried to assure Congress that Marriott had every intention of being a good neighbor to the battlefield park and the surrounding community by accepting their suggestions and following them "within any kind of reason." Other proponents of the theme park emphasized the tax revenue benefits the project would give Prince William County. Porter, LeKander, Simpich, and other concerned individuals expressed their misgivings about the effects of traffic, pollution, and crime. Raymond Humphreys, a neighbor of the park, fervently argued that to desecrate the hallowed ground of the battlefield by the "infringement of crass commercial enterprise" was to "trample the most sacred" of all American institutions. Porter especially worried that ancillary facilities springing up around the Marriott park would destroy the aesthetic and historic values of the Manassas National Battlefield Park and the surrounding areas. In response to these different concerns, theme park opponents reintroduced the idea of the federal government acquiring the Marriott tract.[22]

During his testimony on 3 April, NPS Director Walker drew criticism from Congress and theme park opponents for not taking a stand on the Marriott proposal. Subcommittee Chair Roy A. Taylor (D-N.C.) noted that in his thirteen years as head of the national parks committee, Walker was the first director to say Interior could not take a position because it did not have enough facts. Walker explained that Marriott had been cooperative in holding initial meetings with the Park Service, but the agency needed detailed site plans to determine with confidence the theme park's potential impact on the battlefield. This explanation failed to satisfy. Civil War Round Table representative Simpich concurred with Congressman Taylor's observation and requested that the subcommittee urge Interior to be creative in its thinking rather than be content to tell Congress why it could not act. LeKander ended his testimony with the cutting observation that former NPS Director Conrad Wirth knew how to protect the park system, implying that Walker did not.[23]

Outside the hearing room, other members of Congress supported the National Park Service's decision to delay taking a stand on the Marriott proposal. Speaker Tip O'Neill (D-Mass.) saw the political value of seeking information and establishing dialogues among the different parties until all the needed data became available. In recognition of Berry's particular role in this process, O'Neill asked that Berry be considered for a superintendency of two historical parks in Boston in which O'Neill had a special interest. Berry accepted the offer and left the Manassas National Battlefield Park in late spring 1973.[24]

The National Park Service continued its neutral stance when Richard Hoffman replaced Berry as superintendent. Hoffman, a self-described "down-home, crusty type of guy," met on several occasions with both preservationists and Marriott officials to obtain information. His unpretentious appearance made him seem approachable. His previous experience at the Glen Canyon National Recreation Area, Fire Island National Seashore, and Isle Royale National Park provided him with an understanding of conflicting use patterns. He was also the first nonhistorian appointed to the superintendency at Manassas, furthering the change in management style that Berry had initiated. In his initial meetings with theme park opponent Annie Snyder, now recovered from her accident, and ardent Marriott supporter Ralph Mauller, Hoffman succeeded in leaving each person uncertain of the Park Service's leanings on the issues, thereby retaining the agency's neutral position. Hoffman also managed to garner help from Prince William County supervisor Mauller on other issues affecting the battlefield park, including information about a proposed community college on the park's borders. In discussions with Marriott's David Brown, Hoffman continued Berry's efforts to obtain further clarification of plans for the theme park.[25] With the NPS remaining neutral, events played themselves out on the local and national level. Resolution of the Marriott controversy is a significant barometer of a similar debate fifteen years hence.

Marriott Stalled: The Local Level

While the administration at the battlefield park was changing, Prince William County rushed forward with its review of the Marriott proposal. In what opponents called a "crash program," Prince William officials quickly addressed the different points of the county's 16 February letter of intent with Marriott. Two significant aspects of the letter involved adequate sewer and water facilities and the necessary rezoning and special permits. By the end of February the board of supervisors had begun negotiations with the state Water Control Board to obtain certification of additional capacity in the Upper Occoquan Sewer Authority. The board also pushed to hold meetings with the towns of Manassas and Manassas Park to investigate borrowing some of their projected sewer capacity and water supplies for the Marriott theme park. The county would need these sanitation and water facilities to meet the anticipated demand.[26]

To address the rezoning and special use issues, the supervisors asked the county planning commission to report on expected effects of the Marriott complex on Prince William County. In mid-March the planning department issued a preliminary report which indicated a "positive attitude" toward Marriott despite the lack of sufficient data for immediate recommendation of the proposal. Two weeks later, on 3 April, the planning commission issued its revised report, which recommended passage of the rezoning request but listed a series of conditions for the special use permit. These conditions reflected the remaining unanswered questions about the complex, including adequate access roads, protection of water quality, and the need to buffer the national battlefield park from the theme park by the planting of trees. County planners also wanted assurances from Marriott that construction of a hotel and other amenities would wait until economically justified and that both Marriott and the county would work out a mutually agreeable rezoning if the corporation decided not to build the theme park.[27]

Driving the approval process was the realization that Marriott might soon abandon Prince William County. The corporation's options with ten property owners to buy the designated 513 acres expired on 7 April. Marriott had previously encountered opposition in Howard County, Maryland, twenty miles north of Washington, and had decided to consider Prince William County as an alternative. Having won this coveted opportunity, county officials did not want the corporation to renew its search. The planning commission accepted good faith efforts on the part of the county and Marriott to work out such remaining problems as protection of water quality and construction of adequate roads.[28]

Fully aware of the 7 April deadline for land options, the board of county supervisors met on 5 April to review the rezoning and special use permit request. The supervisors asked Marriott to clarify a range of issues, including sewers and road access, before voting unanimously in favor of the proposal. The board rezoned 335 acres next to the Manassas National Battlefield Park for the Great America theme park and an adjacent 178-acre tract for a light industrial park. For the special use permit, the supervisors attached the conditions that the planning commission had placed in its 3 April report. Individual board members also wanted assurances that the Marriott project would not divert road construction funds from other districts in the county.[29]

Perceived benefits from the Marriott theme park and light industrial complex countered the unresolved issues noted in the planning commission's April report. Certainly the projected $35-million Great America park and its expected multi-million-dollar tax revenues swayed supervisors toward approval. But social factors also played a role. Prince William supervisors cited Marriott's reputation as a "root-beer-to-riches, wholesome, family-oriented business" as a significant factor in granting the rezoning. Here was a company seen to be economically successful and committed to the same values as county residents. Such an image made Marriott attractive as a kind of antidote to rapid changes in the county. Significant population increases in the county over the past decade had led to an increase in crime. Fifty-seven people had been arrested recently in the county's largest drug raid. Marriott's promises of jobs, tax revenues, and a recreational outlet for county residents provided the needed assurances that the bad effects of county growth could be counterbalanced with promising economic development.[30]

The county supervisors' ideas about the beneficial aspects of the Marriott proposal failed to convince the Prince William League for the Protection of Natural Resources. Porter and Snyder continued to oppose construction of the theme park and light industrial complex. They wanted to protect the battlefield park from what they saw as uncontrolled development. They also wanted to preserve some of the last open spaces in the county. In an attempt to nullify the rezoning decision, the league filed a lawsuit against the county, arguing that supervisors had not given ample time to opposing viewpoints during the board's 5 April meeting. County officials had allowed nine people opposing the Marriott proposal and twelve supporters to speak. Almost ninety people had attended the April hearing, including Anthony Lapham, attorney for the Prince William League, who called the board's actions "prejudged and preferential" toward Marriott. The league also alleged that the county had violated a state code by advertising the date of the meeting for fifteen days instead of the required nineteen.[31]

These issues temporarily halted work on the Marriott project. In January 1974, in the midst of addressing the charges in the lawsuit, the county's legal advisers determined that the rezoning and special use permit were invalid because of insufficient advertising for the April 1973 meeting. Supervisors, unaware of a 1968 state code that set a minimum of nineteen days for advertising a board meeting, questioned whether the rest of their post-1968 zoning determinations could go unchallenged. County officials wanted the Marriott decision grouped with all the other questionable rezonings and either set aside or validated by passage of special legislation in the Virginia General Assembly.[32]

Meeting the conditions of the special use permit proved more difficult to overcome. To address concerns over water quality, Marriott proposed to build its own spray sewage irrigation facility, which would handle waste until the expected 1980 opening of the Upper Occoquan Sewer Authority plant. The sewer authority, the agency that would review and approve Marriott's sewage treatment proposal, tabled discussion of the independent plant until Marriott could provide detailed engineering plans. Questions over access to the Marriott tract also stalled construction. In November 1974 the Federal Highway Authority approved the requested additional interchange at Interstate 66 but indicated that no federal interstate funds were or would be available for the project. The authority also placed four conditions on its approval, including the preparation of a full environmental impact statement. The state of Virginia also indicated its approval of the proposed interchange, although it refused to provide funding.[33]

The federal request for an environmental impact statement signaled the end for the Marriott proposal. When questions arose in 1973 and 1974 over freeway access and the legality of the county rezoning decision, corporate officials delayed the anticipated opening of the theme park from the original date of 1976 to 1978. Marriott had planned to open the theme park in time for the nation's bicentennial celebrations, recognizing that tourists traveling to Washington, D.C., for special festivities would consider spending a day at the theme park. Although Marriott had to delay the opening, the company remained committed to the project until the request for the environmental statement. The federal government wanted a detailed statement, which would require at least a year to complete. Marriott had theme park projects in the works in California and Illinois, and the corporation decided to focus on these sites until they were "well off the ground." Without the National Park Service ever stating a position, Marriott placed its Virginia Great America on the "back burner" and proceeded with other more promising projects. The threat to the park appeared dead, or at least moribund.[34]

The National Park Service's decision to stay neutral on the Marriott proposal saved the agency from taking a potentially controversial stand against local governing boards and politically influential individuals. The agency gained experience in addressing adjacent land-use controversies while also defending the lands under its charge. Yet nagging issues remained. At what point should the Park Service take a stand and embroil itself in heated debate? How should the agency approach opposing sides once it has taken a stand? To what extent should political realities shape the Service's steps to protect its parks? Over the next fifteen years, the Manassas National Battlefield Park and National Park Service would confront each of these questions as the abandoned Marriott tract generated new controversies.

Chapter 8

EXPANDING THE BOUNDARIES

In a 1973 letter to the chairman of the House Subcommittee on National Parks and Recreation, Civil War historian Bruce Catton wrote: "Parks like [Manassas] are of profound importance. They are not obtrusive tourist traps, clamoring for attention, baited by the arts of honky-tonk; they are just quiet bits of land preserving the memory of scenes where heroic men of the north and south displayed a bravery, a devotion and a capacity for self-sacrifice that still have the power to move us." Catton's intention was to justify incorporating the Marriott tract into the Manassas National Battlefield Park, but his words reflect the reasons driving the federal government to expand the battlefield park's boundaries in the 1970s. The Park Service recognized that the 1954 boundary legislation had been effective in incorporating key tracts principally associated with the First Battle of Manassas. The experience of the Marriott theme park proposal accentuated the need to acquire the remaining historically significant lands before they were lost and to obtain buffers to shield the heart of the park from the threat of "honky-tonk" development.[1]

In the embattled route toward park expansion, the Park Service made two key decisions that would have long-lasting repercussions in the field of historic preservation. First, the Service decided to exclude the Marriott tract, including Stuart's Hill where General Robert E. Lee had his headquarters, from consideration. This left the door open for future development on the tract; later proposals would electrify a large and politically influential preservation-minded public.[2] Second, the Park Service failed to present a unified policy with respect to Stuart's Hill. Although NPS historians spoke of the land's importance for interpretive efforts, the Service made no official pronouncements on acquisition. Confusion resulted, with the Park Service sometimes working at cross-purposes to itself. The delay in boundary expansion cost the federal government dearly because of the steadily rising property values and the inability to address effectively future development proposals.[3]

Why Save More Lands?

Richard Hoffman realized the value of adjusting the battlefield park's boundaries soon after arriving in 1973. Three days before he officially took up his post as superintendent, he wandered the park as an anonymous tourist. Unable to find clear demarcations of where the protected areas ended and private property began, he concluded that the park had a "lousy boundary line." In some cases, national park land appeared to be private because the Park Service had leased the land to local residents to farm. This arrangement was beneficial for the Park Service as it allowed the land to be used as it was during the Civil War. Local residents also benefited from the opportunity to produce and sell more agricultural products. In Hoffman's view, though, interpretation suffered. Because many visitors could not distinguish between park land and private property, they did not explore all the park's resources.[4]

Hoffman's concern over the park's boundaries fed into additional worries over park interpretation and resource management. This combination of factors led him to support boundary expansion legislation. For example, he knew from his historians that many of the park's natural resources did not match the lay of the land at the time of the two Civil War battles. A solid stand of pine trees had grown up near the embankment of the unfinished railroad and obscured the clear view that had existed during Second Manassas. A diorama in the visitor center, which showed Confederate troops fighting Union forces with stones in open fields, emphasized the incongruity between the historical facts and existing reality. Hoffman decided to tear down the pine trees, but he found himself locking horns with Annie Snyder.[5]

Snyder, "just madder than hops" about the prospect of losing the beautiful forest, demanded that Hoffman defend his decision. After showing her the diorama, Hoffman took Snyder to the unfinished railroad and explained that the pine trees contradicted the history of the battle told in the visitor center. Snyder agreed that the pine trees presented visitors with historical inaccuracies, but she also felt the trees were valuable to the community. The tall stand of pines offered a natural barrier, separating residential areas and the park from traffic along the major roads. The trees cleaned the air of pollutants and acted as deterrents to erosion. The tall dense pine trees were also aesthetically pleasing, blocking views of the urban developments slowly moving into the area and providing a parklike atmosphere. Snyder wanted to preserve some of these qualities and sought a balance between strict historical accuracy and local interests. She asked Hoffman if he would "thin" the trees, and Hoffman responded by encouraging her to work with him on a mutually agreeable resource management plan. As the tree-cutting example suggests, Snyder's park advocacy encompassed the needs of both historic preservationists and park neighbors. She had stated in the 1969 House hearings on the national cemetery that the Manassas National Battlefield Park had a value to historical purists who wanted to see the woods and pastures "precisely as they were" during the battles and to urban dwellers who wanted to "hike, picnic, ride horseback, or simply enjoy" the open space.[6]

This dual-purpose view of the battlefield park was shared by others, and this became apparent as Hoffman met more residents, including Gilbert LeKander, and learned of their concerns. LeKander had joined Snyder in opposing the 1969 national cemetery proposal and had spoken against the Marriott theme park at a 1973 congressional hearing. The completion of Interstate 66 brought suburban developments to the once quiet town of Manassas, of which the Marriott theme park and office complex proposal was only the most visible example. Longtime residents like Snyder and LeKander wanted to preserve the rural feeling of their community and protect the historical associations of the battlefield park. Before the Marriott proposal, most of the land along the park's boundaries had been farmed. With Marriott came the prospect of twentieth-century office buildings, entertainment complexes, and shopping centers built up to the edges of the park. From Snyder's and LeKander's point of view, these intrusions jarred the historical sensibility and disrupted the open feeling of the landscape. For Hoffman, whose principal task was park protection, the proposed construction threatened the park's integrity and highlighted the importance of acquiring all significant land before the opportunity was lost forever.[7]

Manassas boundary expansion was under consideration in 1971 when the Department of the Interior sought a "less cumbersome means" than individual legislation to obtain increases in appropriation ceilings and to adjust boundaries for a range of parks. Interior proposed umbrella legislation that would allow the Park Service to meet the conditions expressed in each national park unit's authorizing legislation in a timely fashion. Senate Subcommittee Chairman Alan Bible (D-Nev.) spearheaded the congressional effort to obtain passage of this legislation. He asked the Park Service to review its park units and list those areas needing adjustments. The National Capital Regional Office, which soon afterwards obtained jurisdiction over the Manassas National Battlefield Park, recommended that Congress extend the Manassas park boundaries. These proposed changes shed further light on what became the agency's *implied policy* on the Manassas battlefield park, which combined historical idealism with the practicality of dealing with twentieth-century intrusions. Reflecting historical purity, the boundary adjustments included extending the park's western border to incorporate lands known to have significance to the Second Battle of Manassas, including Stuart's Hill and the Brawner Farm, located on either side of Lee Highway west of Groveton Road–Featherbed Lane. Another historically informed boundary change included Stony Ridge, where Jackson's lines fought in Second Manassas. National Capital Region officials recommended acquiring the Wheeler Farm, both for its historic value and its ability to protect the southeastern corner of the park. From the pragmatic side, the regional office suggested placing a buffer of 750 feet along Bull Run in Fairfax County and a scenic easement on the Bacilli tract, which was located near the northeast section of the park and was being threatened with residential development. The Park Service also recommended buying land around Stone Bridge in Fairfax County to remove a gas station.[8]

When the National Capital Region voiced its recommendations in 1971, the idea of incorporating Stuart's Hill into the battlefield park met with instant opposition from the county supervisors. Prince William County officials had identified the area along both sides of I–66 between Gainesville and Route 234 as a regional employment center and did not want its economic plans thwarted by the Park Service. Wanting to ensure the economic health of the county, the board of county supervisors favored development that was consistent with the county's master plan.[9]

The county's opposition to the recommended boundary changes forced the Service to reconsider. In an effort to avoid stalling the entire park bill under consideration by Senator Bible's committee, the agency dropped Manassas, allowing for passage of the umbrella legislation in 1972. Resolution of what lands should be added to the Manassas battlefield park remained. The decision centered on the controversial Stuart's Hill, especially after

Marriott announced its intention in 1973 to build the Great America theme park on that tract, a proposal the economic-minded Prince William County officials warmly embraced.

Historical idealism did not offer a clear-cut position for the Park Service to follow. Former superintendent Wilshin described Stuart's Hill as crucial for understanding the events of Second Manassas. Bearss, a recognized expert within the Park Service on the Civil War, wrote in 1973 that the Marriott theme park would occupy "key and critical sites" associated with the Second Battle of Manassas. Yet, as other historians pointed out, blood was not shed on the land in any significant military actions. How should the Park Service evaluate this tract? Was it sufficient to preserve only lands where soldiers died in battle? Or did the Park Service have a responsibility to provide visitors with lands that help explain why certain military actions were taken? If the latter, then what definable limits existed for the Park Service to preserve historically significant lands that had not seen significant battle action? In the 1970s the Park Service avoided addressing these questions directly; instead it followed an implied policy of what could be called *pragmatic authenticity*, seeking a balance between historical significance and practical considerations about local land use. Areas marked for inclusion had either seen fighting during the two Civil War battles or would act as a buffer to outside development. The agency's official policy stayed undefined, leaving open the opportunity for negotiation as events unfolded.[10]

Finding a Congressional Ally

Opposition from the Prince William Board of County Supervisors squashed the Park Service's initial foray into boundary expansion in the early 1970s. Still committed to the idea of preserving more lands at Manassas, LeKander and Snyder decided to take another tack. In late 1974 they approached Stan Parris (R-Va.), their U.S. Representative who had recently lost his bid for reelection, and asked that he introduce a bill in Congress. Parris agreed and submitted a bill that LeKander helped draft. No action resulted, but, as Snyder later remembered, "at least we got it on the books." Then in early 1975, Snyder and LeKander, both lifelong Republicans, "swallowed [their] pride" and talked to their new congressman, Democrat Herb Harris.[11]

What Snyder and LeKander quickly discovered was that Herbert E. Harris II, a transplanted Midwesterner, had gained a great appreciation for history and the environment while living in Virginia. Born and raised in Kansas City, Missouri, Harris had moved to the Washington, D.C., area in 1951 and practiced international and antitrust law. He became active in Fairfax County politics, helping to establish community parks and preserve green space, and served on that county's board of supervisors from 1968 to 1974. From there, he won election to the U.S. Congress. Although he had established himself on the East Coast, Harris never lost the sense of fascination in history "that you can only get as a Midwesterner [who] comes to Virginia." He found that many Virginians took much of this history and "precious, precious heritage" for granted because they had been near it for so long. The longer Harris lived amidst the past, the more committed he became to its preservation.[12]

Snyder and LeKander did not know what to expect in their initial meeting with Harris. They had some trepidation about how they would be received by their Democratic congressman, especially since they had lobbied for the Republican Parris during the election campaign. But their ardent belief in saving the battlefield park and the surrounding countryside from outside development guided their presentation and made a convert of Herb Harris. All three shared an interest in preserving historical areas and open space. Harris later admitted that "it's impossible to talk to people like [Snyder and LeKander] without being instilled with the same fervor that they have." He responded to their plea in a very businesslike fashion and sent one of his legislative aides to the park to investigate. What Harris learned convinced him to act, first by proposing a boundary expansion bill to Congress and then by addressing a revived attempt to build a national cemetery at the battlefield park.[13]

In June 1975 Harris introduced legislation that authorized the Department of the Interior to acquire 1,500 acres for the Manassas National Battlefield Park. Lands listed for acquisition included the Brawner Farm, which was located north of the Marriott tract along Lee Highway and was the site of the opening engagement of the Second Battle of Manassas. The Harris bill extended the southern park boundary to Interstate 66 by designating tracts for purchase or for scenic easements. Harris included lands near the Stone Bridge to protect this structure from commercial development. Privately owned tracts designated for inclusion under the 1954 boundary legislation had scenic easements placed on them.[14]

Harris adopted a pragmatic approach and did not include Stuart's Hill, which was then owned by the Marriott Corporation, in his legislative proposal. Snyder and LeKander had argued for its incorporation, noting its historic significance to Second Manassas and the threat the Marriott development posed to the park and its rural surroundings. Strident opposition from the Prince William Board of County Supervisors, however, kept Snyder's and LeKander's pleas at bay. The county saw the Marriott land as an important source of tax revenues and refused to support its transfer to a tax-exempt status under the federal government. This unremitting resistance, along with opposition by Marriott, forced Harris, like the National Park Service in 1973, to remove Stuart's Hill from consideration. Harris realized he would not succeed in adding any new land to the battlefield park if he refused to compromise on the Marriott land.[15]

With Stuart's Hill excluded, Harris proceeded to guide his bill toward law. He held public meetings and obtained input from the Prince William County historical commission. Harris oversaw its passage by the Committee on Interior and Insular Affairs and the full House, which sent it to the Senate as part of a park omnibus bill. There Harris encountered opposition from Sen. William Scott. As the representative for Virginia's Eighth Congressional District in the late 1960s, Scott had proposed building a national cemetery at the Manassas park. Responding to concerns raised in the local community, Scott opposed including some of the lands designated in the 1975 Harris bill. Harris worked with Scott to obtain a compromise bill and achieved some success. Scott reportedly agreed to the adjustments just as the congressional session ended, but he placed a hold on the legislation and left for the Philippines. When contacted overseas, Scott refused to lift the hold, and Harris's first attempt at Manassas battlefield park boundary expansion came to naught. Over the next five years, Harris tried three more times, always balancing historicity and practical exigency.[16]

As the 1975 expansion bill fizzled, the idea of placing a national cemetery at the Manassas National Battlefield Park resurfaced. The need to find an extension to Arlington remained pressing, and in 1975 the U.S. Veterans Administration (VA) revisited the idea of using the Manassas battlefields. The Park Service reluctantly agreed to have soil tests done at the park, and these determined it would make an "outstanding national cemetery." Veterans Administration representatives put Manassas at the top of their list for a cemetery, noting its proximity to Washington, D.C., and its gently undulating, aesthetically pleasing landscape of woods and open lands. Its historic associations with past military conflicts and the fact that the land was federally owned added to its attractiveness.[17]

Realizing that the VA's recommendations to Congress might have sufficient weight to win, the Park Service reiterated former director Hartzog's 1969 statement on the cemetery question and unequivocally refused further consideration of the park's land for the cemetery. Citing a 1975 Suitability/Feasibility Study that Park Superintendent Hoffman had completed, Director Gary Everhardt argued that the cemetery would destroy the historic scene of the fields and woods, which aided in the interpretation and understanding of the two Manassas battles. The Park Service considered the alteration of the historic sites by the cemetery as inappropriate to the mission of the national park. Everhardt and the secretary of the interior, as Hartzog had done, encouraged the VA to buy land adjacent to the national park. The Park Service's firm stand on the national cemetery proposal shows the limits of its historical pragmatism. The NPS may have been willing to compromise on development outside existing park boundaries, but the battlefield park itself continued to focus on history and interpretation.[18]

The Veterans Administration might have let the issue die and considered an alternative site, but some members of Congress favored the Manassas National Battlefield Park for the cemetery. During hearings in November 1975, Rep. George Danielson (D-Calif.) argued that the land proposed for the cemetery did not serve "any useful purpose" in the Civil War. He viewed Second Manassas, which took place on the land slated for the cemetery, as a rerun of the First Battle of Manassas. Danielson also defended the national cemetery proposal on the grounds that not many visitors came to the park and thus the area would be better served as a cemetery. He offered to "sound out" his colleagues on the appropriate committees to pursue the Manassas site. One person who supported Danielson's position was Senator Scott.[19]

Within this climate of opinion, Snyder and LeKander pressed Harris to come to the battlefield park's aid. In a letter to Harris, LeKander argued that the national cemetery threat to Manassas was as ludicrous as placing "Disneyland in the heart of Yosemite." For LeKander, the cemetery would destroy the historicity of the battlefield park and bring unwanted development to the area. Harris agreed, but he faced a dilemma. He understood that the Arlington National Cemetery needed an annex soon, and he would "feel great pride" if the new cemetery were located in northern Virginia. But the idea of losing the "precious historical resource" at the Manassas battlefield park also seemed "very wrong." To resolve this conflict, Harris scouted for other suitable locations and found the Marine Corps Base at Quantico, Virginia. Quantico, which LeKander had touted in 1969 and which the VA had rated just below Manassas as a potential site, offered a considerable amount of unused acreage close to a major interstate. Its soil was also suitable for burial purposes. With these favorable characteristics, Quantico seemed the best alternative location for the national cemetery.[20]

Harris acted quickly to secure this site and remove any consideration of the Manassas National Battlefield Park as the place for a national cemetery. In December 1975 he submitted H.R. 11140, which designated 620 acres at Quantico as an annex to Arlington. Harris then went to the public to garner support. In a town meeting at Dumfries, Virginia, on 16 January 1976, Harris heard "not one single voice of opposition or resistance" to his newly proposed bill. Further unified assistance came from a hefty number of local and state organizations and the two local newspapers serving the area. More remarkable, the Prince William Board of County Supervisors voted unanimously on 6 January to adopt a resolution of support. The board recognized that the national cemetery, now slated for land already federally owned, would not adversely affect the county's real estate tax structure. The fact that the county would not have to build additional transportation, water, and sewer services also made Quantico attractive to the supervisors. Congress responded favorably to the broad base of support Harris had amassed and voted to make Quantico a national cemetery. The Manassas National Battlefield Park escaped another threat to its mission of preserving and interpreting Civil War history.[21]

Maneuvering the Roadblocks

With the integrity of the battlefield park assured, Harris reentered the fight for expanded boundaries. His persistence went hand-in-hand with an acknowledgement that he could not achieve his objectives without the cooperation of others. As he stated later, anybody could propose good things; the "job is to figure out how to get it done." For Harris, the job involved listening to the range of interests in the county and in the Park Service and working to find mutually beneficial compromises. Once agreement was reached, Harris believed "you can move and adjust and thereby accomplish very, very fundamental things." [22]

As Harris proceeded to meet these objectives, the management of Manassas battlefield park changed: in 1977 R. Brien Varnado replaced Hoffman as superintendent. Hoffman admitted later that he had been "pretty burned out" over the boundary expansion legislative process and it was time to bring in people with "other talents and ideas and brand new energy" to steer the park. Varnado's appointment represented a return to the previous tradition, the park superintendent being a historian. Varnado, who held undergraduate and master's degrees in history, decided that he could reach more people at a single park than in any classroom and joined the Park Service. Fittingly, Varnado came to Manassas, the location of the first major land battle of the Civil War, after serving as chief of interpretation and resource management at Fort Sumter in South Carolina, where the opening volleys of the Civil War were fired. Manassas was his first superintendency.[23]

While Varnado settled into his new position, Harris conducted meetings with Park Service officials, the board of county supervisors, and community groups in anticipation of redrafting his legislation. In these meetings, he heard arguments on both sides of the preservation issue. Some people believed that enough land had been removed from the county's tax base, while others argued that another $8 million should be spent on land acquisition for the park. Harris came to understand both sides and sought to balance them in his new boundary expansion bill, H.R. 2437, submitted in 1977, calling it a "realistic approach" for assuring preservation of the Manassas battlefields.[24]

This bill delineated the same boundaries as the 1975 bill with two changes. First, H.R. 2437 added an 800-foot-wide scenic easement along the eastern side of Bull Run, in Fairfax County. This buffer zone along the north and east sides of the existing park was in a flood plain that local zoning regulations prohibited from being developed. Harris and the National Park Service, however, believed that the existing land use controls were inadequate for controlling such activities as tree cutting, which would open the park to visual encroachment from development on the other side of the flood plain. Complicating matters was the fact that park land on the western side of Bull Run stood higher than that on the northeast side of the stream, making the 800-foot buffer a minimum for protecting the battlefield park's vistas. The Fairfax Board of County Supervisors unanimously endorsed Harris's proposed buffer zone, thus paving the way for its acceptance during the debate over H.R. 2437. This 800-foot buffer represented Harris's and the Park Service's belief that some lands warranted protection more for their ability to preserve the heart of the historic battlefield than for purely historical reasons.[25]

Second, Harris excluded from the bill the Northern Virginia Community College campus, located south of the park's boundary and north of the Interstate 66–Route 234 interchange. The state of Virginia had first identified this land for the community college in the early 1970s. Then-superintendent Hoffman had tried to convince Virginia to consider an alternative location. The Park Service had wanted to acquire the land to protect the southern entrance to the battlefield, the most historic area of the park. The NPS saw the 1977 legislative proposal as one more chance to control development and noise at the community college campus. Recognizing the educational and aesthetic benefits of having a national park site next to the college, state officials proceeded with their plans and built their campus, which included facilities to test aircraft engines. The community college had opened by the time Harris drafted H.R. 2437 in 1977.

After the community college and the Manassas battlefield park became neighbors, the Park Service continued to express concern over the college's impact on the park. To control the expected rise in noise pollution from the engine testing and to restrict the construction of tall buildings, the Park Service asked Congress to incorporate the community college campus into the battlefield park. State officials, who wished to retain control over future developments at the college, protested the Park Service's stance. Harris sought to address this opposition and gain the needed support of the college for his bill. For this reason, he agreed to remove from his revised bill any language that would allow the federal government to direct the affairs of the community college.[26]

Harris's legislation also sought to balance Park Service, county, and community college concerns over the proposed Route 234 bypass, which Prince William County officials planned to build through a corner of the Brawner Farm, a key tract included in H.R. 2437. Since 1964, the county had recognized the need to reroute Route 234 to the west to alleviate traffic congestion between the town of Manassas and the battlefield park. By 1977, county studies reported that more than 6,800 vehicles per day traveled the two-lane Route 234 through the national park and more than 8,000 swelled the four-lane road to the south, heading from I–66 to the town of Manassas. To ensure the future health of residential and commercial development in Prince William County and the town of Manassas, county officials knew they had to alleviate the congestion and improve accessibility. The Route 234 bypass addressed these needs.[27]

Uncertainty over the exact route of the 234 bypass led Harris to leave the subject open in his bill to a mutually derived decision by all relevant parties. The secretary of the interior had jurisdiction to "negotiate and consummate arrangements with appropriate authorities" to reroute or remove roads within the park in an effort to reduce adverse impacts. This language made it possible for both the Park Service and county officials to support this aspect of the bill. To protect the battlefield park's integrity, the Park Service had express authority to participate in local road decisions. And because the bill avoided designating particular tracts of land that would or would not be part of the rerouting, the county continued to have a full range of options available for consideration. The county asked only that the bill's language be clarified so there would be no question of directing the bypass through a corner of the Brawner Farm, if that land became part of the park and if the county determined this route to be the most advantageous for the bypass. Again, Harris showed his willingness to find politically advantageous compromises in an effort to garner support for his bill.[28]

Despite these efforts, Harris still encountered some opposition. Community college officials expressed their disagreement with the bill's language, fearing that the National Park Service would close Route 234 at the I–66 interchange once the bypass was completed. The Interior Department gave credence to this interpretation when it indicated in a 27 June 1977 letter to the Senate Committee on Energy and Natural Resources that the federal government wanted to close the existing Route 234 from the I–66 interchange to a point where it joined the bypass to the north. By closing Route 234, the Park Service hoped to reduce intrusive traffic and retain the park's historic integrity. Community college officials reminded Harris that Route 234 was the only mode of access to the college and were "appalled to think that anyone would even think of isolating the Campus from the community it serves." Although Harris emphasized in the hearing that it had "never been the intention" of his bill to close the main artery to the college, this concern fed opposition to the bill.[29]

Department of the Interior authorities aroused further anxieties among residents of the so-called Battlefield Community, a residential area located near Groveton Road south of Lee Highway and next to the Marriott tract. Interior wanted to add a section to Harris's bill that placed scenic easements on this seventy-five-acre subdivision to protect the remaining woods and prevent more intensive use of the land. General Longstreet had staged his historic flanking attack on this land during Second Manassas. Memory Porter, speaking on behalf of the Prince William League for the Preservation of Natural Resources, argued in the congressional hearing that the Battlefield Community touched the land lightly. The expensive single-family homes, set along quiet private streets, nestled into the existing woods. In Porter's opinion, only massive development next door on the Marriott tract would drive these residents to sell their homes and make the scenic easement worthwhile. Since Interior did not request scenic easements over the Marriott land, Porter reasoned that it was unnecessary to use easements on the residential area. Interior's recommendation left the residents in fear that the federal government would eventually convert the easements into fee simple, or land designated for purchase by NPS. E. Clay Hollingsworth, who lived in the Battlefield Community, expressed this concern, worrying that he would be forced to leave the home he had built. Community members had not forgotten the Park Service's previous record of land acquisition, especially during the 1950s and 1960s, when homeowners were forced to leave their lands.[30]

Placement of scenic easements on Sudley Church, located at the northern edge of the battlefield park's boundary, precipitated more protest against Harris's bill. Like the Stone House, an earlier Sudley Church had been converted into a field hospital during the battles, and Harris wanted to preserve the location. Harris agreed with the Park Service, in this case, that the historic significance of the land required some protection, despite objections by parishioners. Church members pointed out that the original building had been replaced twice since the Civil War and no longer represented the structure that had served as a field hospital. In addition, they opposed the easement, fearing that the park might eventually condemn the land.[31]

The concerns raised by the Northern Virginia Community College, the Battlefield Community residents, and Sudley Church could have been addressed by Congress without significantly altering H.R. 2437. Harris's interest in obtaining a politically viable bill made him amenable to clarifying its language and removing the scenic easement on Sudley Church. But a lingering fear that Congress, acting in partnership with the Park Service, would add the Marriott tract to the final bill fueled overwhelming opposition to Harris's proposed legislation.

Prince William County supervisors knew that the Park Service favored acquiring the old Marriott tract. One board member had been informed in Congressman Harris's presence that the Interior Department "intended to have the bill amended to take the entire Marriott tract." Some members of the full congressional committee were sympathetic to the idea of acquiring the Marriott tract, and this made the county supervisors more sensitive to any suggestion of federal acquisition of this land. In addition, in his December 1976 historical evaluation of the Marriott tract, park historian Michael Tennent had written that it contained several areas of major significance to Second Manassas. Tennent believed that the Marriott property provided "potential key sites for proper interpretation" of the battle. The combination of these opinions gave the supervisors reason to continue their opposition to the entire bill, which they formally announced in a 10 May 1977 statement.[32]

Senator Scott listened to this rising furor against H.R. 2437, and he effectively blocked its passage. Rep. Phillip Burton (D-Calif.), coming to Harris's aid, tried to hide the bill in his proposed legislation on parks in New Orleans. Senate staffers spied the reference to Manassas in the New Orleans bill and demanded its exclusion. H.R. 2437 was effectively defeated, and Harris returned to drafting legislation for the next congressional session. The defeat of this bill would have significant financial consequences in later years.[33]

There was one benefit from the delay in passing the park boundary expansion. By the time the Senate had a chance to review H.R. 5048, the 1979 incarnation of the Manassas National Battlefield Park boundary legislation, Scott had retired from the Senate; John William Warner won his seat in the 1978 elections. Senator Warner proved crucial for overcoming the opposition to park expansion. In statesmanlike fashion, Warner sat down with Harris soon after the elections and listened to his argument on the value of acquiring more land for the Manassas National Battlefield Park. Unlike his predecessor, Warner agreed to look at the proposal. Five years of congressional debate had left the local community unable to plan its economic future, and it kept the Park Service uncertain about the park's future development. To resolve this stasis, Warner went to Prince William County residents to learn their concerns. He also sought the advice of Civil War historians to ensure that all historically significant land be protected in his bill, S. 1857.[34]

Warner's version of the park expansion legislation resolved the long-standing resistance of Prince William officials. The Senate bill, which reduced the total acreage for inclusion in the park to 661 acres, versus the 1,681 acres included in H.R. 5048, was attractive to the county supervisors. The supervisors also appreciated the fact that S. 1857 excluded a section of the Brawner Farm, providing a clear right-of-way for the still proposed

Route 234 bypass. Warner's bill removed the scenic easement that Harris's bill had placed on the area around the I–66 and Route 234 intersection, allowing the county to develop this land for commercial purposes. Finally, Warner promised that this park expansion would be the last one at Manassas. By this admission, Warner allowed the old Marriott tract, which had caused so much contention in the past, to remain in private hands and available for development. In recognition of these concessions, and particularly because of the exclusion of the Marriott land, the board of county supervisors voted unanimously in 1979 and 1980 to support S. 1857. Prince William County supervisors recognized the importance of adding some historically significant lands to the battlefield park. But they also wanted assurances that these acquisitions would be balanced with the county's need to find diverse avenues for generating tax revenues. Warner's bill fit these requirements.[35]

With this critical support in hand, the Senate passed S. 1857. A conference of both houses produced a final bill that President Jimmy Carter signed on 13 October 1980. Public Law 96-442 looked most like Harris's original proposal, allowing the addition of almost 1,500 acres to the park and increasing the park's size by one-third. Its component parts reflected the input and wishes of many different interests. Key areas designated for purchase in the 1980 legislation included the Wheeler tract in the park's southeastern corner, land to the east of the Stone Bridge, and an area to the west of Route 234 bordering the interstate highway. These had been lands the Park Service wanted either for their historical significance or for their ability to buffer the park. All of the Brawner Farm, a key historic area, came into the park, because the Virginia Department of Highways determined that the proposed bypass would go around the tract. Not wanting to lose county support, the legislation retained a clause giving a right-of-way to the county if at a later date it decided to route the bypass through the Brawner tract. To address the fear of condemnation raised by many park neighbors, P.L. 96-442 specifically forbade the Park Service from acquiring land without the consent of the owner, so long as the land continued to be used in a fashion similar to its use in September 1980. The law included an 800-foot scenic easement along the eastern side of Bull Run and an easement around Sudley Springs Ford, giving the Park Service the added buffering protection it wanted for these sections of the park. Sudley Church, the Battlefield Community, and the commercial district near the I–66 and Route 234 intersection remained outside the authorized boundaries, satisfying the requests of church parishioners, local residents, and the county. The Marriott tract also continued to sit outside the park, a specific bow to Prince William County.[36]

Implementing the Boundary Expansion Law: Brawner Farm

The "third battle" of Manassas, as many people dubbed the park boundary expansion debate, ended with the daunting challenge to acquire the newly designated lands. Varnado, living in the front lines of the park expansion battle, had experienced firsthand the political infighting and turmoil created by park neighbor arguing against park neighbor. Even before the legislation was passed, he accepted a promotion to the National Capital Regional Office Headquarters. Rolland Swain, former unit manager of Lookout Mountain at the Chickamauga-Chattanooga National Military Park and thirteen-year veteran of the Park Service, arrived in September 1980 as the Manassas National Battlefield Park's eighth superintendent. Swain had majored in botany at the University of Colorado, but his own interest in history and his seven years at the Chickamauga and Chattanooga National Military Park gave him the background he needed to address his new assignment.[37]

Swain expected to start land acquisition immediately and drew up a detailed review of the seventy-two designated parcels in preparation for purchase or scenic easement, which had been approved under the 1980 legislation. With the 1980 election of Ronald Reagan and his appointment of James Watt as secretary of the Interior, Swain's orders changed. In February 1981 Watt placed a temporary moratorium on land acquisition in the National Park System, thereby suspending immediate attempts to implement the 1980 Manassas boundary expansion legislation. Watt justified this action by noting that the Park Service did not have sufficient economic and human resources to manage the lands already under its protection. The secretary also needed to address Reagan's call for slashing domestic program budgets while increasing defense spending.[38]

In response to the changed political climate, Swain developed a land protection plan that categorized tracts for acquisition, easement, or special protection. Land protection plans replaced the previous Park Service format of a land acquisition plan. The new plans were a way for the Reagan administration to minimize federal ownership by designating only the most essential tracts necessary to protect park resources for fee simple purchase. Swain's land protection plan necessarily reflected this new attitude and identified only the Brawner Farm and a few small isolated tracts for fee purchase. Most of the Wheeler tract and the land around the Stone Bridge, which P.L. 96-442 designated for fee, were recommended for easement, purchase and sale with covenants, or continued occupancy. With the land protection plan in place, Swain had authority to begin its implementation.[39]

Swain proceeded to hold meetings with the appropriate landowners to purchase those tracts approved for fee simple under the new land protection plan. The Brawner Farm, having top priority, proved difficult to acquire because the approximately seventeen heirs of late owner, Walker Davis, could not agree on a price. Talks stalled until April 1984 when George McDaniel, one of Davis's nephews, informed park temporary historian John Hennessy that he had uncovered friction primers, the small metal tubes used to spark the cannon, during recent relic-hunting trips to the farm. The location of the friction primers, spaced regulation distance apart, indicated the position of Col. S. D. Lee's artillery on 30 August 1862. More important, in July McDaniel and other relic hunters discovered an unmarked battlefield grave containing the skeletal remains of a soldier wrapped in a uniform, several Virginia Military Institute buttons, and a bullet that may have killed the young man. Park Service historians visited the Brawner Farm on several occasions, each time finding "abundant evidence" of relic hunting by friends and relatives of deceased owner Davis.[40]

The removal of artifacts from the Brawner Farm represented a "real and immediate threat" to the historic resources. Items critical to determining the placement of battle lines during Second Manassas were being taken for personal collections and for sale. "Diggers" showed no signs of stopping their activities, with one Davis relative proclaiming he would "take a backhoe to the trenches" to find more artifacts. The Park Service did not have any legal authority to stop the relic hunting because the land was privately owned. Talks with the heirs continued to leave the selling price undetermined, so Swain recommended that the Park Service file a declaration of taking to allow the courts to decide on a fair price and the federal government to take possession of the land by condemnation.[41]

Determination of a fair price and acquisition of the Brawner property proceeded slowly. The Park Service filed its official request for the declaration of taking in October 1984. Transfer of the land came in May 1985, after both houses of Congress approved the measure. The federal government spent the next year deciding on the price for the land. During the condemnation proceedings, Hazel/Peterson Companies, a local real estate development firm, purchased the Marriott tract, which sat across the road from the Brawner property, and announced its intention to build a residential-office complex. Land prices skyrocketed, and the jury reviewing the Brawner case awarded the heirs $4.2 million in 1986. The government unsuccessfully appealed this decision. The delay in obtaining the Brawner Farm was costly. In 1977 the cost of the 312-acre Brawner Farm tract was estimated at $1.5 million. The need for full and honest dealings with all involved parties was apparent. The Park Service would prove it had learned the lesson when it dealt with the next crisis on the former Marriott land.[42]

The 1980 expansion, which allowed the Park Service to acquire the Brawner Farm and most of the remaining historically significant tracts at the Manassas battlefield park, should have changed the park's boundaries for the last time. Thanks to this legislation, the Park Service largely achieved its objectives. The federal government protected the most significant lands where battle action had occurred. At the same time, the park's borders had been rounded out so that its outer limits shielded the heart of the park from outside development. Modern intrusions continued to plague the park, including the traffic at the Stone House intersection, but the Manassas National Battlefield Park finally represented a viable entity. The Park Service could proceed with its mission to interpret this Civil War landscape for increasing numbers of visitors. Yet the entrance of the Hazel/Peterson Companies on the scene cut short the celebrations by park expansion proponents, and questions over the historical significance of Stuart's Hill, which sat on the far edge of the old Marriott tract, resurfaced.

Chapter 9

SEEKING PARTNERSHIPS

"The Park Service does its best to protect these national treasures [national parks], but it needs the partnership of local governments and local citizens, those who have the most at stake to fully achieve this objective." National Park Service Director William Penn Mott Jr. used his speech at the 125th anniversary ceremonies for the First Battle of Manassas to remind his audience of park concerns. In July 1986 Mott's words seemed especially pertinent to the Manassas National Battlefield Park. Just a few months earlier, the Hazel/Peterson Companies, a northern Virginia real estate development firm, had announced its plans to build a corporate office park and residential district, called the William Center, next to the battlefield park. The way the National Park Service handled the ensuing situation reflected Mott's call for partnerships.[1]

Seeking partnerships outside the park was not entirely new for superintendents at the Manassas National Battlefield Park. Joseph Mills Hanson and James Myers had been active in community affairs during the 1940s and 1950s and had used these connections to obtain important acquisitions, including the Dogan House. Francis Wilshin had made it a point to talk with park visitors and enlist their aid in fighting threats to the park. Annie Snyder, a park neighbor recruited by Wilshin, remained an influential ally. Russell Berry took a similar approach when he held discussions with the Marriott Corporation in 1973.

The Service's handling of William Center marked an important change from previous efforts. For the first time, the Park Service became an active negotiator in affairs outside the park. For Hanson, Myers, and Wilshin, contacts with the local community had the sole purpose of adding lands to the

Fig. 12. Amidst musket firing demonstrations and period dress displays commemorating the 125th anniversary of the First Battle of Manassas, National Park Service
Director William Penn Mott Jr. reminded attendees of present-day concerns when
he called for the National Park Service to develop partnerships with local governments and local citizens to protect such national treasures as Manassas National
Battlefield Park from outside development. (Photo by John McDonnell. © 1988,
The Washington Post. Reprinted with permission)

park or protecting existing lands. Outside developments that did not touch
historically significant land were noted but not formally opposed. During
the Marriott theme park controversy, Berry did voice some concerns in his
talks with the developer, but he purposely remained a neutral party. With
William Center, the Park Service launched a new era of partnership that
engaged the park as an active institutional player in the regional business
environment.

It is unfortunate that it took until the 1980s for the Park Service to advocate active negotiations. In the 1970s Prince William County officials had
made clear that they intended to encourage development up to the national park's borders. Neither the park superintendents nor their regional
supervisors contacted county representatives or local business interests to
discuss the park's concerns at that time. Such conversations, initiated be-

fore any specific development proposals surfaced, could have headed off damaging projects and avoided later protracted battles. Instead, the Park Service addressed each crisis as it appeared, without the benefit of long-range planning or allies in the local business community.

Interpretive Improvements

During the early 1980s, Superintendent Swain oversaw the first significant revisions in interpretation at the battlefield park since the closing of the Mission 66 era and the 1969 retirement of Wilshin. In early summer 1980, just before Swain's arrival, facilities at the visitor center underwent a major rehabilitation. An expanded lobby and new information desk were added to improve contacts with the public, ramps made the building accessible to handicapped visitors, and new administrative offices with refinished furniture brought much needed space for park employees.[2]

As part of the 1980 rehabilitation, display space for the nonprofit Eastern National Park and Monument Association increased threefold, allowing the Manassas battlefield park to become one of the best sources of Civil War literature in the area. The association served as a friends group to various national park sites on the East Coast, using space in visitor centers to sell educational and travel materials related to the specific parks. Sales at the bookstore, which had hovered around $30,000, jumped more than 10 percent in 1981 and rose steadily thereafter, amounting to more than $120,000 in 1985. According to the contract between the association and the NPS, receipts went to Eastern and then were distributed to the individual participating parks through a competitive grant process. Later, Eastern adopted a method that gave a standard 5 percent of gross sales to the participating park and 1 percent of sales to the regional office for discretionary use. As Manassas was the only park in the National Capital Region with an Eastern agency, Swain convinced the region to forward its percentage automatically to the battlefield park. This 6 percent of sales augmented the park's interpretation budget.[3]

Aside from the money it provided, Swain considered the expanded Eastern sales area in the visitor center an important part of the park's interpretive program. Each piece of quality information carried away by visitors extended their stay, allowing them to "interact with the resource, with the story of Manassas, days later, weeks later, months later." This "portable interpretation" elaborated on the Civil War battles and kept people in touch with the past. To aid in this effort, Swain avoided "rubber tomahawk" items and instead focused on book reprints, histories, and other educational materials.[4]

The improvements to the visitor center helped offset the understaffing of the park's interpretive program in 1980. For five months after the departure of R. Brien Varnado and before the arrival of Swain, chief historian Stuart Vogt assumed the duties of acting superintendent. Two park technicians left before the start of the traditionally busy summer season, leaving the interpretive program further shorthanded. Supervisory park technician David Ruth, who became the acting chief historian, and seasonal Michael Andrus, who coordinated the Volunteers-in-the-Park program and later became a full-time employee, made up the difference admirably, presenting guided tours, living history demonstrations, and Stone House self-directed tours. Further assistance came from James Burgess, who joined the interpretive staff later in the year.[5]

More enhancements to park interpretation followed. In 1982, prompted by the belief that the existing audiovisual program was the "worst interpretive film in the Park Service," the Sons of Confederate Veterans donated $7,000 to the park for a new one. Members of the Confederate organization pointed out to NPS Director Russell E. Dickenson that the old slide program, developed at the end of Wilshin's superintendency, failed to relate the significant events of the two Manassas battles, particularly Second Manassas, and instead gave a general overview of the entire Civil War. They also argued that the multiple causes for the Civil War needed explanation, not just the issue of slavery.[6]

The Park Service's Harpers Ferry exhibit planning center began designing a new audiovisual program, based on input from park and agency historians. Although recognizing the inadequacies of the former program in conveying specifics about the two Manassas battles, Swain stressed that he wanted a ten-to-twelve-minute show that appealed more to the general public than to the Civil War buff, who represented a small portion of the overall visitation at the park. Edwin C. Bearss, a well-known Civil War authority and then NPS chief historian, emphasized the need for augmenting the discussion on Second Manassas, especially making clear that this battle became a high-water mark for the South.[7]

The new slide program opened in the park's auditorium in time for the annual national camp of the Sons of Confederate Veterans in mid-August

1983. Reconstructing the narrative from diary entries, the show revolved around a Confederate soldier from the Stonewall Brigade and a Union soldier from the Iron Brigade who had fought at both First and Second Manassas. Period photographs, engravings, and Civil War music set the tone for the presentation. Visitors now had the opportunity to learn about the experiences of the men who had fought at Manassas.[8]

Another correction to the park's interpretive program came in 1985 when temporary historian John Hennessy completed sixteen Second Manassas troop movement maps, accompanied by 380 pages of supporting text. As Bearss later recalled, these maps should have been completed during the 1956–66 Mission 66 parks improvement program, but Wilshin had failed to recognize their usefulness as management and interpretive tools and did not pursue them. Hennessy's maps assisted Swain and the park historians in recognizing the significance of certain tracts of land and in enhancing Second Manassas interpretation. Some battle lines that had been "fogged in conjecture" were now clarified with solid documentation.[9]

Hennessy displayed his avid interest in Second Manassas and his thorough understanding of historical scholarship in his work on the troop movement maps. Swain had hired him as a temporary employee in 1980, and although Swain tried to obtain funding for upgrading the position to full time, Hennessy completed the maps as a temporary park historian. Swain later characterized the arrangement as outright exploitation because temporary employees did not receive full benefits. Swain did convince the Eastern National Park and Monument Association to fund a portion of Hennessy's travel research, which enabled him to conduct background research across the country. With this information in hand, he drew mockups of the maps, which the Denver Service Center then refined and prepared for publication through the Eastern park cooperating association. Bearss called the complete 380-page study a "model of its kind," representing "exceptionally high quality."[10]

Swain also encourage wayside exhibits. These trailside markers, positioned at key stops in the First and Second Manassas walking and auto tours, gave visitors information on the significance of a specific site to the two battles. Using the revised audiovisual program as a model, Woody Harrell, the chief park historian who had replaced Vogt in 1982, promoted the concept of letting "voices from the past . . . speak to the visitor today." As the waysides evolved, they included quotations from soldiers, troop position maps, photographic reproductions, and supporting text. The new exhibit markers, which were not installed until after Swain left in 1988, replaced what had been a hodge-podge of markers installed over the previous thirty years.[11]

More interpretive changes came in 1985 when Edmund Raus transferred from the Fredericksburg and Spotsylvania County Battlefields Memorial National Military Park to Manassas to take over Harrell's position of chief historian. With funding from Eastern National Park and Monument Association, Raus initiated bus tours of Second Manassas during summer 1986. This was so successful that it was repeated in subsequent years. Raus broadened the focus of the Stone House exhibits, which had centered on the building as a field hospital, to show the impact of the battles on civilians living on or near the battlefield. He also introduced special outreach programs to enhance the park's image in the community. He organized Saturday lectures and films in the visitor center auditorium, an annual Christmas open house, and five-mile guided hikes through the battlefield each spring and fall. With a $25,000 grant, Raus initiated a new park education program designed to meet state school curriculum standards and the needs of Prince William County school teachers. To encourage older children to learn about Civil War history, the park renewed its student intern program.[12]

Raus also helped organize the park's observances of the 125th anniversaries of the First and Second Battles of Manassas in 1986 and 1987. In keeping with the policy that NPS Director Conrad Wirth had established after the 1961 First Manassas Reenactment, the battlefield park hosted only special artillery firing demonstrations, leaving the large-scale reenactments to private organizations on non-national park lands. Civil War music programs and guided Second Manassas tours by Hennessy, who had since left the park, gave visitors an opportunity to learn about the battles and the time period. Many people from the local community returned several times to participate in the commemorative activities.[13]

William Penn Mott Jr., who followed Dickenson as NPS director in 1985, used the opportunity of the First Manassas anniversary gathering to address a modern-day threat to the integrity of historic sites. He noted that interstate highways, high-rise complexes, housing subdivisions, and other developments threatened to encircle protected national park areas. For a place like the Manassas battlefield, Mott warned that such intrusions could "destroy the historical atmosphere of the parks just as surely as adverse development within their boundaries." Scenic buffers and land acquisition were some avenues the National Park Service could pursue to protect national

parks, but the example of the 1980 boundary expansion at Manassas demonstrated the high cost and protracted amount of time needed.[14]

Mott recognized that each national park site relied on the zoning and
building permit system established and enforced by local jurisdictions for
the effective control of the surrounding land. In an effort to build bridges
with these officials and their voting publics, Mott invited his listeners to
join in partnership with the Park Service to serve the needs of both the local community and the national parks. He defended this arrangement by
pointing to the benefits of having a place like the Manassas battlefield park
in Prince William County. Tourist spending helped the local economy while
residents could enjoy the attractive open space maintained by the federal
government. The national park also enhanced the quality of life in the
county by attracting new industry and employers to the area. By considering
the relationship as a partnership in which everyone benefited, Mott hoped
to address development threats in a nonconfrontational manner. His olive
branch offering was ignored by Prince William County officials but accepted by the William Center developer, Hazel/Peterson Companies.[15]

Planned Mixed-Use Development

Director Mott's call for partnerships between the local community and the
National Park Service faced its first test in 1986 when Prince William County
representatives reviewed a new zoning category, at Hazel/Peterson Companies' request, called a planned mixed-use district (PMD). This category,
which would "encourage and accommodate a mix of commercial, office
and residential development," represented a changing trend in real estate
development. Pioneered in Houston by developer Gerald D. Hines, planned
mixed use linked a range of commercial and business enterprises together
in an integrated space that economically offset the high cost of the land.
The Houston Galleria joined for the first time a retail mall, a hotel, and an
office tower, all interconnected and serviced by multilevel parking garages
that allowed consumers to park once and walk to their different destinations within the larger complex.[16]

Hazel/Peterson, along with other developers nationwide, adopted this
plan for suburban development and added a residential component, giving
people the opportunity to live close to where they worked and shopped.

This mix became a powerful draw for corporations, which were always seeking the best and brightest employees they could afford. People liked the idea of working in a setting that was close to home with nearby shopping alternatives, and businesses responded in growing numbers by moving to planned mixed-use areas, with the Hazel/Peterson Fair Lakes development in Fairfax County, Virginia, being one notable example.[17]

Fair Lakes is a complex combination of imposing development and park-like settings. Its 657 acres contain more than 5 million square feet of office, retail, and hotel space, an amount comparable to the city of Dayton, Ohio. Winding roads pass walking paths and ponds where Hazel/Peterson encouraged waterfowl to nest. Plenty of trees and shrubbery soften the contours further, making Fair Lakes seem more like a park than the economically driven business community it is. Small shopping centers are located within the development, and a full-scale regional mall called Fair Oaks sits only five miles down the road. Houses complete the mix. According to Milt Peterson, who had joined forces with John T. ("Til") Hazel in 1970 to create what would become one of the largest real estate development companies in northern Virginia, Fair Lakes residents and workers have the sense of living and working in the country, a pleasing alternative to commuting from suburban subdivisions to crowded downtown office buildings.[18]

Hazel/Peterson wanted to build the same type of mixed-use development in Prince William County on the old Marriott tract. Although this tract had A-1 agricultural zoning, the county had designated the site for corporate park development in its 1982 comprehensive plan. Superintendent Swain opposed this designation during the public review process, asking for more specific information on the type of development that might be approved, such as height restrictions and level of density. Prince William representatives left these questions unanswered until a definite proposal was made.[19]

Two development plans were presented during the first half of the 1980s, both of which were warmly received by the county. First, the state of Virginia considered building the Center for Innovative Technology in Prince William County, and the county convinced Marriott, still the landowner, to offer 150 acres toward a package bid. The state instead chose a site along the Dulles Toll Road. Then in 1985, Centennial Development Corporation purchased the entire tract from Marriott and announced its plans to build a high-technology office park. In December of that year, however, Centennial backed out, citing high investment costs. Exact descriptions of these development projects were never completed, leaving Swain with the uncomfortable belief that the county would support almost any type of corporate park development next to the battlefield park. His fears were confirmed in spring 1986 when the Hazel/Peterson Companies obtained an option on the same land and pursued its vision of building a Fair Lakes-type community in Prince William County.[20]

Before Hazel/Peterson could begin developing the land, the planned mixed-use district zoning—a category that did not exist in Prince William County—had to be approved. Although eager to have the planned office park, the board of county supervisors had less interest in the residential component, which demanded more government-funded services and produced less net tax revenues than commercial developments. Fearing that Hazel/Peterson would otherwise abandon the site, the supervisors finally acquiesced and approved the PMD zoning in April 1986. Having the complete development was more important to the supervisors than losing everything over one of its components. Their fears were well-grounded. A month later Hazel argued that it was "totally absurd" for his company to build the office park without the further incentives a residential-retail area would provide.[21]

With the required zoning in place, Hazel/Peterson announced in May what it envisioned for William Center, the 542-acre development that would sit next to the Manassas National Battlefield Park. Modeled after Fair Lakes, William Center would include an office park of about 275 acres; a residential neighborhood consisting of 975 townhouses, garden apartments, and single-family homes; and a small shopping center. Hazel expected the project to take ten years to build, and although he would not set a figure on its value, development officials estimated its cost as exceeding $100 million. Hazel did boast that William Center would be a "catalytic agent" for a commercial boom in Prince William County, blazing the way for expanded economic development along the I–66 corridor.[22]

Negotiations with Hazel/Peterson

When Swain saw the newspaper headlines announcing the William Center proposal, he considered his options. He knew that because the county had approved mixed-use district zoning at the request of Hazel/Peterson, it would view favorably the company's specific proposal for William Center. Making any opposing statements during the public review process seemed fruitless. Swain based this judgment on his past experiences at county public hearings: developers had unlimited time in which to present their proposals at zoning hearings, but Swain had a three-minute time limit to make his case. After three minutes, the county representatives would cut him off.[23]

It had become Swain's custom to pack as much information as possible on the visual impact of new buildings along the park's periphery into these three-minute presentations. He felt the Manassas National Battlefield Park had the potential to be "self-buffering" because its rounded shape allowed visitors the opportunity to escape the heavy development in northern Virginia and step back into a nineteenth-century countryside. Tall buildings along the boundaries would disrupt this historic presence, constantly reminding people of the present. During the zoning hearing over the proposal to build a ten-story Holiday Inn near the park's southern entrance, Swain showed its potential visual intrusion by running helium balloons at the proposed height of the building and then photographing the balloons from different places in the park. By restricting the height of the Holiday Inn and using trees to hide the building, Swain argued that the development would not interfere with the historic preservation mission of battlefield park.[24]

In an ideal world, Swain would have liked no new buildings near the park, but he understood the county's need to diversify its tax base. By asking for height restrictions, he offered what he thought was a compromise. But the county ignored Swain's pleas and in November 1985 amended the regulations for its commercial zoning category to increase the height restriction from forty-five to seventy feet. As Swain wrote in his weekly report at the time, "it appears that Prince William County is going out of its way to accommodate the wishes of developers." [25]

In view of the county's history toward developers and the park, Swain gained permission from the regional director to contact the Hazel/Peterson Companies directly to discuss park concerns over the William Center proposal. Swain began these negotiations in June 1986, one month before Director Mott's speech encouraging active partnerships between the Park Service and local jurisdictions. These negotiations also came before Hazel/Peterson presented its proposal to the Prince William Board of County Supervisors for review and approval. Swain found the developer a willing listener and negotiator. As Til Hazel later stated, "it wasn't our intention to be hostile to the Park Service. . . . [It was] simply a good faith effort" to keep an interested neighbor informed. Hazel had obtained the option on the Marriott tract with some trepidation, knowing that the Park Service had once considered acquiring the tract. He had reviewed the 1980 Senate hearings over the boundary expansion and felt assured that the Service no longer had an interest in obtaining the land. Sen. Dale Bumpers, who headed the Interior subcommittee that approved the 1980 legislation, later agreed with Hazel's characterization, saying that the 1980 park expansion was supposed to be the final one. Hazel, wanting to avoid contests with the park or park advocates, welcomed the opportunity to talk with the park superintendent.[26]

These discussions between Hazel/Peterson and Swain resulted in the developer adopting several proffers that largely addressed the Park Service's major concerns about William Center. One series of proffers dealt with the visual impact of the development on the battlefield park. First, Swain asked for and obtained an extended buffer zone along Lee Highway, including plantings, berms, or other suitable methods to screen the development from view, thereby protecting the park's Brawner Farm tract from being overwhelmed by its neighbor across the street. Unfortunately, Hazel/Peterson planned to use deciduous trees as a screen, which would fail to hide the development during the winter. Second, Hazel/Peterson agreed to limit the height of all buildings to forty-five feet. Although the planned mixed-use district zoning (which was separate from the commercial zoning category) already contained this restriction, special use permits could be granted by the county for a particular development. Swain convinced Hazel/Peterson of the importance of staying within the forty-five-foot limit for the sake of reducing the visual impact on the park.[27]

Four additional proffers related directly to traffic concerns. First, Hazel/Peterson agreed to provide $2,250,000 toward the design and construction of an interchange at Interstate 66 and the proposed William Center Boulevard, the main artery for the development. This interchange would relieve traffic on Lee Highway through the battlefield park and provide easy access for residential and commercial residents of William Center. Swain expected this interchange to become part of the larger Route 234 bypass that the county had proposed building. Hazel/Peterson also agreed to direct William Center Boulevard traffic south onto Groveton Road, an existing road that separated the proposed William Center from the battlefield park. This arrangement would prevent overloading the Route 234–Lee Highway intersection. Another nod toward traffic concerns included eliminating Lee Highway access to the community shopping center, meant to decrease use of this already heavily traveled road. Finally, the developer agreed to construct storm water retention ponds to limit drainage to the predevelopment rate. This action would prevent frequent flooding of the Lee Highway–Route 234 intersection, where the Stone House stood.[28]

Hazel/Peterson addressed other concerns raised by local residents with additional proffers. The Northwest Prince William Citizens Association (NWPWCA), of which Annie Snyder was a member, persuaded Hazel/Peterson to decrease the number of residential units in the William Center development from 975 dwellings to 560, thereby reducing the county's burden to provide adequate schools and other services for these new residents. To further assist the county, the developer agreed to contribute $50,000 toward public school site acquisition and construction and another $100,000 for public school purposes. Hazel/Peterson included a community trail system to facilitate pedestrian movements throughout the development. Recreational facilities proffered by the developer included a community swimming pool and center, two tennis courts, two multipurpose courts, and a multipurpose ball field. Five acres were dedicated for a fire station and a commuter parking lot. With these concessions in hand and knowing that they had made the best of a bad situation, the NWPWCA spoke in favor of the William Center rezoning.[29]

Tough Decision

Satisfied that he got "the best deal he could," Swain spoke at the county hearing in support of rezoning the William Center tract from agricultural to planned mixed use. As Swain expected, the board of county supervisors voted six to one in favor of the application (the local representative voted against the rezoning), making the rezoning and the attached proffers legally binding. Swain did not want the William Center development next to the park, but he knew that his negotiations with Hazel/Peterson, along with those by the NWPWCA, resulted in a proposal that would have much less impact than other possible developments. He had toured the Fair Lakes development with one of Hazel/Peterson's landscape architects and felt that the same kind of "campus like office park" could be done at Manassas without being overwhelmingly intrusive. Swain also knew that the county could not have negotiated the same types of concessions with Hazel/Peterson that he obtained. According to Virginia state law, Prince William County could accept proffers, but it could not demand them as a condition for approving a development.[30]

Swain made a tough decision to enter into negotiations with Hazel/Peterson Companies, and many members of the preservation community attacked him for appearing to favor development over the battlefield park's integrity. Jerry Russell, national chairman for the Civil War Round Table Associates, advocated in his organization's monthly newsletter Swain's reassignment to another park where he would "not need to be sensitive to history, or be a strong representative of NPS." Russell's call prompted many of his readers, all Civil War enthusiasts, to write the National Park Service or their congressional representatives demanding explanations for Swain's action. Other preservationists argued that if Swain had resolutely stood for protection of the battlefield park, the Prince William Board of County Supervisors would have taken his stance into account when determining the fate of the old Marriott tract. Preservationists believed that the Park Service managers should aggressively defend park sites from outside assaults. Talking with developers and local landowners was acceptable, especially because so many parks were becoming islands in a sea of development, but preservation of park resources should remain paramount.[31]

National Park Service representatives defended Swain's negotiations with Hazel/Peterson Companies. Susan Moore, who came to the Manassas National Battlefield Park in the fall of 1985 as a management assistant and had worked closely with Swain on land-use and land protection issues, including the William Center development, later argued that the Park Service had to talk with developers and county planners to protect the park. Moore stated that unfortunately "it looked like we were in cahoots with the developer," which she insists was never the case. Chief Historian Bearss also defended Swain to Russell and other Civil War enthusiasts, pointing out that Swain had "stuck his neck out" for the Service and had negotiated an honest deal that was in the park's best interests. Bearss considered Swain a "first-class manager" who discharged his responsibilities at the Manassas battlefield in a "conscientious and satisfactory manner." National Capital Regional Director Jack Fish and NPS Director Mott echoed these statements in support of Swain. For Mott, Swain had implemented the very call for partnerships that he had proposed.[32]

Swain may have appeared less committed to preservation because of his quiet manner in handling issues. Bearss characterized him as low key: "He doesn't lose his temper. He is viewed as somebody that can talk reasonably with both sides." Moore stressed Swain's nonconfrontational nature, his "voice of reason" in which he thought things through very carefully and then acted in the way he felt best preserved the park's resources. And

Moore perceptively pointed out that this was new territory for the Park Service: the agency had not been an active negotiator with developers in the past. To Bearss and Moore, Swain's personality and management style were assets when addressing Hazel/Peterson's proposal. To Russell and other preservationists, though, Swain appeared more like an "automaton bureaucrat" who "rolled over and didn't do anything."[33]

Swain had also generated some bad press in spring 1986. When the park had acquired land to the east of the Stone Bridge, as allowed under the 1980 boundary expansion legislation, the NPS had to remove an old gas station. Swain brought in contractors to demolish the building and remove the debris. To save money, Swain agreed to let the contractors place the waste on the northern slope of Henry Hill as opposed to hauling it to the county dump. Swain chose the side of Henry Hill because his maintenance chief had complained that ground depressions there had made the hill difficult to mow. The debris and added top soil would have helped fill in the depressions. The local newspaper reported the event and included a photograph showing the "battlefield eyesore" within sight of the Stone House. In response to public pressure, Swain had the debris moved, but his decisions raised doubts about his commitment to historic preservation.[34]

Despite his poor judgment on the gas station debris, Swain's actions following the William Center rezoning demonstrate his continued commitment to preserve the historical integrity of the Manassas battlefield park. Just days after the rezoning approval, Swain wrote Regional Director Fish and requested immediate assistance in reidentifying the exact park boundaries around the Stone House intersection. Swain needed this information to show that the state did not have sufficient right of way to add left and right turn lanes to the intersection, an idea pushed by the local county supervisor. Swain feared that adding turn lanes would ultimately result in the widening of Lee Highway and Route 234 through the park, an idea that the county and state came to support in 1987. The park's historic flavor would be lost in the noise and pollution of thousands of commuters traveling the high-speed multilane roads through the park. The fact that the county had failed to support funding for the William Center interchange at I–66, thereby making Lee Highway a major access road to the new development, added extra urgency to Swain's request for help.[35]

Swain's strategy worked. Years before, the county had straightened out a dogleg on Route 234 just south of the intersection and in the process had placed the current 234 shoulder on park land under a special use permit. The county then deeded to the park the land vacated by the straightening.

Once it became clear in 1987 that Prince William County and Virginia wanted to improve the Lee Highway–Route 234 intersection by widening both roads, Swain called them on the special use permit. He warned that the Park Service would not give a permit to expand the road and that the Service would not renew the special use permit, which was due to expire in 1989. This meant that the county could widen only three of the four arms of the intersection, making the entire endeavor unprofitable. Talk of upgrading Lee Highway–Route 234 quieted, keeping the historic crossroad intact. Yet the quiet around the Manassas National Battlefield Park was only temporary: in 1988 the Hazel/Peterson Companies dropped a bombshell.[36]

Chapter 10

STONEWALLING THE MALL

"It is not easy for a Republican, particularly a conservative Republican, to advocate the taking of land, particularly when that is bound to be expensive, but it seems warranted in this emergency case," said Gordon J. Humphrey, a senator from New Hampshire in response to the January 1988 announcement by the Hazel/Peterson Companies of the addition of a regional shopping mall to the William Center's residential-office complex. In Humphrey's opinion, the mall and its accompanying traffic and parking lots would turn the Manassas National Battlefield Park into "little more than a pastoral backdrop for another metropolitan concrete complex." To prevent this, Humphrey supported a legislative taking bill, which would automatically put the land under federal ownership, leaving resolution of its cost to later discussions. Senator Humphrey's remarkable stand, especially under the Reagan administration's call for less government interference in local affairs, demonstrates the far-reaching effects of this third battle of Manassas.[1]

These effects have been enduring. Manassas battlefield park became a household word in the late 1980s and continues to have star power. Congressional budget battles threatening to shut down the federal government prompt news reporters to trek out to Manassas and show viewers what they would lose if this park (and others like it) were forced to close. This name recognition has had other effects. Public interest in Manassas has translated into millions of dollars donated to battlefield preservation efforts and expanded membership in preservation organizations. Congress has aided the work of private groups by protecting sites and expanding boundaries at existing parks. The Manassas mall controversy raised public awareness about historic preservation in ways no other previous issue had.

Initial Reaction

In late January 1988 Bob Kelly, Hazel/Peterson's vice president for public relations and the company's principal contact person for the park, casually announced to Swain and park management assistant Susan Moore that Hazel/Peterson Companies wanted to build a regional shopping mall on top of Stuart's Hill. As Moore remembered it, Kelly just dropped by park headquarters and said "Oh, by the way, we've changed our plans slightly. Will this cause you any concern?" Swain and Moore immediately recognized the import of this news: more traffic needing more interchanges and upgraded roads, a highly visible megastructure on top of the hill. The proposed campuslike office park set within a heavily landscaped setting and joined by residential homes and a small community shopping center had now become a bustling shopping mecca for northern Virginia. Swain "cried foul" as the Park Service evaluated its response to this change in plans.[2]

Til Hazel and his company proposed to build a 1.2 million-square-foot mall, anchored by five major department stores, as the centerpiece of the 542 acre William Center. Hazel/Peterson obtained the services of the Edward J. DeBartolo Corporation, one of the country's leading owners and operators of shopping centers, for the project. Construction was expected to start in two years, once stores had been signed up. To show the importance of the mall, William Center literature proudly boasted that in its first ten years of operation, the mall and the other nonresidential components of the tract would generate $27.3 million in net fiscal benefits for the county. After twenty years, Hazel/Peterson estimated the total fiscal benefit to be almost $180 million, a healthy infusion into county coffers.[3]

Mindful of these tax revenues, Prince William officials welcomed the idea of having a huge shopping mall built on the William Center property. Supervisor Robert Cole relished the prospect that his county would no longer have to "stand in the shadow of Fairfax County," an adjacent county that had experienced a massive building boom in recent years. With the mall in place, other quality development, including corporate offices and headquarters, would logically follow, ensuring the economic health of the

western portion of the county. Although the chairman of the board of
county supervisors, Kathleen K. Seefeldt, voiced concerns over the shape
of the resulting transportation network, she remained generally in favor of
the mall.[4]

The mall announcement caught the NPS off guard. Swain remembered
the feeling as playing a "bait and switch game" and wondered if Hazel/
Peterson had always intended to build a mall but waited to announce it
until after the rezoning had been approved. In fact, Hazel had wanted to
include a mall in the William Center development from the start and had
sought the planned mixed-use district zoning because this zoning category
permitted such a retail center. The PMD description allowed for unspeci-
fied retail development. Hazel waited to make the mall announcement until a developer had been identified and signed onto the project. This delay
in fully disclosing the extent of development planned for the William Center left Swain and many others feeling deceived. As Annie Snyder wrote
in early February, western Prince William County residents felt "deceived,
cheated and defrauded" by the Hazel/Peterson Companies. For many, the
developer showed an apparent disregard for the good faith agreements it
had made with the Park Service and the Northwest Prince William County
Association (NWPWCA).[5]

For the Park Service and mall opponents, adding a regional shopping
mall to the original campuslike office park created an entirely new situation, one that threatened the existing Manassas battlefield park. First,
the Park Service and county residents believed that William Center traffic
would increase considerably with the mall, with as many as 80,000 cars per
day traveling to the shopping center. Lee Highway and Route 234 through
the battlefield park would be especially attractive for handling this traffic,
thereby putting the battlefield park in jeopardy. Hazel disagreed, saying
that only the sixteen shopping days preceding Christmas would bring this
level of mall visitation. The rest of the year, the mall would generate lighter
traffic than office complexes, which create heavy rush hour demands.
Second, the Park Service worried about the road widenings the increased
mall traffic would necessitate, specifically at the Stone House intersection.
Third, building a mall on top of Stuart's Hill would make the complex visible
from many points in the battlefield park. Swain had worked hard to reduce
this type of visual intrusion in his 1986 negotiations with Hazel/Peterson.
The mall proposal made those negotiations seemingly immaterial.[6]

Finally, for many residents, the regional mall seemed incompatible with
the historical and environmental value of the surrounding countryside.

Malls represented blatant twentieth-century commercialism and materialism. They ate up land with acres of parking lots. It seemed that a mall could
be built anywhere, whereas the few remaining pieces of open land should
be saved. Many mall opponents also questioned the plan's economic sound-
ness. Fair Oaks, a similarly sized mall, was located only eight miles east of
the William Center site. Tyson's Corner, with two huge shopping centers,
was not far from Fair Oaks. With so many regional shopping opportunities
located close by, the Manassas mall might be the economic loser.[7]

Seeking a way to address this situation, NPS Director Mott turned to
Prince William County. Mott reinvoked his call for partnerships between
federal and local governments. In a 5 February letter to Kathleen Seefeldt
of the board of supervisors, Mott asked the county to join with the Park
Service to consider the impact of the mall on both the county and the
battlefield park. Mott knew that the landscape surrounding the battlefield
park would inevitably change and that the Park Service could not acquire
all lands, and he understood the "heavy burdens born by county officials
in rapidly developing areas," yet he believed that through partnerships,
county officials and the Park Service could achieve mutually beneficial
goals. By reducing the visual impact of outside developments, the park's
historic integrity would be preserved, and the county would have a valuable
resource. "In the spirit of full and friendly" cooperation, Mott asked Seefeldt to give the mall proposal a "thorough review."[8]

Mott may have been honest in his attempt to forge a working relationship with the county, but he exacerbated the situation by publicly releasing
the letter at the same time he mailed it to Seefeldt. Seefeldt sent an angry
reply, accusing Mott of trying to "inflame" citizens and prevent a rational
and substantive discussion of the issues. Seefeldt called Mott's gesture toward partnerships with local government "neither useful nor wise" and
questioned the Park Service's commitment to preservation. She contended
that Prince William officials were "extremely proud" of their county's heritage and had done "nothing, nor will it, to desecrate or damage" the battlefield. In addition, Seefeldt questioned the Park Service's stewardship of its
own park in light of the 1986 dumping of the gas station debris on Henry
Hill and the continuing proposal to cut down acres of mature trees to restore the historic scene. In her opinion, the mall would bring more visitors
to the battlefield park, and thus the two facilities would likely "complement each other, and not necessarily compete." Hazel/Peterson's "extensive measures" to place buffers and upgrade roads would help ensure the
historic integrity of the park.[9]

Fig. 13. Annie Snyder got her gun figuratively when she took on Til Hazel and his proposal to build a shopping mall next to Manassas National Battlefield Park. (Photo by James A. Purcell. © 1984, *The Washington Post*. Reprinted with permission)

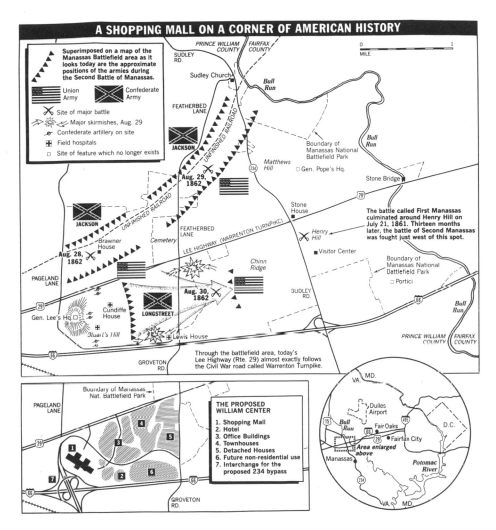

Map. 1. Approximate positions of Union and Confederate forces during the Second Battle of Manassas are superimposed on a map of the existing battlefield park and adjacent land earmarked for the William Center development, graphically illustrating the land's historical significance. (Map by Dave Cook. © 1988, *The Washington Post*. Reprinted with permission)

contacts with the Department of the Interior, the Environmental Protection Agency, and other federal agencies, forcing them to respond to the coalition's concerns.[14]

While Boasberg initiated legal proceedings, Bruce Craig brought into the fold the first national organization. Craig, who became an ardent supporter of Snyder's work after attending the 5 February rally, went back to the National Parks and Conservation Association (NPCA), where he worked as a cultural resources program coordinator, and convinced its president to make the NPCA the first national organization to oppose publicly the William Center project. Craig then convinced Ian Spatz from the National Trust for Historic Preservation to consider taking on the Manassas mall issue. From these discussions, the National Heritage Coalition formed in mid-May. Sponsored by the NPCA and the National Trust, this organization became an umbrella for Civil War, conservation, historic preservation, military, and other preservation-minded groups. The National Heritage Coalition pooled resources and helped make the Manassas mall a national issue. In the process, the coalition brought preservationists together in a way that had never been achieved in the past.[15]

More people quickly enlisted in the Save the Battlefield Coalition. Jody Powell, former press secretary for President Jimmy Carter and head of a Washington public relations firm, had read the *Washington Post*'s coverage of the mall and had told himself "this sounds outrageous." A phone call from Boasberg, whom Powell had met several months earlier, turned Powell's thoughts into action. Powell brought to the coalition his contacts with the media as well as the expertise to generate interest in the mall. Stories about the plight of the Manassas battlefield park soon rolled off the presses and onto the radio and television airwaves.[16]

When the Manassas mall story went national, it centered on Annie Snyder and her Save the Battlefield Coalition. Snyder's "absolute forthrightness and ability to carry a message" made her a logical focus for the campaign. Her command of theater, including an uncanny ability to cry in public at just the right moment, inspired millions of Americans to consider the emotional side of the issue. For Snyder, the battlefield park was hallowed ground, where soldiers, many of whom were barely teenagers, lost their lives. She wanted to preserve the battlefield as a national park for all time, so that present and future generations could visit it and learn from it. Having the William Center mall so close to the parklands appeared as a real threat to the park's integrity.[17]

Snyder, as well as many prominent historians, had long believed that

Stuart's Hill, site of the proposed mall, had enough historic significance to warrant inclusion in the battlefield park. Stuart's Hill had been Robert E. Lee's August 1862 headquarters, where he masterminded one of his most successful battles in the Civil War. Further research indicated that some minor skirmishing occurred on the eastern side of the William Center tract and that unmarked graves may have surrounded a field hospital used during the battle. This information added extra urgency to Snyder's opposition to the mall. Hazel/Peterson Companies hired a Civil War historian, Dr. James A. Schaefer, to conduct a historical investigation of the tract. Schaefer reported in August 1987 that no significant military actions occurred at the site, paving the way for the developer to proceed with construction. In 1988, however, Schaefer reassessed his conclusion and joined the preservationists, saying that it was ludicrous to consider Stuart's Hill as just another one of Lee's headquarters. Schaefer's reversal was prompted by the "keen sense of betrayal" he felt over the mall announcement, which had caught preservationists and the Park Service off guard. These historical opinions strengthened the conviction of Snyder and others that Stuart's Hill and the rest of the tract was hallowed ground and should have National Park Service protection.[18]

Snyder's commitment to preservation of the Manassas battlefields and Stuart's Hill was joined by her wish to save the semirural area where she had lived for forty years. Her farm sat within a few hundred yards of the William Center development, close enough to hear the bulldozers and see the steady construction work. This churning of the earth, particularly around Stuart's Hill, disturbed Snyder greatly. She saw land as a resource, not a commodity. Open space, in her opinion, gave urban populations a place to recreate and commune with nature. Undeveloped land provided ecological benefits to the surrounding communities. She wanted to preserve some of these advantages before unchecked development overwhelmed all of northern Virginia.[19]

Unlike many of her neighbors, Snyder did not believe that progress in and of itself was beneficial for Prince William County. She weighed the economic value of a particular development against the natural resource benefits of preserving the land. In the case of the campuslike office park Hazel/Peterson had proposed in 1986, Snyder had resisted pulling out her public relations artillery to fight the project. She did not welcome Hazel/Peterson with open arms, but she did work with the NWPWCA to obtain proffers and make the William Center as compatible as possible with the surrounding landscape. But for Snyder, all agreements were voided when Hazel/Peterson announced the addition of the regional shopping mall. The mall represented the kind of unchecked damaging growth that she had long opposed. For the sake of the battlefield park and for the sake of the rural countryside embracing the park, she resolved to fight.[20]

Park Service and Interior Negotiations

Aside from Mott's letter to Seefeldt, the National Park Service delayed taking a formal position on the mall issue until the end of April. As the Save the Battlefield Coalition gathered national attention, the NPS quietly reviewed the situation and determined that mall traffic through the battlefield park at the Stone House intersection represented the most serious threat to the historical integrity of the park. To accommodate the expected surge in vehicular traffic, Prince William County officials favored widening the two crossroads—Lee Highway and Route 234. This proposed widening would destroy whatever historic presence the intersection still had. The park would be effectively divided into quadrants, and interpretive efforts would suffer because visitors would be constantly crisscrossing the intersection to get to the historic park areas. The proximity of this traffic to the Stone House would also severely endanger its structural integrity.[21]

Director Mott presented this information to Secretary of the Interior Donald Hodel and asked for his assistance in reopening communication with the county and the developer. Mott rightly believed that the Park Service had to continue negotiations with the interested parties to ensure protection of the battlefield park. The NPS's active negotiations with Hazel/Peterson during the 1986 William Center rezoning had set the tone of the agency's involvement and made it difficult for the Service to stay on the sidelines with regard to the mall proposal. The neutral stance taken during the 1973 Marriott theme park proposal had been replaced by discussion and cooperation. Mott and Hodel sat down and discussed the mall situation with Prince William County representatives, Hazel/Peterson, the Virginia state highway authorities, the state historic preservation officer, congressional representatives, and the U.S. Department of Transportation. These initial meetings resulted in a compromise that Hodel and Mott announced on 28 April 1988.[22]

At the April press conference, Hodel and Mott noted that the proposed widening of the Stone House intersection would destroy the historical in-

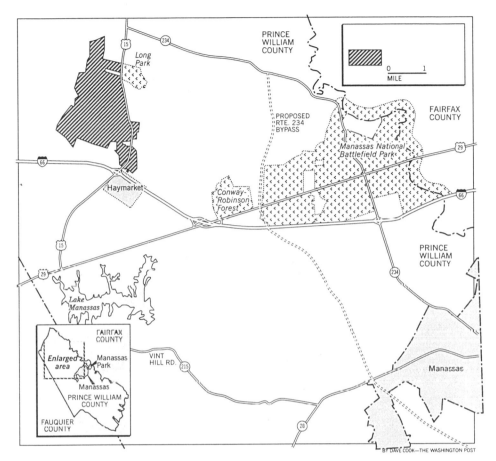

Map. 2. Interior Department officials proposed a compromise to the William Center mall controversy by supporting the Route 234 bypass, which they argued would funnel traffic out of the battlefield park and allow the National Park Service to close the roads inside the park. (Map by Dave Cook. © 1991, *The Washington Post*. Reprinted with permission)

tegrity of the battlefield park. As an alternative, they described how mall traffic could be rerouted. The compromise, which they emphasized was still a general concept and not an accomplished fact, involved relocating the mall to a lower elevation, thus making it less visible from the park. Deciduous trees would help screen the development from the road, at least during the warmer months. The Park Service would provide text for Stuart's Hill interpretive displays, to be placed prominently near the buildings, to assist visitors in understanding its significance to Second Manassas. Hazel/Peterson would build two-story office buildings on the remainder of Stuart's Hill. The NPS would support efforts to route traffic out of the park, including building the Route 234 bypass, with a major interchange at the William Center tract, to accommodate north-south traffic, and widening Interstate 66, to remove east-west traffic from Lee Highway. Lee Highway and Route 234 would then be closed to through traffic and returned to gravel as they existed during the Civil War.[23]

The compromise plan excluded a key interest group, the Save the Battlefield Coalition. Prince William County officials accepted the offer for further negotiations, with Seefeldt commenting that "positive suggestions" had been made. Hazel/Peterson supported the proposed plan because it kept the mall and offered a solution to the traffic problem. Park Service officials agreed that the park's historical integrity would be best preserved by closing the roads, on which the compromise focused. Snyder and the Save the Battlefield Coalition, though, were outraged that Interior and the Park Service had not asked the preservationists, who had brought national attention to the issue, to the negotiating table. This affront seemed especially curious since the compromise plan implied that Stuart's Hill was of sufficient historic significance to warrant moving the mall and placing interpretive displays on the hill. Bolstered by this indirect admission, the Save the Battlefield Coalition rallied more attention to its cause.[24]

Wanting to reach an agreement acceptable to everyone, including the Save the Battlefield Coalition, the Park Service and Interior invited the involved parties to a series of task force meetings. The first conference ended with the hope that the compromise could be implemented, but subsequent meetings deteriorated as it became clear that the federal government could not force a negotiated compromise. Several factors influenced this deadlock. The Department of the Interior and the Park Service had no trump to bring the opposing parties into line. Their delay in responding to Hazel/Peterson's proposal, waiting until the SBC had attracted national attention to the mall, impaired the federal government's ability to take control of the situation. This situation worsened on 19 May when the Save the Battlefield Coalition irretrievably divorced itself from Interior's compromise plan and at a national press conference announced its continued opposition to the mall. The historical significance of the tract became a key issue, with former park historian John Hennessy arguing that Lee's planning on Stuart's Hill was critical to the outcome of Second Manassas.[25]

Fig. 14. Northern Virginia developer John T. ("Til") Hazel, whose motto was "never give up," had construction crews working twenty-four hours a day on his William Center shopping mall-residential-office complex next to Manassas National Battlefield Park, despite protests from preservationists. (Photo by James A. Parcell. © 1988, *The Washington Post.* Reprinted with permission)

Other reasons contributed to the deadlock over the Park Service's compromise plan. Hazel/Peterson exercised its legal right to proceed with construction on the site, twenty-four hours a day, seemingly bypassing any agreements that may have been made in the recent meetings. Coalition supporters wondered how the developer and Interior could be committed to reaching a compromise if Hazel's construction crews continued working at the site. And although everyone, including the SBC, agreed that closing Lee Highway and Route 234 was necessary to the long-term health of the park, they also recognized the high costs involved. Hefty financial commitments by state and federal highway authorities were needed, which SBC lawyer Boasberg acknowledged publicly during the 19 May press conference, and this increased skepticism about the feasibility of the Park Service's compromise plan. Finally, members of Congress became involved, effectively removing the mall issue from the control of the Interior Department and the Park Service.[26]

Congressional Involvement

In mid-January 1988 Mike Andrews (D-Tex.) gladly accepted the opportunity to tour the Second Manassas battlefield with his friend, noted Civil War historian Dr. Frank Vandiver. They tramped around the Brawner Farm and discussed the pivotal actions taken by the South to win a second resounding victory at Manassas. A few days later, while flying home to Houston, Andrews read in the *Washington Post* that the Hazel/Peterson Companies planned to build a shopping mall on Stuart's Hill. Astounded by the incongruity of having a regional mall where Lee had had his headquarters, Andrews called his colleague Bob Mrazek (D-N.Y.) and enlisted his support in stopping the mall.[27]

For Andrews, the mall threatened to change forever the nature of the Manassas National Battlefield Park. With this "monstrous behemoth development next door," Andrews believed that the park's integrity would be lost. Mall traffic on the fragile park roads would be "devastating, insurmountable," and a critical part of the battlefield—Stuart's Hill—would be destroyed. The fact that the battlefield was in a congressional district other than that of Texan Andrews or New Yorker Mrazek did not stop Andrews. In his opinion, everyone in the federal government had a responsibility to ensure the protection of national parks. And Andrews did not agree with Interior Secretary Hodel that the compromise plan of closing the roads and allowing construction of the mall would preserve the historic Manassas landscape.[28]

Andrews and Mrazek first tried to talk with Til Hazel to resolve the controversy. Hazel's determined response, "no one is going to stop me from building this mall," convinced them to look elsewhere for support. They established contacts with the Save the Battlefield Coalition and exercised their legislative authority within the House of Representatives. In April they inserted language into a supplemental appropriations bill for the Department of Transportation that prohibited federal funds from being used to plan, design, or construct an interchange on I–66 at the William Center. Without the vital interchange, Andrews and Mrazek reasoned, the mall would not be able to survive and thus would not be built. Then, in May, they introduced H.R. 4526, which would have authorized the federal government to purchase the entire William Center tract and incorporate it into the Manassas battlefield park.[29]

But H.R. 4526 did not offer much hope of meeting the immediate threat of Hazel/Peterson's twenty-four-hour construction crews at the William Center. Before the House Subcommittee on National Parks and Public Lands would hold a hearing on the bill and thus begin the review and approval process, its chairman, Bruce Vento (D-Minn.), required that Andrews and Mrazek obtain 200 cosponsors for the bill. The two junior congressmen walked the House floor every time there was a vote and convinced members to sign on, even as Virginia's congressional representatives kept silent. The media attention generated by the SBC and the resulting flood of letters from concerned citizens across the country to their representatives helped Andrews and Mrazek in their task. In short order, they had well over the needed 200 cosponsors.[30]

Despite this initial success, H.R. 4526 faced an uphill battle. Congress was scheduled to recess in August and adjourn in October for election-year campaigning, leaving little time for discussion and passage of the bill. If, miraculously, the bill was passed and signed by the president, Hazel/Peterson would retain the right to develop the tract until Congress appropriated money for its acquisition and the Park Service completed a land protection plan justifying the purchase. Previous experience suggested that ultimate federal government acquisition of the William Center tract could be five years distant. This would give Hazel/Peterson time to construct the mall, irretrievably scar the landscape, and increase the land's value, making it prohibitively expensive.[31]

Frank Wolf (R-Va.) broke the Virginia congressional delegation's silence and offered a solution. For Wolf, "if this land [was] so important," as demonstrated by the national outcry and the professional opinions of historians, then "the government should have it." On 25 May, Wolf introduced H.R. 4691, which utilized a rarely used procedure called a "legislative taking" to allow the federal government to take immediate control of the property and to compensate the landowners at a later date. Legislative takings had been used in 1968 and 1978 for the Redwood National Park in California and in 1974 for the Piscataway Park in Maryland. H.R. 4691 also included $30 million for studying the feasibility of rerouting Lee Highway and Sudley Road out of the battlefield park, thereby addressing some of the concerns of the Interior Department. Hearings in Vento's subcommittee proceeded in rapid fashion on both H.R. 4526 and H.R. 4691 on 21 June.[32]

Congress's response to these bills depended on its reaction to the continuing war being played out in the national media over the William Center. By the end of May, Interior Secretary Hodel had joined the fray, publishing blistering attacks against Andrews, Mrazek, and other Democrats who had indicated support for H.R. 4526. In a letter to the *Houston Chronicle,* Hodel accused Andrews of using the Manassas battlefield issue to gain media attention at the expense of the U.S. taxpayers, who would have to foot the estimated $70 million bill for the William Center tract. Hodel accused Andrews of playing politics, although observers noted that none of the Republican sponsors of H.R. 4526 saw similar letters published in their districts.[33]

Aside from attempting to make the controversy a partisan issue, Hodel did raise two important points for Congress to consider before passing the proposed legislation. First, the cost of the William Center tract continued to escalate as Hazel/Peterson Companies proceeded with nonstop construction work. When discussions with the Interior Department and the National Park Service on the compromise plan had deteriorated, Til Hazel followed his maxim, "never give up," and pushed ahead. He decided that if Congress passed the legislative taking, he would make it an "expensive take." Congress thus had to justify the expected high price for the land.[34]

Second, Hodel wondered how far national park boundaries should extend to provide adequate protection of their natural and cultural resources. Hodel felt there had to be a reasonable limit that took cost into account. This issue had been debated during the previous boundary expansion attempts at the Manassas National Battlefield Park. Historical significance had been a primary factor, along with the desire to have the park shield itself by acquiring tracts between historic areas. With the William Center land, both its historical significance with regard to Second Manassas and the effect of large-scale development on the battlefield park warranted, in the eyes of SBC supporters, federal acquisition. Mott's call for partnerships between the federal government and local interests had shown its strengths and weaknesses during the William Center controversy. When Superintendent Swain had entered into negotiations with Hazel/Peterson Companies in 1986, the resulting office park complex addressed the Park Service's most serious concerns. But these negotiations proved insufficient once the developer announced the mall. Congress had to decide if it should rely on such partnerships in the future.[35]

As Hodel tried to undercut the efforts of the Democratic members of Congress with his articles in local newspapers, the Save the Battlefield Coalition organized a huge rally at the battlefield park on a steamy Saturday in mid-July. This kept the mall issue in the media as Congress recessed for the Fourth of July holiday. The coalition ensured television coverage by using a special "TV blue" backdrop for the stage, which is most compatible with television cameras, and having as many celebrities as possible participate. These efforts paid off. As one of Jody Powell's associates at Ogilvy & Mather stated, the rally was "critical because we got such incredible media." An estimated 5,000 people joined Snyder, Powell, Representative Mrazek and other members of Congress, and radio and newspaper personalities for a day of speeches and commemoration. Willard Scott, an NBC-TV weatherman, spoke on the meaning of the Manassas National Battlefield Park to him, a resident of Virginia and a Civil War enthusiast. Scott had long been interested in the outcome of the William Center controversy, aiding publicity by televising one of his weather broadcasts from the park during the controversy's early stages.[36]

Celebrities helped draw media attention, but the incongruity of having a shopping mall—that bastion of twentieth-century materialism—next to the battlefield park drew ordinary people. They traveled from as far away as Ohio, California, and even Puerto Rico to sport buttons reading "Stonewall the Mall, Save Manassas" and participate in the protest. Civil War reenactors, braving the 104-degree heat in their heavy woolen uniforms, gave demonstrations for the crowd. Participants joined the SBC in a rendition of the organization's theme song, "Manassas There's No Need for You to Die," performed by the artists who had recorded it, Dusty Rose and Tom Lofgren. Written by David Lowe and released to area radio stations in May, this song created an emotional appeal that drew people together. Its last stanza, sung against the backdrop of a Civil War fife and drum, encapsulated the issue for many:

> So I drove out to Manassas, stood alone and watched the sunset
> I imagined I would see grandfather fall
> Behind the place where he was standing
> Just before the bullet took him
> Is where they're going to build a SHOPPING MALL.

The bluntness of the image of a shopping mall standing where a Civil War soldier had fallen personalized the struggle and contributed to the rally's success.[37]

This overwhelming support for saving the battlefield, along with the potential for political exploitation, drew an immediate response from one of

Fig. 15. Youths dressed in Civil War–era costumes, reminders of the youngsters
who had served and died during the 1861–62 battles, dotted the estimated 5,000-
strong crowd of supporters at Manassas battlefield park who gathered one steamy
Saturday in mid-July 1988 to demonstrate their opposition to the William Center
mall. These boys, Thomas and Stephen Edgar, pictured with their father Tomas,
were members of the United Youth Army of the North and South. (Photo by Andres Alonso. © 1988, *The Washington Post*. Reprinted with permission)

Virginia's silent congressional leaders. Sen. John Warner had first declined
an invitation to participate in the rally, but as the date neared and the publicity increased, he realized the political value of attending. He still did not
intend to address the audience, but a lengthy conversation with Willard
Scott changed Warner's mind. Responding to the crowd's enthusiasm, Warner promised to introduce legislation to preserve a portion of the William
Center tract from development. When Congress reconvened in September,
he laid out his plan: federal purchase of 136 acres, or one-quarter of the
land, using a legislative taking; mall construction banned on the rest of
the tract; $11.9 million to build an interchange on Interstate 66 for the
Route 234 bypass; and a study of new roads needed to replace Lee Highway

and Sudley Road, should they be closed to through traffic in the battlefield park. Warner later scaled back the amount of land to 80 acres by eliminating some of the buffer along Lee Highway and thereby reducing the estimated cost of his proposal. In the Senate subcommittee hearing Warner argued that his plan protected the most historic areas of the tract, allowed the developer to build the office park as originally proposed, addressed the Park Service's concerns about traffic through the battlefield park, and saved the taxpayers the high cost of buying the entire tract.[38]

Some preservationists see Warner's announcement at the July rally as turning the tide toward acquisition. Having the senior member of the Virginia congressional delegation—and a Republican—admit that Stuart's Hill should be federal land strengthened the cause against the mall. In remarkably speedy fashion, in August before its recess, the House voted overwhelmingly for Andrews's and Mrazek's H.R. 4526, which had been amended to include Wolf's language of a legislative taking and the $30 million road study. The highly publicized rally and Warner's presence in the debate certainly influenced the outcome of this vote.[39]

Legislative Taking

The legislative taking gained momentum in the early fall: Sen. Dale Bumpers (D-Ark.), chairman of the Senate Subcommittee on Public Lands, National Parks and Forests, devoted his subcommittee's work to the mall controversy. Bumpers toured many western national parks during the summer recess. Amidst the magnificent scenery, he found several disturbing things. Condominiums and shopping centers abutted the Rocky Mountain National Park, threatening winter range critical to the park's wildlife populations. The Church Universal and Triumphant planned to develop lands adjoining Yellowstone National Park for their geothermal potential, possibly disturbing the most significant natural geyser basin in the world. Although, Bumpers admitted, Congress could not stop all these threats to the national parks, some land could be saved.[40]

One piece of land that Bumpers could preserve was the William Center tract. He brought the House's legislative taking bill and Warner's compromise plan before his committee members. He set the tone of the hearing by flatly stating his support for the taking bill, later calling Warner's compromise a "fig leaf" offering. Bumpers had been reading James M. Mc-

Pherson's Pulitzer Prize-winning account of the Civil War, *Battle Cry of Freedom,* and had talked with historic preservationists about the significance of the William Center land. He had also talked with Hazel/Peterson and Prince William County representatives, to gain an understanding of their reasons for allowing the mall to proceed. What he saw in the western national parks, though, confirmed that he had to take action before development made it impossible to act. The example at Gettysburg, where the battlefield park was surrounded by tacky commercial development, further prompted him to act.[41]

Determining how to act became the issue at the 8 September subcommittee hearing. Interior Secretary Hodel reiterated his position that the most serious threat to the battlefield park came from the traffic problems on Lee Highway and Route 234, a situation the legislative taking proposal did not directly address. If Congress took the William Center land, traffic might temporarily be abated, but only until another development went in down the road. The estimated $70-million price tag for the William Center would be better spent, in Hodel's opinion, by redirecting traffic out of the park and converting the park roads to their historic nonpaved appearance. Hodel so strongly believed that the legislative taking was the incorrect action that he stated he would recommend a presidential veto it if it did pass the Congress.[42]

Other people testified at the September hearing in support of Interior's compromise plan, which allowed mall construction and offered the Route 234 bypass as a solution to expected traffic increases through the park. Kathleen Seefeldt reminded Congress of the gravel trucks that barrel down the park roads and disturb places set aside for quiet reflection, such as the New York monuments located along Lee Highway. Congress could best protect the battlefield from such invasive noise, Seefeldt argued, by providing funding to build the Route 234 bypass. Seefeldt also noted that the county's growing population required the type of commercial development the William Center would offer. The tax revenues, estimated at $23 million a year, would allow the county to provide education, health, and other services to residents. Til Hazel reiterated the tax benefits of his development. No-growth residents who opposed the mall, he argued, had "thwarted all planning and growth and all effective development" in the county for twenty-five years, leaving the county without sufficient funding to support its burgeoning population. The William Center was a "quality project, [that would] serve Prince William and make a little money on the way." He saw Interior's plan as a "win-win" solution that Congress should support.[43]

Further testimony revealed significant flaws in Interior's plan. James M. McPherson, Edwards Professor of American History at Princeton University, made the unequivocal statement that "the very fate of the nation" was at stake at Second Manassas. In his opinion, the William Center tract had "the same kind of historical significance as Seminary Ridge does at Gettysburg." Lee and his generals James Longstreet and J. E. B. Stuart had their headquarters on the William Center land. Forty thousand Confederate and Union troops had congregated on the tract over the course of the three days of the battle. Some skirmishes resulted. Two Confederate field hospitals had stood on this land, and "probably hundreds of Confederate and some Union soldiers [were] buried on this property." McPherson stated that there was no evidence that these bodies had ever been reinterred.[44]

McPherson's testimony demonstrated that Interior's compromise plan was untenable because the historical significance of the William Center property warranted its protection. And there were other problems with the plan. William Leighty, the deputy secretary of transportation for Virginia, noted that the state had designated money in its six-year plan for design work on the 234 bypass, but not construction. This meant at least a six-year delay before the road work could begin. When questioned on the amount needed to build the bypass and widen I–66, Leighty stated that the cost would exceed $100 million. As the entire construction fund for all of northern Virginia was only $78 million, the state would require substantial federal assistance to complete the road program proposed by the Interior Department, but the compromise plan contained no specific provisions for financing road construction. In addition, the plan did not require that the mall's opening coincide with the road closures, thereby assuring the park's protection from mall traffic. Combined with McPherson's testimony, this information gave subcommittee members considerable reason to doubt the merits of Interior's compromise plan.[45]

The death knell of the compromise plan was the petition urging a halt to mall construction signed by 75,000 people from across the nation, which Annie Snyder presented to Congress. The Save the Battlefield Coalition had collected these signatures in only seven months, whereas during the boundary expansion debate in the 1970s, it took four years to obtain 9,000 signatures. The Coalition's efforts against the William Center property had effectively reached a broad segment of the country in a remarkably short period of time. A local zoning question had been transformed into a national issue. The senators responded and voted in favor of the legislative taking, both in the subcommittee and the full Energy and Natural Resources Committee. Warner's compromise proposal to buy only a portion of the tract and prohibit mall construction was seen as insufficient for protecting the historically significant land included in the William Center.[46]

On 7 October 1988, in the waning hours of the 100th Congress, Bumpers engaged in a debate on the legislative taking bill with James A. McClure (R-Idaho). Senators settled into their chairs after dinner as Bumpers began, with accompanying maps and charts, a decidedly Southern history lesson on the Civil War and Second Manassas. His "absolutely rhapsodic" retelling of the importance of a Southern win at Manassas captured the Senate's attention. In August 1862 General Lee thought the Confederacy's future rested on a victory at Manassas, as Britain and France had indicated that a decisive victory might lead them to provide much-needed industrial support to the South. Bumpers emphasized this fact to his spellbound audience. National Parks and Conservation Association representative Bruce Craig, who viewed the proceeding, stated that "it was one of the most amazing things where the floor of the Senate actually became a place for education and debate." Many senators made up their minds on this issue based on what they learned from Bumpers and McClure that night.[47]

McClure, intending to defuse his opponent's argument with hard realities, instead added fuel to Bumpers's fire. The conservative Republican reminded his colleagues that "there is not a single battlefield free" from the pressures of development. One-hundred-foot microwave towers threatened Bolivar Heights and Antietam. Richmond, Virginia, was inching its way over the Civil War battlefield of Cold Harbor. At what point, asked McClure, will this battle over land end? McClure concluded with the observation that "perhaps the most significant battle of the entire Manassas Battlefield with respect to the William Center tract is that being fought now"—not the Civil War battles. And so McClure unknowingly summed up the position taken by mall opponents: the William Center property required federal protection because it represented one of the few places Congress could save from the seemingly relentless attack of development. The senators voted 50 to 25 for the legislative taking.[48]

Victory in the Senate did not ensure success of the legislative taking. To avoid a certain presidential veto, the chairman of the House Ways and Means Committee, who was a friend of Mike Andrews, attached the taking legislation to the Tax Technical Corrections Bill. But negotiations between

House and Senate conferees on the tax portion of this bill broke down just before Congress adjourned, without much hope of finding a compromise. On 21 October headlines announced what seemed to be the certain failure of the legislative taking. Then, at 1:00 A.M. the next day, the bill passed. On 2 November it reached the White House. On 10 November President Ronald Reagan signed the bill into law, without fanfare or comment. At that very moment, the 558-acre William Center tract became part of the Manassas National Battlefield Park.[49]

Congress proved to be the essential factor in halting the mall and acquiring the William Center tract. Without congressional action, Til Hazel would have proceeded with his development. Prince William County officials offered no resistance to the mall proposal, affirming its legality. The Save the Battlefield's media campaign only made Hazel more determined to continue building, as evidenced by the twenty-four-hour, seven-days-a-week construction schedule that resulted in the near completion of three model homes. Public outcry was important in convincing individual members of Congress to support Andrews, Mrazek, Bumpers, Wolf, and Vento with the legislative taking. But all the media coverage and letters to Congress would not have stopped Hazel/Peterson if these members of Congress had not been convinced of the intrinsic importance of saving Stuart's Hill and the surrounding land from the impending development. Their commitment to preserving the William Center tract made the taking possible.[50]

Was It Worth It?

Two days after Reagan signed the tax bill and its legislative taking into law, Annie Snyder and one hundred devoted followers joined in a victory gathering of prayer and song on the William Center land. Since the beginning of the long fight, Hazel/Peterson's burly guards had blocked their entrance to the tract. As Bruce Craig remembered later, it was "very much an emotional feeling" finally to step on the land they had worked so long to save. A small plane flying overhead tried to break the solemnity of the event with its banner "The taking of private land is un-American." The image of the mall protesters and the plane highlights the mixed lessons from the incorporation of the William Center tract into the Manassas battlefield park.[51]

The National Park Service gained a great deal from the legislative taking. First and foremost, it obtained control of a 558-acre tract of land its

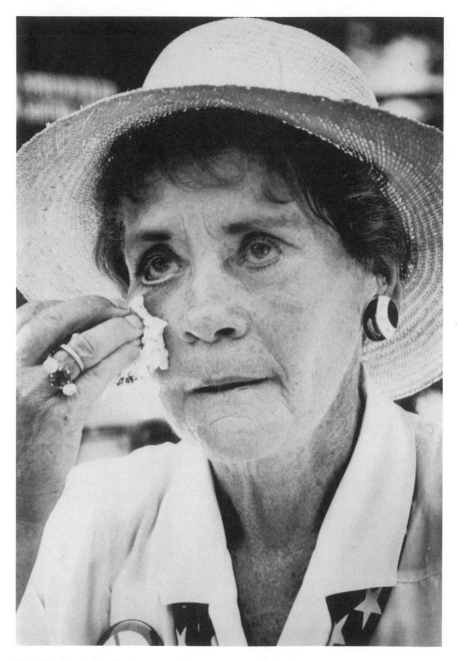

Fig. 16. Annie Snyder's unwavering commitment to the preservation of land associated with the two Manassas battles inspired millions of Americans to voice their opposition to perceived threats to the battlefield park, which ranged from historical theme parks to shopping malls. (Photo by Andres Alonso. © 1988, *The Washington Post*. Reprinted with permission)

historians, beginning in the 1930s, had identified as having sufficient historical significance for inclusion in the battlefield park. Second, the Park Service learned the importance of working with outside jurisdictions to protect its lands. Rolland Swain's discussions with Hazel/Peterson in 1986 resulted in numerous concessions by the developer for the battlefield park.

The Park Service also learned a hard lesson. It needed to act quickly in response to the mall proposal and to include all parties in discussions: the county, the developer, the preservationists, members of Congress, and relevant state and federal officials. By excluding the Save the Battlefield Coalition, which had created a national communications network and support system, NPS and Interior forced the preservationists to defend their position without compromise. The taking became the only viable option.[52]

For Swain and Susan Moore, who were on the front lines throughout, other lessons became apparent. They needed a way to use basic data effectively in analyzing the impact of development on the park. Swain took photographs of red helium-filled balloons to show how the building might be seen by park visitors. This method, the only one available in the Park Service at the time, was ineffective for convincing the county zoning board to impose height restrictions on developments. The newly emergent technology of the Geographic Information System (GIS), a system that uses computer imaging to show how a construction project would appear from different areas, makes a much more compelling argument for restrictions. Since 1988 GIS has become a staple tool for Park Service employees, although demand has often overwhelmed its availability.[53]

Swain and Moore also learned the importance of having good zoning lawyers and technical advice available to the Park Service. During the 1986 rezoning process, they could have used zoning law assistance to understand exactly what a planned mixed-use district allowed. This information would have helped them make informed assessments on potential development next to the park. When in negotiations with Hazel/Peterson before the mall announcement, Swain and Moore also could have used legal expertise to review the proffers and ensure the park's concerns had been addressed. A zoning lawyer could have pointed out that the PMD retail component might include a mall, thus enabling the Park Service to anticipate the development.[54]

Finally, the Park Service learned the importance of taking the lead when confronting difficult issues. Long-range strategic planning following the Marriott controversy would have enabled the NPS to consider the impact of possible future developments and prepare a response before the situation became unmanageable. The lack of a proactive stance made a later controversy inevitable. When confronted with this type of situation, NPS continued its reactive position, with damaging consequences. Aside from a letter to Kathleen Seefeldt of the Prince William Board of County Supervisors, the Park Service remained silent until late April when Mott and Hodel presented their compromise plan. During this period, the Save the Battlefield Coalition established a nationwide media campaign and became, in effect, the voice of the Manassas National Battlefield Park. Interior's compromise plan contradicted what Snyder and her supporters believed about the mall—that the mall would destroy the historic integrity of the battlefield park—and left the public, educated by the SBC's media blitz, uncertain of the Park Service's ability to protect the land. Interior reinforced this perception by negotiating with the developer and the county, not the preservationists.[55]

The $134 million that the federal government has paid for the William Center tract has left some observers wondering if the Park Service gained anything from the legislative taking. This amount, almost twice what was originally predicted, reflects the agreed upon value of improvements Hazel/Peterson made. Til Hazel later commented that for that same sum, the roads at the Stone House intersection could have been closed to traffic. Instead, the park has another piece of land, but the road situation continues to worsen. The federal government, however, would never have allocated such a sum for the battlefield park, for any project. The legislative taking required adequate compensation for the taken land, and Hazel set that price with his nonstop building. Superintendent Swain questioned the appropriateness of the legislative taking, especially considering its cost, because understanding Second Manassas does not require having that land, in his opinion. Betty Duley, a local resident, also noted that the Park Service had money to obtain more land but lacked the resources to care for its existing property, pointing to the rundown buildings and the lack of adequate patrols around the park. Duley and others believed that the NPS should have focused on capital improvements, not acquiring more land.[56]

Others consider the money well spent and in accordance with the park's mission. Craig noted that every year Congress designates a considerable sum, reaching well into the hundreds of millions of dollars, for the Land and Water Conservation Fund, an account designated specifically for land purchases. Since the early years of the Reagan administration, only a small portion of this fund is spent to acquire parklands; most is left to accumulate, in effect to offset a portion of the country's budget deficit. If Congress used the fund to its full potential, Craig believed, expensive takings like the William Center property could be avoided. For Craig, Snyder, Powell, Bumpers, and other preservationists, owning the site from which Lee staged one of the most impressive Confederate victories justified the expense and accorded with the battlefield park's mission.[57]

Prince William County officials believed they lost a great deal with the legislative taking. The anticipated jobs evaporated, the estimated $23 million in annual tax revenues was gone, and the promise of increased investment that would have spun off from the William Center was lost. The tract, designated in the county plan for economic development and thus tax generation, was removed from the tax rolls. With the county's growing population demanding more services, the legislative taking presented a host of economic issues for county officials.[58]

The events leading to the acquisition of the William Center property profoundly influenced historic preservation in the United States. The mall announcement resulted in a highly publicized coalition of preservation groups: conservationists, Civil War enthusiasts, and historic preservationists joined hands. They created a united front, under the Save the Battlefield Coalition and the National Heritage Coalition, which proved unbeatable. Each organization involved in the fight benefited from the heightened visibility and increased membership. Some observers even thought that the national organizations gained more from the exposure than they contributed to the SBC in its particular fight against Hazel/Peterson.[59]

The mall controversy and the expense of the legislative taking made clear to historic preservationists that they had to find alternative means for saving significant lands from development. This realization led to two related efforts: the introduction of the Heritage Preservation Conservation Act legislation and the establishment of Civil War battlefield preservation organizations both within the federal government and in the private sector. The example of the William Center controversy prompted Bruce Craig of the NPCA and Ian Spatz of the National Trust for Historic Preservation to draft the Heritage Preservation Conservation Act as a vehicle for addressing any future land-use conflicts adjacent to national parklands. Although it was never passed, the act would have established an overlay district adjoining a park where development would be restricted and would have provided other safeguards, such as authorizing the federal government to stop a construction project for a period of days while parties tried to negotiate a solution. If the government determined the land should be acquired, money would come from a special emergency fund.[60]

Other successful preservation efforts have been directed toward saving unprotected Civil War battlefield sites. In June 1987, about thirty interested individuals met in Fredericksburg, Virginia, to assess the events at the Manassas battlefield and at the Chantilly battlefield, a site in Fairfax County under immediate threat from development. They realized that a private-sector organization specializing in Civil War preservation needed to act in tandem with the government to save threatened areas. In July they formed the Association for the Preservation of Civil War Sites (APCWS). As the Manassas story played out in 1988, APCWS members, including A. Wilson Greene, a Park Service historian who eventually left his job to serve as APCWS's executive director and later president, grew more convinced that the sort of "eleventh-hour-and-fifty-ninth-minute rescue operation, at a cost that is so astronomical, is simply not a blueprint" for battlefield preservation.[61]

The APCWS developed an alternative. It conducted numerous surveys to identify the core historic areas of battlefields across the country and then assessed each parcel within the core area for its integrity and the level of threat from outside development. From these surveys, the APCWS established a set of priorities to determine which lands to buy. Using funds raised through private sources, the APCWS purchases tracts and holds them in a land trust until the federal government can accept them. In this way, battlefields are preserved before development overwhelms them and before prices make the land prohibitively expensive. Efforts by the APCWS have been augmented by the Civil War Trust, established by Congress at the behest of Secretary of the Interior Manuel Lujan Jr. to work toward preservation, and Jerry Russell, founder of the Civil War Round Table Associates, who has publicized the need to save battlefields in his monthly newsletter.[62]

Congress responded to the lessons of the William Center controversy and established a fifteen-member Civil War Sites Advisory Commission in November 1990. Secretary of the Interior Lujan, Hodel's successor, proposed such a commission at the July 1990 ceremonies for the 129th anniversary of First Manassas. The commission, which included Civil War historians, individuals experienced in preservation and land-use issues, members of Congress, and the National Park Service director, set out to identify historically significant Civil War sites and determine their relative importance. Individual sites were assessed for their existing condition and the threat of impending development. Based on this information, the commission recommended alternatives for preserving and interpreting the sites in its 1993 report, which detailed the status of every significant Civil War battlefield site and proposed cooperation between the public and private sectors to save the highest priority areas before they are lost. Despite early efforts by Lujan to raise money for implementing these recommendations, action has not been taken.[63]

There have been some gains for historic preservation as a result of the William Center controversy, but at a cost. By adamantly opposing any compromise that would have preserved part of the tract and allowed development on the rest, preservationists appeared unwilling to negotiate. Jody Powell later remarked that preservationists must find a reasonable balance between saving aspects of American history and allowing economic opportunity. If they say "no, no, no" all the time, the public will be unwilling to listen to their concerns and they will lose their overall effectiveness in preserving lands. Til Hazel believes preservationists have already bankrupted their credibility: any piece of property for which they can devise historical allegations for saving has become fair game for their efforts. Hazel agrees that some places, such as George Washington's home at Mount Vernon, warrant protection, but price and relative historical significance, according to Hazel, should determine what other areas deserve preservation.[64]

The National Park Service did not have long to assimilate what it had learned from the William Center controversy before an even larger issue developed. In November 1993 the Walt Disney Company announced its intention to build a historical theme park in Haymarket, Virginia, 3.5 miles from the battlefield park. The resulting battle highlighted the shift in concerns facing Manassas National Battlefield Park. During its first thirty years, the park had to contend with development threats on land the Park Service wanted to acquire. Beginning with the 1973 Marriott theme park proposal and ending with the William Center, the NPS had to determine its response to development immediately outside park boundaries on land of some historical significance. In the 1990s the Park Service had to shift its attention to land that did not adjoin the park but could be developed in a way that would detrimentally affect the battlefield park. The Service entered a new area of defining the significance of resources, recognizing that historic resources could not be protected solely by extending park boundaries.

Chapter 11

MORE BATTLES
The Horse and the Mouse

The Virginia piedmont region "has soaked up more of the blood, sweat and tears, . . . has bred more founding fathers, inspired more soaring hopes and ideals and witnessed more triumphs and failures, victories and lost causes" than any other piece of the nation's landscape, wrote Yale University historian C. Vann Woodward. "If such a past can render a soil 'sacred,' this sliver is the perfect venue." These words, written in response to the Walt Disney Company's 1993 proposal to build a history theme park 3.5 miles from the Manassas National Battlefield Park, helped give a national perspective to a local land-use battle.[1]

The proposed site for the Disney theme park lacked historic significance and its lands had never been identified for acquisition in Manassas battlefield park. But Disney's America, as it would have been called, represented a very real threat to places like the battlefield park. Urban sprawl with its encroaching residential developments, office complexes, retail centers, and service facilities have been slowly advancing on rural areas. In most cases, its appearance attracts little notice beyond local preservationists and park officials who want to minimize visual and environmental disruption. The battles are usually fought in local zoning board meetings. The Disney proposal brought the urban sprawl issue to national attention and helped educate Americans about its effects.

Horses

The Park Service had another issue to resolve before it became embroiled in the Disney controversy: its decision to augment the horse program at the battlefield park. Examination of the history of horse use at the Manassas National Battlefield Park demonstrates how a seemingly innocuous recreational activity evolved into a national debate that questioned the Park Service's commitment to preserve and protect its natural and historical resources. Park neighbors had enjoyed riding their horses throughout the battlefield since the park was established in 1940. Eventually some organized events developed. Francis Wilshin had allowed fox hunts in the park when he was superintendent, a concession to the politically powerful people living nearby. When horseback riding began to overwhelm the historic areas, Wilshin's successor, Russell Berry, put in trails, which controlled but did not eliminate this activity.[2]

At some point in the early 1970s regional office representatives decided that horses may serve a worthwhile official function at the park, in addition to recreation for the public. Horses broken in at the George Washington Birthplace National Monument, also located in Virginia, could be trained for Park Service work at Manassas. From Manassas, the horses were assigned to other areas.[3]

Over time, Manassas kept three horses for park protection purposes. Carl Hanson, park ranger under Berry and eventual chief of law enforcement, considered the horses a useful tool for patrolling the park. On horseback, park officials could cover short distances quickly and had a visible presence. In addition, horses provided good public relations because most people like horses. The horses stayed at Sutton Farm, located inside the park boundaries, near the Stone Bridge and north of Lee Highway. Outbuildings suitable for keeping horses had been built by the previous owners.[4]

The horses attracted little public attention until 1986 when National Capital Regional Director Manus J. (Jack) Fish decided to expand the NPS horse program. Fish chose Manassas because he saw a need to enhance equestrian use in the National Capital Region, and Manassas, as part of the region, provided a suitable setting for the program. Originally, Fish wanted to renovate a dairy barn located on the Wheeler tract, a large parcel in the park's southeast corner acquired by the federal government in 1985, to house horses donated to the United States Park Police and train park rangers and individuals in the Volunteers-in-the-Parks program. Marion C. Wheeler donated $50,000 toward the renovation in memory of her husband, William H. Wheeler. By 1987 the renovation had evolved into the proposal to tear down the aging dairy barn and replace it with a fourteen-stall horse barn with an office, tack room, classroom, and showering facilities. This horse remount facility would cost an estimated $120,000. Fish assigned retired U.S. Park policeman Denis Ayres, a noted horseman, to lead the augmented program at Manassas.[5]

John Hennessy, who had served as a temporary park historian at Manassas from 1981 to 1985, led preservationists in an attempt to block construction of the horse remount facility. Hennessy argued that the land identified for the horse facility was historically significant ground that warranted restoration, not development. Hennessy uncovered this new information while doing research on the Second Manassas troop movement maps for the park. Archaeological excavations completed after Hennessy left the Park Service revealed more evidence at Portici, located adjacent to the proposed remount facility site. The combination of these two finds convinced Hennessy that construction on the Wheeler tract would jeopardize the historical integrity of the area. Bruce Craig and the National Parks and Conservation Association joined Hennessy in trying to stop the project.[6]

Hennessy also wondered the effect such a project would have on the Park Service's credibility as an agency dedicated to the protection of historical and natural resources. If it developed historically significant lands within the park boundaries, the Park Service might appear less credible in its objection to intrusive construction outside the park. The William Center complex was only the most recent and most visible indication of continuing pressures to build along the park's borders. In light of the horse remount program, Hennessy believed that "no one will listen" when the Park Service voiced opposition to this and future outside developments.[7]

In late January 1988 Til Hazel announced plans to add a regional shopping mall to the William Center tract. As the Park Service expressed its concerns over the effects of the mall on the battlefield park, Ed Bearss, NPS chief historian, and Jerry Rogers, cultural resources director, among others, recognized that the NPS held a precarious position. Historical information brought to light by Hennessy made clear that construction of the horse remount facility would constitute an impact on the park. By pursuing construction on the battlefield while opposing development outside, the Park Service opened itself up to a potential public relations disaster. Interior officials, including Assistant Secretary for Fish and Wildlife and Parks Brian Horn and Deputy Assistant Susan Reece, a horse enthusiast, disagreed with this assessment and tried to pressure NPS Director Mott into continuing the remount program. They argued that the horse program and the William Center project were separate issues requiring separate analysis and action. Mott took Bearss's position and in March 1988 decided to delay construction of the stable pending further review of the historical evidence. The mounting cost of the new horse facility, which grew to as much as four times the Wheeler donation, helped Mott make his decision. The financially strapped National Park Service would have had to use money from interpretation and other programs to build the horse stable, leaving the agency open to further criticism. Ending the discussion of a horse remount facility on the Wheeler tract, the Service returned Mrs. Wheeler's $50,000 donation.[8]

Ayres, who had been reassigned to the Manassas battlefield, stayed to manage the existing horse program at the Sutton tract, which had increased to about sixteen horses. Considered one of the best horsemen in the country, Ayres attracted attention within the Washington horse community. Many people used the park's volunteer patrol program to receive expert advice from him. The volunteer program allowed citizens to ride government horses or their own mounts through the park as they patrolled the trails.[9]

One family ostensibly in the volunteer program attracted considerable attention beginning in the spring of 1989. Vice President Dan Quayle, wife Marilyn, and their children began making regular visits to the Manassas battlefield park to ride the government horses. This visible presence at the park soon prompted the Secret Service to request that Park Service Director James M. Ridenour, Mott's successor, consent to the construction of six to nine additional stalls at the Sutton Farm to house Secret Service mounts used for the Quayle visits. The mounts would not be used specifically to strengthen the park's law enforcement needs. Opposition to this plan grew after the 1990 Columbus Day weekend when the federal government closed the battlefield park and all other nonessential federal government sites for lack of an approved budget. During this lockout, the Quayle family went riding in the Manassas battlefield, accompanied by three park employees. Newspapers did not mince words over the implications of this ride, calling the national battlefield a "private playground" for the Second Family. Repeated questions surfaced over the apparent use of limited park funds for the singular recreational activities of an already unpopular vice president and other influential individuals. It was becoming clear to observers that the original horse program, which had aided in park law enforcement and protection, had been overwhelmed by recreational use.[10]

After a year's debate in the media, Sen. Dale Bumpers, chairman of the Senate subcommittee on national parks, led Congress in defeating the Sutton Farm stable expansion proposal. Congress amended the National Park Service budget to prohibit funding for the stables for fiscal year 1992. Just before the change of administration from George Bush to Bill Clinton in 1993 and after a new fiscal year had started, outgoing Interior Secretary Lujan, who rode at Manassas, ordered the immediate construction of the stables. This work continued until February 1993 when the newly appointed Secretary of the Interior, Bruce Babbitt, called for its immediate halt. The Park Service then conducted a review of the battlefield park's horse program, including the number of horses, volunteer program, and stable addition. In the meantime, the number of horses was reduced to three, and Ayres stayed at the park to manage them. On 1 March 1995, NPS Director Roger G. Kennedy informed Senator Bumpers that the Service had decided to continue the present level of operation, having a three-horse equestrian program devoted to park protection and law enforcement uses. Recreational riding of park-owned horses would be eliminated, and requests from agencies for assistance in equestrian training would be referred to the U.S. Park Police. This controversy demonstrated that uses acceptable to the public, such as horseback riding in the parks, had narrow limits, which would be challenged. The crisis also made clear that development projects within national park sites, though seen by some federal officials as consistent with the park's preservation mission, would meet with scrutiny from outside observers. Preservation and use was a dynamic duo.[11]

Disney's America

Questions about acceptable uses of park resources, as the horse program highlighted, continued to deserve attention, but concerns over outside development became more pressing: the issue of historic preservation and use extended beyond the park's borders. In the case of the William Center controversy, the belief in the historical significance of the land, the site of General Lee's headquarters, was enough to halt construction. The federal government purchased the land and placed it under the protection of the National Park Service. Future threats would involve development away from the battlefield's historic lands but close enough to cause traffic and other problems for the national park. In these cases, the federal government had no historical reason to acquire more land. Instead, negotiation and education must promote the best interests of the park.

In November 1993 the Walt Disney Company surprised northern Virginians with the announcement of its intention to build a historic theme park called Disney's America in Haymarket, Virginia, 3.5 miles from the Manas-

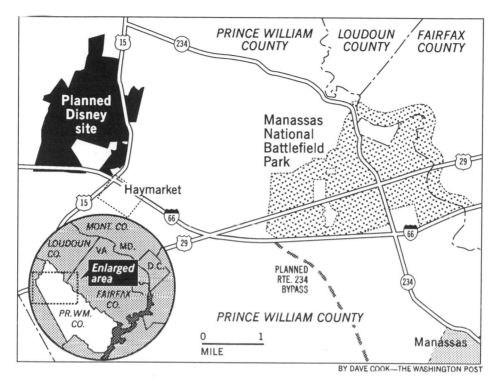

BY DAVE COOK—THE WASHINGTON POST

Map 3. At its proposed location 3.5 miles from Manassas National Battlefield Park, the Disney's America historical theme park promised jobs and tax benefits for financially strapped Prince William County residents while also threatening to spawn uncontrolled development around Manassas National Battlefield Park. (Map by Dave Cook. © 1994, *The Washington Post*. Reprinted with permission)

sas battlefield. Disney executives had been working in extreme secrecy for a few years searching for a new theme park location with a regional market that would not "cannibalize" visitation at either California's Disneyland or Florida's Walt Disney World. The Washington, D.C., area, with its estimated 19 million tourists annually proved attractive. Disney officials narrowed their search to Virginia, which they considered more probusiness than the neighboring state of Maryland, and the Route 66 corridor, which was an important transportation link to the rest of the metropolitan area. When a 2,300-acre site in rural western Prince William County became available, Disney was able to place an option on a single sizable piece of land. This tract became the centerpiece of what would eventually become a 3,000-acre proposed development.[12]

After they had identified the location for the theme park venture, Disney representatives explored the full ramifications of settling near the nation's capital. Peter Rummell had extensive experience in resort development in Hilton Head Island, South Carolina, and in other areas of the Southeast before he joined the Walt Disney Company in 1985 and turned its seven-person Disney Development Company into the multifaceted Disney Design and Development, which included Walt Disney Imagineering. As president of this new subsidiary, Rummell oversaw the creative and development aspects of the new theme park. As he later recounted, the lure of the Washington market had brought Disney to northern Virginia, but once there, "the creative juices started to flow and all of a sudden we realized that there was, we thought, a really interesting opportunity to deal with the story of America." Vignettes of American history became the brush with which to paint, the common thread that would organize the visitor's experience at the proposed theme park.[13]

Disney emphasized the nation's Civil War heritage for its latest venture. As Disney's America was initially conceived, visitors would enter through a re-created Civil War–era village and then ride steam trains to explore nine areas inspired by events in American history, including a Civil War fort portraying the daily experiences of soldiers. Battle reenactments on land would be accompanied at night by a restaging of the naval showdown between the ironclads the Monitor and the Merrimac on a manmade lake called Freedom Bay. In an effort to combine education and entertainment, Disney officials hoped to include "painful, disturbing and agonizing" exhibits on slavery and re-create a piece of the underground railroad through which park visitors would escape. The goal, as Rummell later clarified, was to be "entertaining in the sense that it would leave you with something that you could mull over."[14]

The rest of the park was designed around other themes from America's past. Native American life would be highlighted through the presentation of re-created Indian villages and authentic works of art. A Lewis and Clark raft trip would give park goers an opportunity to experience western exploration. "President's Square" would focus on the War for Independence and the ideas of the Founding Fathers. In "We the People," a reproduction of the port of Ellis Island and an offering of a variety of ethnic foods and music would remind visitors of America's immigrant heritage. A tribute to American ingenuity would include examples of inventions and a high-speed roller coaster ride through a turn-of-the-century mill, simulating an escape from a fiery vat of molten steel. The "Family Farm" area would pay tribute to the nation's farms with barn dances and cow milkings, and the "State Fair" section would look at the Depression era and have a sixty-foot Ferris wheel, a wooden roller coaster, and an exhibit paying homage to baseball. The military theme of the Civil War entrance would be continued with "Victory Field," which would use virtual reality technology to give park visitors the opportunity to experience both flying in and parachuting from a World War II–era plane.[15]

The history theme park would be only part of the development Disney officials envisioned at the Haymarket location. Having such a large tract of land encouraged Rummell and his coworkers to explore further developments to complement the theme park. They considered adding resort hotels with 1,340 guest rooms, an RV park with 300 campsites, a twenty-seven-hole public golf course, and a commercial complex consisting of 1.3 million square feet of retail and 630,000 square feet of office/business space. Rummell expected to sell part of the land—enough for up to 2,300 houses—to a residential developer. Disney planned to donate land for schools and a library, while up to 40 percent of the site would remain green space, acting as a buffer between the recreational core area and outside developments.[16]

Virginia state and county representatives welcomed the Disney proposal, heedful of the attractive fiscal benefits it promised. Governor-elect George Allen unabashedly proclaimed his administration would "kick down any hurdles" Disney encountered on its way toward getting full legal authority to build the theme park and its supporting facilities. Allen believed that the projected $1.18 billion of revenues the state would receive over the next thirty years was well worth the initial investment of taxpayer monies into expanding roadways, building an interstate interchange, and providing adequate sewage and water hookups. Prince William County Executive James Mullen agreed with Allen, stating that there were "no obstacles that cannot be overcome." The anticipated $680 million in tax revenues for the county over the next thirty years and the projected 2,700 new jobs were enough to gain many allies in the county legislature.[17]

Landing just this sort of economic windfall had been a driving force in Prince William County long-range planning for years. The 1980s had taken a financial toll on the county, leaving it with a 50 percent increase in population but without an equivalent growth in business to offset steadily rising property taxes. The loss of the William Center land to the federal government added to the problem. To address the need for more and better schools and county administrative services, the legislature adopted in 1990 an ambitious goal of luring 14,000 new jobs and $1 billion in nonresidential growth to Prince William County by 1997. The county advertised its pro-

Fig. 17. Prince William Board Chairman Kathleen K. Seefeldt, Virginia Gov. L. Douglas Wilder, and Gov.-elect George F. Allen enthusiastically listen as Disney Design
and Development President Peter Rummell (third from left) unveils in November
1993 the initial plans for Disney's America, a proposed historical theme park to be
located in Haymarket, Virginia. (Photo by Frank Johnston. © 1988, *The Washington
Post.* Reprinted with permission)

business stance nationwide, and the electorate backed up this marketing
effort by approving bonds to finance major infrastructure improvements.
The way Prince William officials courted business, including the Danish
firm Lego, which considered building a theme park in the county, drew the
attention of Disney representatives and played a role in their decision to
choose Prince William County for Disney's America. As Kathleen Seefeldt,
chairman of the board of county supervisors, stated when learning of the
Disney proposal, "economic development is the number one goal" for the
county, and the Disney project promises to "exceed all reasonable expectations for economic development" in the near future.[18]

This seemingly single-focused economic-mindedness worried many individuals living in the rural areas surrounding the proposed Disney site. A curious mix of middle-class families and wealthy landowners, whose ranks included such powerful voices as the owners of the *Washington Post* and Hollywood actor Robert Duvall, they were attracted to the quiet and privacy of this horse country in western Prince William and adjacent Fauquier and Loudoun counties and relished the quaint two-lane roads and abundance of open space. "Lousy commutes" into Washington every workday on the heavily traveled but sorely inadequate I–66 highway were tolerable because these people valued a home in the country. Over the years, the wealthier residents had been active in preserving "the traditional character and visual order" of the horse country by organizing as the Piedmont Environmental Council and buying permanent easements over 77,000 acres of open space to bar development. Disney's announcement threatened this peace and seclusion. Visions of clogged roadways and a snarled interstate appeared in their minds as they heard Disney predict an estimated 30,000 visitors daily (6.3 million annually) to the theme park. Along with the traffic, opponents believed the region's already polluted air would get worse with the increased tourist traffic. And, once Disney settled into Haymarket, accompanying developments on the surrounding lands seemed a sure bet, especially given the board of county supervisors' probusiness attitude. The speedy urbanization of this rural outpost appeared a certainty, much to the disliking of many of its inhabitants.[19]

Others opposed Disney's decision to combine proud and painful moments in American history with entertainment. At the initial press conference, Senior Vice President Bob Weis made the mistake of saying that, to show the Civil War "with all its racial conflict," attractions would "make you a Civil War soldier . . . [and] make you feel what it was like to be a slave." Weis meant to refer to Disney's use of the new technology of virtual reality, in which visitors could physically enter an environment and explore it. For instance, Disney had created a ride on Aladdin's carpet in which guests would literally feel as if they were flying through a room. Weis did not intend to suggest for Disney's America the sociological impacts associated with slavery, but many listeners immediately made the connection. *Washington Post* columnist Courtland Milloy did not mince words when he reminded readers that "authentic history," as Weis promised, must include such atrocities as slave whippings and rape. Unamused, Milloy urged Disney to stick with fun and keep history, especially slave history, out of the park.[20]

With the lines of battle already drawn, National Park Service officials entered into negotiations with Disney. The talks centered around potential impacts of the theme park development on the Manassas battlefields; from the federal government's perspective, the lands identified for the theme park were not of sufficient historical significance to warrant acquisition. The Park Service found Disney a ready listener. For example, Disney agreed to limit the height of its structures to 140 feet, which the government determined would probably not be visible from the battlefield. Disney did not want people looking down from high rises into the theme park, and it did not want theme park guests looking up at tall structures. Disney also had an interest in addressing traffic concerns. The company proposed limiting vehicle trips to its theme park and introduced the idea of transporting 20 percent of guests and 10 percent of employees by special transit buses. Although opponents argued that such measures as capping the number of vehicles to the theme park would be unenforceable, Disney's proffers toward reducing the expected rise in traffic were seen by some in the Park Service as at least promising.[21]

What most concerned Park Service and Interior Department officials were traffic and building heights from ancillary development. Already congested roads seemed vulnerable to what Park Service Director Roger Kennedy called "shortsighted quick fixes" by the county. In particular, Kennedy and Interior Assistant Secretary George T. Frampton Jr. worried about Prince William County's apparent decision to widen Lee Highway through the Manassas National Battlefield Park. Long opposed by park officials, this proposed widening would, in their estimation, "violate all accepted criteria for maintaining the dignity and integrity" of the national park. The Park Service wanted assurances that road improvements on I–66 would be completed in time for the theme park's opening, and it wanted "enforceable commitments" to reroute and close the roads bisecting the battlefield park. The NPS had proposed closing Lee Highway and Route 234 in 1988, but this idea evaporated as soon as the furor over the mall subsided. To address concerns about building heights, the Interior Department promoted the idea of establishing a historic overlay district for a distance of two miles from the Manassas park, limiting the height of buildings within that area to sixty feet. Although the existing county land-use plan designated the areas north and west of the national park as semirural residential, the potential existed for tall structures to be introduced, thereby disrupting the historic viewshed. The historic overlay could also act as a tool to guide development, making the county a national example in land-use planning.[22]

Although troubled by the potential for development further encroaching on the battlefield park, some Park Service officials and other preserva-

Fig. 18. A silent sentinel from the First and Second Battles of Manassas, the Stone House overlooks jammed roads crossing the heart of the battlefield park during rush-hour traffic, one of the continuing management challenges facing the National Park Service. (Photo by R. Anthony Todt. © 1996. Reprinted with permission)

tionists saw positive benefits from Disney's America. As Rummell remembered, former superintendent Ken Apschnikat, who left the park in fall 1994, was "tickled to death" with Disney because it promised higher visitation rates. Apschnikat also hoped that having Disney as a neighbor would divert existing recreational traffic to the theme park. Apschnikat and his staff could then direct their attention to interpretation, instead of trying to balance recreation and history. Others believed Disney's focus on history would help the Park Service and other historic preservation interests. Perhaps most influential, Disney's creative genius might spark an excitement about history in many of its visitors that the federal government and schools could never match. Disney had also promised to donate a significant amount of its charitable giving to historic preservation, a pledge it quickly fulfilled by giving money to the Association for the Preservation of Civil War Sites. The company agreed to design and sell special items with a historic preservation theme in the theme park. Finally, Disney expected to

create a separate venue in the history theme park devoted to educating its visitors in historic preservation issues and about Manassas National Battlefield Park. These actions, for some people, showed the opportunities that Disney's theme park promised.[23]

The Disney theme park expected six million visitors annually, and Park Service officials knew they would have to upgrade the battlefield park to handle the many people who would come there as well. Park officials began revising the 1983 general management plan, which laid out the overall interpretive and administrative plans for the park. The existing facilities could not accommodate the expected increase in visitation. The visitor center on Henry Hill needed a larger parking area, more restrooms, and more space for educational exhibits. These deficiencies prompted discussion on whether the visitor center should remain at Henry Hill. Before the Disney announcement, the Park Service had considered developing a full-fledged interpretive program for Second Manassas, including building another visitor center near the newly acquired Stuart's Hill. Park Service representatives renewed their discussions of this second visitor center in response to Disney's plans. All these ideas required extensive planning, increased funding, and speedy implementation to meet the expected opening of Disney's America in spring 1998.[24]

As the Park Service began preparing its response to the Disney proposal, debate over the theme park grew in tenor. The Piedmont Environmental Council (PEC) launched an aggressive lobbying effort against the Disney proposal, sending two full-time representatives, twenty-six-year-old news reporter Hilary Gerhardt and twenty-nine-year-old environmental lawyer Chris Miller, to Richmond, the state capital. Although bankrolled by generous gifts from such prominent families as the Mellons, du Ponts, and Mars (of candy bar fame), the council's efforts failed. Disney's America promised too many financial benefits to the state to be easily dismissed. And, the wealthy connections of the Piedmont Environmental Council fed into pro-Disney media hype, which characterized Disney opponents as being rich and powerful elitists. The fact that Disney was a multibillion-dollar company whose chairman earned $203 million the previous year failed to garner attention. Governor Allen went to bat for Disney, seeing an "economic renaissance" for Virginia from the project, and convinced the state legislature to hand Disney a $163-million package of subsidies, including widening I–66 and expanding or building interchanges to handle the theme park's traffic. Disney seemed unstoppable—until Richard Moe put pen to paper and made Disney's America a national issue.[25]

Moe, president of the National Trust for Historic Preservation for less than a year when Disney made its big announcement, brought the weight of his national organization to the table. Under his stewardship, the National Trust had begun to broaden its focus from saving individual historic properties to fighting what it considered was the devastating effects of urban sprawl, which often ate up the last remaining bits of open land while leaving historic downtowns as ghost towns, unable to compete against megastores like Wal-Mart and Home Depot. Disney's proposed theme park and residential-office-retail complex was exactly the type of development that Moe and the Trust feared: it leapfrogged past the current line of development and settled on a countryside resonant with historical associations. Once in place, Disney's America would, they believed, spawn further development, filling in the remaining green space between Washington and Haymarket. As Moe later stated, "Even though this [Disney's America] wasn't on historic land, it would've had the effect indirectly of destroying historic areas, Civil War battlefields, districts, the whole landscape, because of the sprawl." The example in Orlando, Florida, which was transformed by Walt Disney World and accompanying developments, painfully indicated how extensive this type of low-density, land-consumptive, automobile-oriented development could be.[26]

Moe and others did not want the region where Founding Fathers had trod and Civil War soldiers had fought to suffer the same fate. Believing that review of the theme park proposal belonged in a national—as opposed to a state or county—forum, Moe tapped into the elite circle of Disney opponents living in the northern Virginia horse country. He prepared an article outlining his views and shared it with Julian Scheer, a former newspaperman who had lived for the past thirty years in Fauquier County. Scheer's daughter was Hilary Gerhardt, one of the PEC's Richmond lobbyists. Moe submitted the revised column to the *Washington Post*, where it was published in December 1993. He argued that urban sprawl emanating from Disney's America would "devastate some of the most beautiful and historic countryside in America." With a graceful turn of the pen, Moe transformed the debate from a local land-use issue to one of national historical significance. The country's national heritage was at stake, in Moe's estimation, and action was needed now.[27]

Many prominent historians, led by Pulitzer Prize-winner David McCullough, answered Moe's call. In spring 1994, after talking with an old friend who was active in the Piedmont Environmental Council, McCullough visited the Disney site and met with local residents opposed to the project.

Fig. 19. National Trust President Richard Moe brought nationwide attention to the Disney's America proposal, arguing
that the theme park would unleash a tidal wave of urban
sprawl, which would engulf Manassas National Battlefield
Park and obliterate the historic character of the surrounding
rural countryside. (National Trust photo)

Appalled by what he saw and heard, McCullough soon began volunteering
hours of his time toward the anti-Disney effort. McCullough's national repu-
tation, gained from his appearance as narrator on the Ken Burns series on
the Civil War and his many connections within the historical community,
brought increased visibility to the issue. Other historians soon joined the
movement and organized in May 1994 as Protect Historic America. The

luminaries in Protect Historic America included Princeton University Professor James M. McPherson, whose Pulitzer Prize-winning book *Battle Cry of Freedom* is considered one of the best single-volume histories of the Civil War. McPherson had previously contributed his talents to the fight against the Manassas mall. Yale University Professor Emeritus C. Vann Woodward and Duke University Professor John Hope Franklin served as spokespersons for the organization. The PEC handled much of the organizational work for the historians in Washington, including financial support. On May 2, the National Trust published an open letter to Disney Chairman Michael Eisner in the *Washington Post*, asking him to consider an alternative site for the theme park. Nine days later, Protect Historic America sponsored a news conference at the National Press Building, with Woodward leading the call by characterizing Disney's America as "an appalling commercialization and vulgarization of the scene of our most tragic history." Newspapers across the country covered the story, and people began writing their congressional representatives demanding action.[28]

Moe and his fellow preservationists obtained their desired result. National attention, similar to that generated by Annie Snyder and the Save the Battlefield Coalition in 1988, focused on Disney and its plans to build a theme park on what was now seen as historically significant land. Snyder, not surprisingly, joined Protect Historic America and participated in a June rally in Washington, D.C., at the opening of Disney's animated movie *The Lion King*. Snyder and about 100 protesters chanted to Eisner "Take a hike, Mike" in front of television cameras. Also in June, Sen. Dale Bumpers asked McCullough, McPherson, and Moe, along with Governor Allen and Disney executives, to testify on the potential impact of Disney's America on the "scores of historic sites scattered throughout the farms and hillsides of the Virginia Piedmont." Rep. Michael Andrews, the Texas Democrat who had spurred the House into action against the mall, introduced on June 16 a House resolution asking Disney to relocate its theme park. Newspapers throughout the country publicized the debate (producing more than 10,000 items on the subject), with many editors and syndicated columnists coming down on the side of the historians. George Will labeled Eisner a "Hollywood vulgarian" who should follow the example of Gen. Robert E. Lee and surrender. Cartoonists delighted in picturing Honest Abe with mouse ears. These cuts at Disney were not lost on Disney's chief executive officer, Michael Eisner.[29]

Location was the most significant factor driving opposition to Disney's America. The Piedmont Environmental Council adopted a classic not-in-my-backyard (NIMBY) stance, opposing Disney because it believed that the region's traditional character, its peace and seclusion, would be lost to fast-food restaurants and endless traffic snarls. When the council's efforts to thwart Disney at the state level failed, its members sought alternative means for defeating Disney's America. The National Trust offered the promising avenue of gaining a national audience, and the PEC embraced this opportunity. Once Protect Historic America joined the opposition, the council provided significant financial and organizational resources to ensure its continued success. However, the membership within Protect Historic America had joined in opposition to Disney's America for differing reasons. Officially, Protect Historic America followed the lead of the Piedmont council and the National Trust and opposed Disney's America on the basis of its location. The historians believed that building the theme park in Haymarket would destroy historically rich lands and trigger later development that would encroach on the Manassas National Battlefield Park. Prince William County officials tried to address this concern, pointing out that the type of project Disney proposed would generate less traffic than the existing mixed-use development zoning allowed. Beyond the site of the proposed development, the zoning remained low-residential density, and the county did not expect this designation to change. The county's proactive stance toward attracting business, however, left many people questioning whether such zoning would withstand future development proposals.[30]

Some historians supported Protect Historic America because they were skeptical about how Disney would interpret and present the past. Disney's record at Disneyland had shown that fantasy often crept into its interpretation of historic events. As custodians of the nation's history, American historians were especially sensitive to its presentation because of recent attacks on the profession. When the Smithsonian's National Air and Space Museum began developing a fiftieth-anniversary exhibit on the atomic bombing of Japan, using the B-29 aircraft *Enola Gay* as a central feature, veterans' groups opposed the preliminary exhibit plan, arguing that the text was offensively anti-American and overly apologetic to Japan. Lengthy negotiations ensued, involving the Smithsonian, the American Legion, and members of Congress. Historians wondered, who owned history? Did the curators have the right to plan exhibits without interference from the public? Did public institutions like the Smithsonian have a responsibility to give voice to organized groups having special stakes or expertise in the nation's past? Smithsonian Secretary I. Michael Heyman resolved the debate by removing all text and displaying the airplane alone, with only a brief statement as to its significance.[31]

This action was a politically astute move, but the question of how history should be presented to the public remained a hot issue. As multiculturalism flourished in the university, inviting scholars to explore the nation's diverse cultural heritage, right-wing critics questioned the advisability of teaching the writings and history of underrepresented groups. Former National Endowment for the Humanities Chair Lynne Cheney blasted the newly released *National Standards for United States History* in October 1994, arguing that it produced an unbalanced focus on victims and oppressors without affirming the greatness of the nation. Such attacks, widely reported in the media, forced historians to confront how their work was adopted by others. Disney's America unleashed questions about how to make accurate history fun and entertaining. McPherson worried that Disney's version of the past might be "an artificial and probably sanitized version" of reality. Civil War historian Shelby Foote agreed, stating that Disney would do to history what it had already done to the animal kingdom—take out the complexity and leave visitors with a rose-colored glasses' view, this time of the past.[32]

On the other side of the debate, some historians questioned whether location should be an issue at all. James Oliver Horton, professor of history and American studies at George Washington University and director of the Afro-American Communities Project at the Smithsonian's National Museum of American History, pointed out that historical significance depended on what stories you focused on: "Do we commemorate Ellis Island as the gateway for immigration or as an ancient site sacred to Native Americans?" Why were no voices raised against the obliteration of slave pens near the White House? Why did no one fight the replacement of historically significant sites to southern and African-American peoples by luxury resorts in the Sea Islands of South Carolina and Georgia? A particular location has many potential stories to tell, requiring historians, archaeologists, preservationists, community leaders, and the public to explore fully together.[33]

For Horton, the promise of Disney using its command of technology to do good history in an entertaining way was enough to gain his critical support. Horton decided to work with Disney as a historical adviser, saying later that historians have a responsibility to convince the public and corporations like Disney that "really good history sells as much, maybe even better than fantasy." Admitting that most people will learn their history in national parks, museums, and historical theme parks, Horton urged historians to be "in those places to the extent [they] can and [to] encourage people who are doing history in those places to do good solid history based on the latest most sound research." To address concerns that such history is ultimately boring, Horton argued that "good education is really entertaining." As an example, he thought Disney's America might explore the historical themes of urbanization and race by recreating New York's Savoy Ballroom. While playing variants of jazz as performed in Chicago and New York, the setting could teach theme park guests about the Great Migration of African Americans from the South to northern cities and how different African-American communities interacted. What historians should remember, Horton later stated, was: "all of this would call for a great deal of imagination, but the point is that that ought to be part of our business. If we want to educate people . . . then we have to use a little imagination to make [history] engaging." At stake, in Horton's mind, was nothing less than the survival and flourishing of democracy. History has shown that monarchy lasts—it has lasted for thousands of years. Democracy has survived a test of only a couple hundred years. To maximize the success of democracy, Horton believed that "we need to educate our people and we need to do that in a variety of places. We can't count on the schools or the universities or even formal mainstream traditional museums to do the education . . . alone." Horton saw promise with Disney's America, but many others saw standstill traffic and urban sprawl lapping at Manassas National Battlefield Park.[34]

The growing national opposition to the historical theme park caught Disney by surprise. The company had sailed through the Virginia statehouse, developed public-private partnerships, conducted environmental and archaeological studies, and argued that the theme park would not degrade the environment or the traditional character of the region. Yet, these studies and partnerships mattered little. For Peter Rummell, "the problem was that the people that owned those farms just didn't want us there. And there's nothing you could do or prove that would ever change that." What most impressed Rummell about the Piedmont Environmental Council was its sophistication, its ability to turn an essentially NIMBY argument into a national discussion about Disney's right to present history. The council's membership used its extensive contacts to educate others about the Disney's America proposal and provided initial organizational and financial support to the historians when they joined to form Protect Historic America. Although location of the theme park remained a concern for both groups, the council sought to protect a rural twentieth-century lifestyle while the historians wanted to preserve a historically poignant landscape. Once Disney's America attained national significance, its fate was sealed by public opinion and action. Previous development confrontations related to Manassas battlefield park had ended either with compromise, as in the routing of the interstate south of the national park instead of through it, or with preservation triumphant, as in the case of the legislative taking. Unlike the determined Til Hazel who refused to give up until forced by the taking, Disney chose another route.[35]

Mounting public opinion against Disney, bad press, and challenges within the company prompted action. Still amazed by the strength and intensity of opposition to Disney's America, company officials were reluctant to defend their theme park proposal. As Rummell later stated, "We didn't feel comfortable as a company having to go out and defend ourselves against something that we really didn't think needed a defense." In addition, in 1994 Euro Disney reported a $900 million loss, the Walt Disney Company's first major financial trouble since Eisner's arrival in 1984. The corporation suffered further when Frank Wells, its president and CEO, died in a helicopter crash and Eisner himself underwent emergency quadruple bypass heart surgery. Eisner returned to shake up the corporate leadership by firing one of the rising stars in the film and animation divisions. The combination of internal turmoils and public outcry convinced Eisner that it was time to cut his losses. He asked Disney Channel President John F. Cooke to open discussions with Moe, McCullough, and McPherson in an attempt to forge a compromise. When these talks failed to produce an agreement, Eisner recommended to the Disney board that the Haymarket location be abandoned. Leaks to the press forced Eisner to announce his decision earlier than planned.[36]

On 28 September 1994, less than one year after its initial announcement, Disney concluded that the theme park hurt the company's treasured public image too much to warrant continued fighting for the Haymarket location. Although it had obtained incentives from the state of Virginia and approval from the county's zoning board, Disney killed the project. Rummell later remarked: "It was just not worth it. We're a big company, we've got a lot of things going on, and at some point the abuse, combined with the time it was going to take, just weren't worth it. . . . I'm convinced in the end we could've won but it just takes time, it takes management, it's a distraction, and frankly in the end it wasn't worth it. The potential rewards were just not worth either the time or the continued abuse."[37]

For the Manassas National Battlefield Park, Disney's withdrawal meant that the spring 1998 deadline for upgrading visitor services could be extended. But the same problems existed—overloaded roads, inadequate visitor facilities. Without the money and cooperation that Disney promised, these problems would likely continue well into the future. The Disney tract in Haymarket would eventually bring in other development, as allowed under the county comprehensive plan, though the developers might not be as willing as Disney to deal on a friendly basis with the Park Service. As had happened when the mall controversy was resolved, constructive talks about improving roads and even shutting down the two bisecting the national park halted without promise of renewal. A county task force report, commissioned in 1993 in response to the Disney proposal, met with underwhelming interest when it was released more than a month after Disney's retreat from Haymarket. The report's suggestions for channeling growth around the battlefield park and building multilane highways into Loudoun and Fairfax counties appeared "slated for obscurity," although the underlying issues remained.[38]

What lessons do we take with us from the story of the horse and the mouse? We know that preservation of our national treasures requires vigilance and commitment in the face of a range of challenges. Yet, *preservation* becomes a slippery term when applied to real circumstances and changing ideals. Three horses in the Manassas National Battlefield Park were acceptable for law enforcement purposes, but sixteen for the same reason were found to be inappropriate. Any developments on parkland today, whether for horse remount centers or for visitor centers, must meet exacting but changing criteria to ensure that the land where they are sited has less national significance than other areas within the park. Having too much development inside a park raises questions about the Park Service's commitment to preservation. But how much is too much? Finally, what right does the Park Service and the public have to question development outside a park's boundaries? At what point does this outside development reach the point of unacceptability and require action?

With the Disney controversy, fears of ancillary development surrounding the battlefield park and forever altering its character prompted action by citizens nationally. Disney retreated and so the historians and their followers disbanded, but the slow advance of development continues. More than likely, there will be no national outcry if a filling station is put here or a small residential subdivision there, but the end effect for the national park will be the same: the replacement of the last bits of open fields with modern life; the steady stream of more and more cars on the fragile two-lane roads. With Disney as one of the players, debate and negotiation seemed promising. Without such a nationally known player, the opportunity for open and extended conversation seems uncertain. What park managers and the public must remember is that participation and discussion at all times are needed to achieve necessary objectives.

APPENDIXES

Appendix 1. Order Designating the Manassas National Battlefield Park, Virginia

Whereas the Congress of the United States has declared it to be a national policy to preserve for the public use historic sites, buildings and objects of national significance for the inspiration and benefit of the people of the United States; and

Whereas certain lands and structures in Manassas Magisterial District, Prince William County, Virginia, because of their historical importance as the battlefield site of the First and Second battles of Manassas during the war between the States, have been declared by the Advisory Board on National Parks, Historic Sites, Buildings and other monuments to be of national significance; and

Whereas title to the above-mentioned lands with the buildings and structures thereon is vested in the United States:

Now, therefore, I, Harold L. Ickes, Secretary of the Interior, under and by virtue of the authority conferred by section 2 of the act of Congress approved August 21, 1935 (49 Stat. 666), do hereby designate all those certain tracts or parcels of land, with the structures thereon, containing approximately 1,604.575 acres and situated in Manassas Magisterial District, Prince William County, Virginia, as shown upon the diagram hereto attached and made a part hereof, to be a national historic site, having the name "Manassas National Battlefield Park."

The administration, protection, and development of this area shall be exercised by the National Park Service in accordance with the provisions of the act of August 21, 1935, *supra*.

Warning is expressly given to all unauthorized persons not to appropriate, injure, destroy, deface or remove any feature of this park.

In witness whereof, I have hereunto set my hand and caused the official seal of the Department of the Interior to be affixed, in the City of Washington this 10th day of May, 1940.

Signed Harold L. Ickes
Secretary of the Interior

of such acquisition, retain for himself and his heirs and assigns a right of use and occupancy of the improved property for noncommercial residential purposes for a definite term of not more than twenty-five years or for a term ending at the death of the owner or the death of the spouse of the owner, whichever is later. The owner shall elect the term to be reserved. Unless this property is wholly or partially donated to the United States, the Secretary shall pay the owner an amount equal to the fair market value of the property on the date of its acquisition less the value on such date of the right retained by the owner. If such property is donated (in whole or in part) to the United States, the Secretary may pay to the owner such lesser amount as the owner may agree to. A right retained pursuant to this section shall be subject to termination by the Secretary upon his determination that it is being exercised in a manner inconsistent with the purposes of this Act, and it shall terminate by operation of law upon the Secretary's notifying the holder of the right of such determination and tendering to him an amount equal to the fair market value of that portion of the right which remains unexpired.

"(b) No property owner who elects to retain a right of use and occupancy under this section shall be considered a displaced person as defined in section 101(6) of the Uniform Relocation Assistance and Real Property Acquisition Policies Act of 1970 (84 Stat. 1894). Such owners shall be considered to have waived any benefits which would otherwise accrue to them under sections 203 through 206 of such Act.

"Sec. 4. For purposes of this Act—

"(1) The term 'improved property' means a detached, one-family dwelling, construction of which was begun before January 1, 1979, which is used for noncommercial residential purposes, together with not to exceed three acres of land on which the dwelling is situated and together with such additional lands or interests therein as the Secretary deems to be reasonably necessary for access thereto, such lands being in the same ownership as the dwelling, together with any structures accessory to the dwelling which are situated on such land.

"(2) The term 'park' means the Manassas National Battlefield Park established under this Act.

"(3) The term 'Secretary' means the Secretary of the Interior.

"(4) The term 'owner' means the owner of record as of September 1, 1980.

"Sec. 5. (a) In addition to sums heretofore expended for the acquisition of property and interests therein for the park, from funds available for expenditure from the Land and Water Conservation Fund, as established under the Land and Water Conservation Fund Act of 1965, not more than a total of $8,700,000 may be expended for the acquisition of property and interests therein under this Act.

"(b) It is the express intent of Congress that, except for property referred to in subsection 2(b), the Secretary shall acquire property and interests therein under this Act within two complete fiscal years after the date of the enactment of the Manassas National Battlefield Park Amendments of 1980.

"Sec. 6. (a) Authorizations of moneys to be appropriated under this Act from the Land and Water Conservation Fund for acquisition of properties and interests shall be effective on October 1, 1981.

"(b) Notwithstanding any other provision of this Act, authority to enter into contracts, to incur obligations, or to make payments under this Act shall be effective only to the extent, and in such amounts as are provided in advance in appropriation Acts."

SEC. 3. (a) The Secretary of the Interior shall conduct a study to determine appropriate measures for the protection, interpretation, and public use of the natural wetlands and undeveloped uplands of that portion of the Hackensack Meadowlands District identified as the DeKorte State Park on the official zoning maps of that District. The Secretary shall, in the course of the study, consult with and seek the advice of, representatives of interested local, State, and other Federal agencies. As a part of the study, the Secretary shall determine the suitability and feasibility of establishing the area as a unit of the national park system, including its administration as a unit of Gateway National Recreation Area, together with alternative measures that may be undertaken to protect and interpret the resources of the area for the public. Not later than two complete fiscal years from the effective date of this Act, the Secretary shall transmit a report of the study, including the estimated development, operation, and maintenance costs of alternatives identified therein, to the Senate Committee on Energy and Natural Resources and the Committee on Interior and Insular Affairs of the House of Representatives, together with his recommendations for such further legislation as may be appropriate.

(b) There is authorized to be appropriated from amounts previously authorized to study lands for possible inclusion in the national park system not to exceed $150,000 to carry out the provisions of this Act.

Approved October 13, 1980.

Appendix 4. Public Law 100-647, 100th Congress, 2d Session

Title X—Manassas National Battlefield Park

SEC. 10001. SHORT TITLE.

This title may be cited as the "Manassas National Battlefield Park Amendments of 1988."

SEC. 10002. ADDITION TO MANASSAS NATIONAL BATTLEFIELD PARK.

The first section of the Act entitled "An act to preserve within Manassas National Battlefield Park, Virginia, the most important historic properties relating to the battle of Manassas, and for other purposes," approved April 17, 1954 (16 U.S.C. 429b), is amended—

(1) by inserting "(a)" after "That"; and

(2) by adding at the end thereof the following:

"(b)(1) In addition to subsection (a), the boundaries of the park shall include the area, comprising approximately 600 acres, which is south of U.S. Route 29, north of Interstate Route 66, east of Route 705, and west of Route 622. Such area shall hereafter in this Act be referred to as the 'Addition.'

"(2)(A) Notwithstanding any other provision of law, effective on the date of enactment of the Manassas National Battlefield Park Amendments of 1988, there is hereby vested in the United States all right, title, and interest in and to, and the right to immediate possession of, all the real property within the Addition.

"(B) The United States shall pay just compensation to the owners of any property taken pursuant to this paragraph and the full faith and credit of the United States is hereby pledged to the payment of any judgment entered against the United States with respect to the taking of such property. Payment shall be in the amount of the agreed negotiated value of such property or the valuation of such property awarded by judgment and shall be made from the permanent judgment appropriation established pursuant to 31 U.S.C. 1304. Such payment shall include interest on the value of such property which shall be compounded quarterly and computed at the rate applicable for the period involved, as determined by the Secretary of the Treasury on the basis of the current average market yield on outstanding marketable obligations of the United States of comparable maturities from the date of enactment of the Manassas National Battlefield Park Amendments of 1988 to the last day of the month preceding the date on which payment is made.

"(C) In the absence of a negotiated settlement, or an action by the owner, within 1 year after the date of enactment of the Manassas National Battlefield Park Amendments of 1988, the Secretary may initiate a proceeding at anytime seeking in a court of competent jurisdiction a determination of just compensation with respect to the taking such property.

"(3) Not later than 6 months after the date of enactment of the Manassas National Battlefield Park Amendments of 1988, the Secretary shall publish in the Federal Register a detailed description and map depicting the boundaries of the Addition. The map shall be on file and available for public inspection in the offices of the National Park Service, Department of the Interior.

"(c) The Secretary shall not allow any unauthorized use of the Addition after the enactment of the Manassas National Battlefield Park Amendments of 1988, except that the Secretary may permit the orderly termination of operations on the Addition and the removal of equipment, facilities, and personal property from the Addition."

SEC. 10003. VISUAL PROTECTION.

Section 2(a) of the Act entitled "An Act to preserve within Manassas National Battlefield Park, Virginia, the most important historic properties relating to the battle of Manassas, and for other purposes," approved April 17, 1954 (16 U.S.C. 429b–1), is amended—

> (1) by inserting "(1)" after "(a)"; and
>
> (2) by adding at the end thereof the following:

"(2) The Secretary shall cooperate with the Commonwealth of Virginia, the political subdivisions thereof, and other parties as designated by the Commonwealth or its political subdivisions in order to promote and achieve scenic preservation of views from within the park through zoning and such other means as the parties determine feasible."

SEC. 10004. HIGHWAY RELOCATION.

(a) STUDY.—The Secretary of the Interior (hereafter in this section referred to as the "Secretary"), in consultation and consensus with the Commonwealth of Virginia, the Federal Highway Administration, and Prince William County, shall conduct a study regarding the relocation of highways (know as routes 29 and 234) in, and in the vicinity of, the Manassas National Battlefield Park (hereinafter in this section referred to as the "park"). The study shall include an assessment of the available alternatives, together with cost estimates and recommendations regarding preferred options. The study shall specifically consider and develop plans for the closing of those public highways (know as routes 29 and 234) that transect the park and shall include analysis of the timing and method of such closures and of means to provide alternative routes for traffic now transecting the park. The Secretary shall provide for extensive public involvement in the preparation of the study.

(b) DETERMINATION.—Within 1 year after the enactment of this Act, the Secretary shall complete the study under subsection (a). The study shall determine when and how the highways (known as routes 29 and 234) should be closed.

(c) ASSISTANCE.—The Secretary shall provide funds to the appropriate construction agency for the construction and improvement of the highways to be used for the rerouting of traffic now utilizing highways (known as routes 29 and 234) to be closed pursuant to subsection (b) if the construction and improvement of such alternatives are deemed by the Secretary to be in the interest of protecting the integrity of the park. Not more than 75 percent of the costs of such construction and improvement shall be provided by the Secretary and at least 25 percent shall be provided by State or local governments from any source other than Federal funds. Such construction and improvement shall be approved by the Secretary of Transportation.

(d) AUTHORIZATION.—There is authorized to be appropriated to the Secretary not to exceed $30,000,000 to prepare the study required by subsection (a) and to provide the funding described in subsection (c).

Approved November 10, 1988.

Appendix 5. Maps of Manassas National Battlefield Park

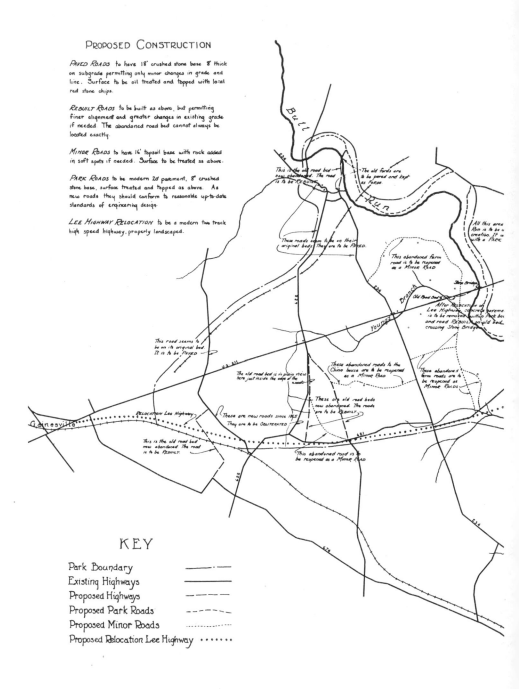

Map A-1. Drawing 1068. Battlefield of Bull Run, preliminary study for roads and paving. 10 June 1935

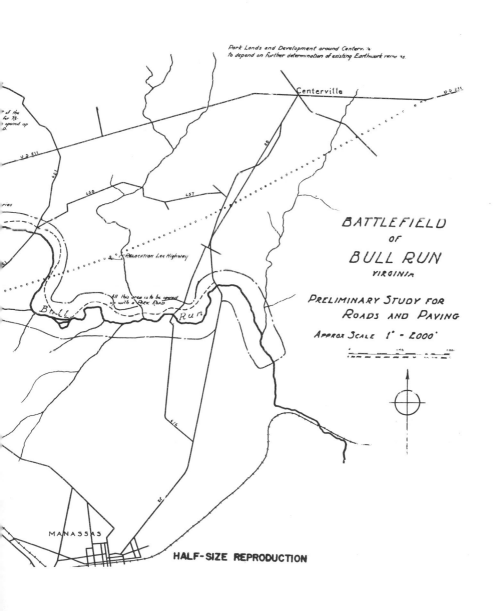

Park Lands and Development around Centerv. le
to depend on further determination of existing Earthwork rema us.

Centerville

BATTLEFIELD
of
BULL RUN
VIRGINIA

PRELIMINARY STUDY FOR
ROADS AND PAVING

APPROX SCALE 1" = 2000'

MANASSAS

HALF-SIZE REPRODUCTION

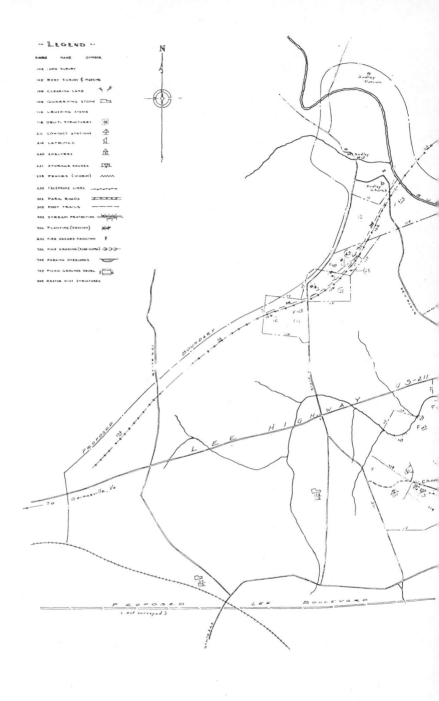

Map A-2. Drawing 1071C. Bull Run Battlefield. 13 November 1935

BULL RUN BATTLEFIELD

KEY MAP
No scale

Bull Run

To Washington, D.C.

Centerville
3½ miles

Matthews
House

Henry
House

BULL RUN

BULL RUN

To Manassas 2 mi.

UNITED STATES DEPARTMENT OF THE INTERIOR
NATIONAL PARK SERVICE
RESETTLEMENT ADM.   DIVISION LAND UTILIZATION
BULL RUN BATTLEFIELD
Area LB-VA-3
FAIRFAX COUNTY   VIRGINIA

GENERAL DEVELOPMENT PLAN

SCALE   1"=1000'

MANASSAS NATIONAL
BATTLEFIELD PARK
VIRGINIA

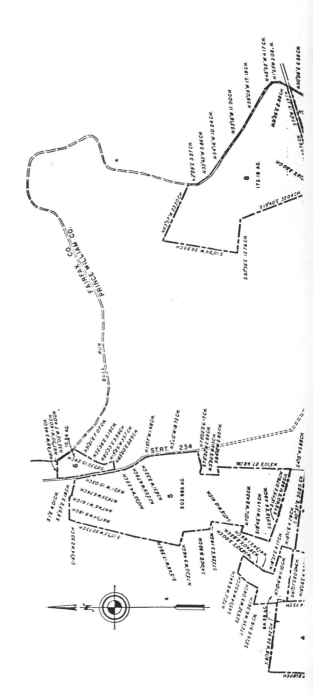

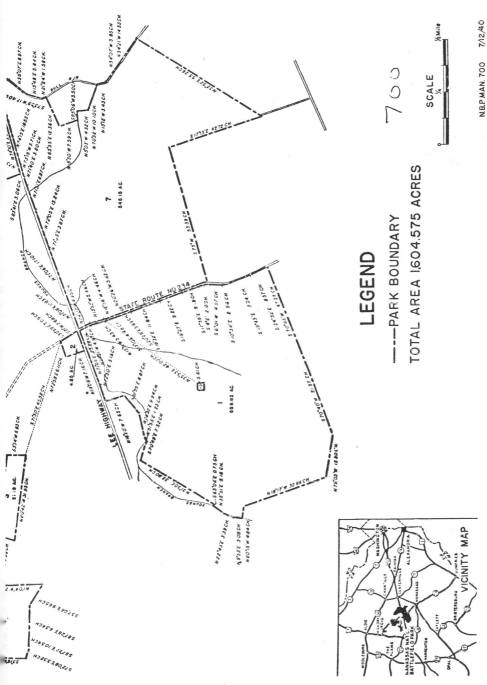

LEGEND

----- PARK BOUNDARY

TOTAL AREA 1,604.575 ACRES

SCALE

N.B.P. MAN. 700   7/12/40

VICINITY MAP

Map A-3. Drawing 700. Manassas National Battlefield Park, 12 July 1940.

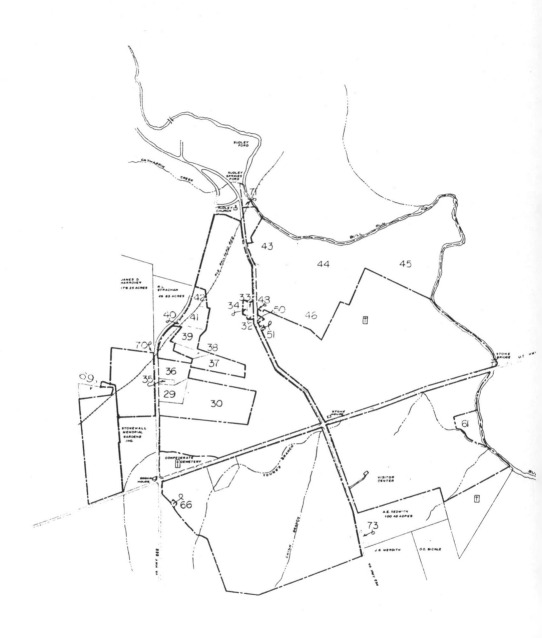

Map A-4. Drawing 2027B. Untitled boundary map. 1 July 1963

PROPERTY LIST

TRACT NO.	OWNERS	ACRES
29	W. L. DISBROW	14.75
30	M. J. PETERS	119.00
32	Wm. E. LINTHICUM	1.00
33	R. H. DOWNS	4.00
34	R. J. PEARSON	2.50
35	S. M. JONES	2.60
36	K. C. WHITE	22.00
37	M. J. PETERS	21.00
38	JAMES PETERS ESTATE	7.00
39	R. F. GARZA	19.05
40	R. E. CATON	2.42
41	E. N. WALKER	15.95
42	SHELLINGTON DEAN	8.75
43	H. J. BAUSILI	66.43
44	E. H. LINDSEY	137.56
45	S. A. MULLIKIN	189.41
46	C. E. CORNELL	100.50
48	JOE SMITH	1.00
50	W. P. DUNBAR	1.00
51	S. A. MOSS	1.19
61	McKINLEY ROBINSON	12.00
66	R. L. ELGIN	1.00
69	ENOCH HARRIS ESTATE	15.00
70	J. D. HARROVER	1.00
71	H. R. WOODWARD	7.00
73	A. E. SEDWICK	10.00

LEGEND

EXISTING NPS BOUNDARY & AREA ————————————
PROPOSED NPS BOUNDARY & AREA —— —— —— ——
SCENIC EASEMENT ————————————

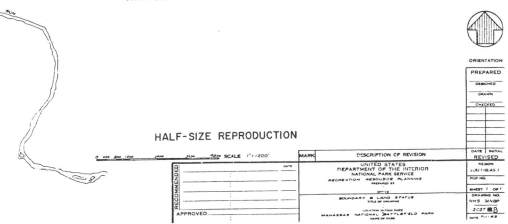

HALF-SIZE REPRODUCTION

0 400 800 1200   2400   3600   4800 SCALE 1"=1200'

MARK	DESCRIPTION OF REVISION			

RECOMMENDED
DATE

APPROVED

UNITED STATES
DEPARTMENT OF THE INTERIOR
NATIONAL PARK SERVICE
RECREATION RESOURCE PLANNING
PREPARED BY

OFFICE
BOUNDARY & LAND STATUS
TITLE OF DRAWING

LOCATION WITHIN PARK
MANASSAS NATIONAL BATTLEFIELD PARK
NAME OF PARK

ORIENTATION

PREPARED
DESIGNED
DRAWN
CHECKED

REVISED
DATE | INITIAL

REGION
SOUTHEAST

PCP NO.

SHEET 1 OF 1

DRAWING NO.
NHS MNBP

2027 B

DATE 7-1-63

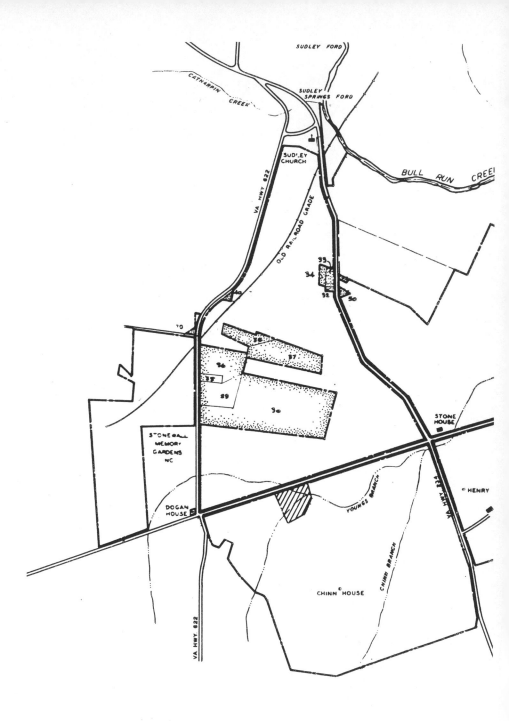

Map A-5. Drawing 7012. Manassas National Battlefield Park.
December 1965

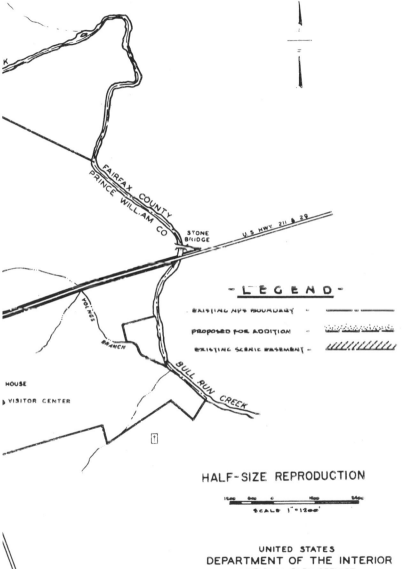

- L E G E N D -

EXISTING NPS BOUNDARY
PROPOSED FOR ADDITION
EXISTING SCENIC EASEMENT

HALF-SIZE REPRODUCTION

SCALE 1"=1200'

UNITED STATES
DEPARTMENT OF THE INTERIOR
NATIONAL PARK SERVICE

MANASSAS
NATIONAL BATTLEFIELD PARK
PRINCE WILLIAM COUNTY
VIRGINIA

NBP-MAN-7012   12/65

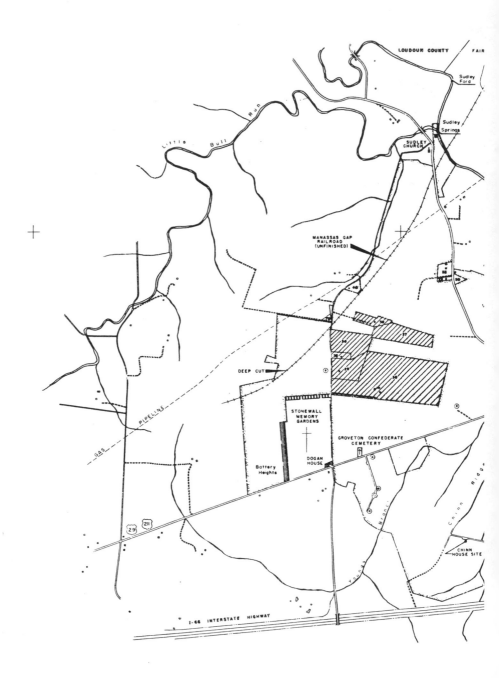

Map A-6. Drawing 379-20015. Untitled boundary map. 14 October 1966

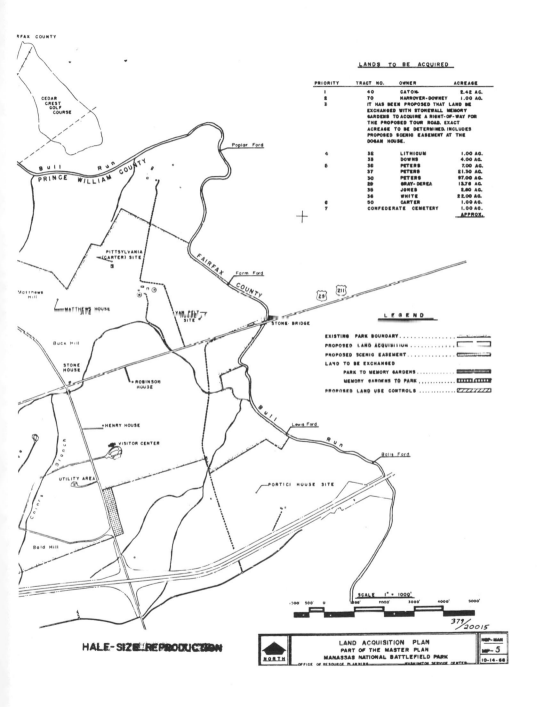

LANDS TO BE ACQUIRED

PRIORITY	TRACT NO.	OWNER	ACREAGE
1	40	CATON	2.42 AC.
2	70	HARROVER-DOWNEY	1.00 AC.
3		IT HAS BEEN PROPOSED THAT LAND BE EXCHANGED WITH STONEWALL MEMORY GARDENS TO ACQUIRE A RIGHT-OF-WAY FOR THE PROPOSED TOUR ROAD. EXACT ACREAGE TO BE DETERMINED. INCLUDES PROPOSED SCENIC EASEMENT AT THE DOGAN HOUSE.	
4	32	LITHICUM	1.00 AC.
	33	DOWNS	4.00 AC.
5	36	PETERS	7.00 AC.
	37	PETERS	21.30 AC.
	30	PETERS	97.00 AC.
	29	GRAY-DEREA	13.78 AC.
	35	JONES	2.60 AC.
	36	WHITE	22.00 AC.
6	50	CARTER	1.00 AC.
7		CONFEDERATE CEMETERY	1.00 AC.
			APPROX.

LEGEND

EXISTING PARK BOUNDARY	
PROPOSED LAND ACQUISITION	
PROPOSED SCENIC EASEMENT	
LAND TO BE EXCHANGED	
PARK TO MEMORY GARDENS	
MEMORY GARDENS TO PARK	
PROPOSED LAND USE CONTROLS	

SCALE 1" = 1000'

379/20015

LAND ACQUISITION PLAN	MSP-MAN
PART OF THE MASTER PLAN	MP-5
MANASSAS NATIONAL BATTLEFIELD PARK	
OFFICE OF RESOURCE PLANNING WASHINGTON SERVICE CENTER	10-14-66

NORTH

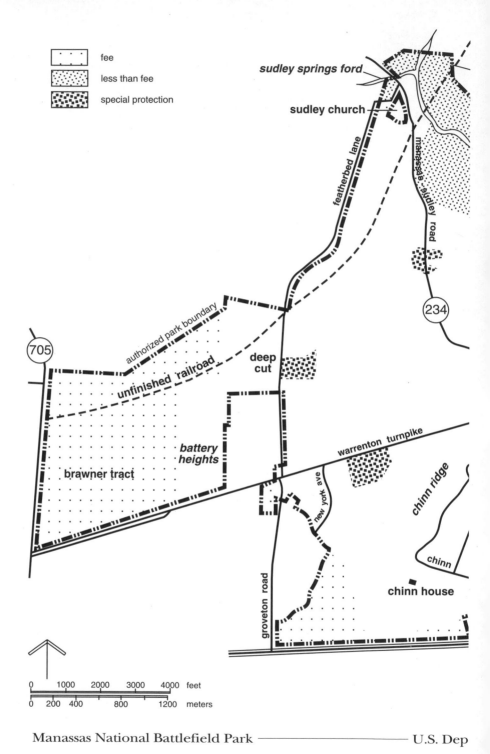

fee

less than fee

special protection

sudley springs ford

sudley church

featherbed lane

manassas-sudley road

234

authorized park boundary

705

unfinished railroad

deep
cut

battery
heights

warrenton turnpike

new york ave

chinn ridge

brawner tract

chinn

chinn house

groveton road

0   1000   2000   3000   4000 feet

0   200 400   800   1200 meters

Manassas National Battlefield Park ———————————— U.S. Dep

Map A-7. Drawing 20047. Land protection as authorized—1980.
September 1983

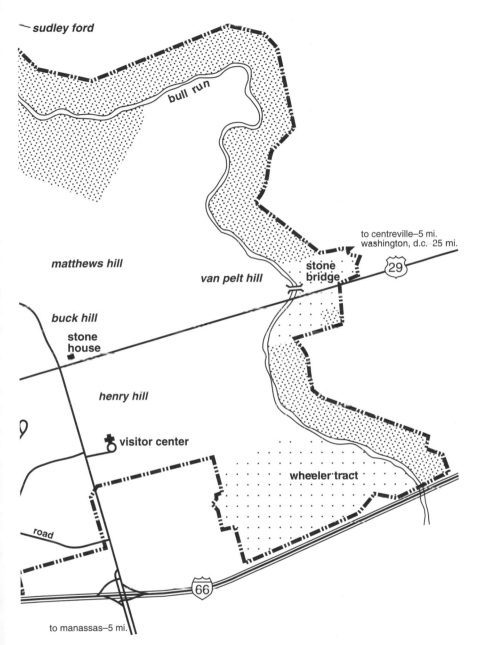

sudley ford

bull run

matthews hill

van pelt hill

stone
bridge

to centreville–5 mi.
washington, d.c. 25 mi.

29

buck hill

stone
house

henry hill

visitor center

wheeler tract

road

66

to manassas–5 mi.

Land Protection as Authorized • 1980

artment of the Interior ——————————— National Park Service

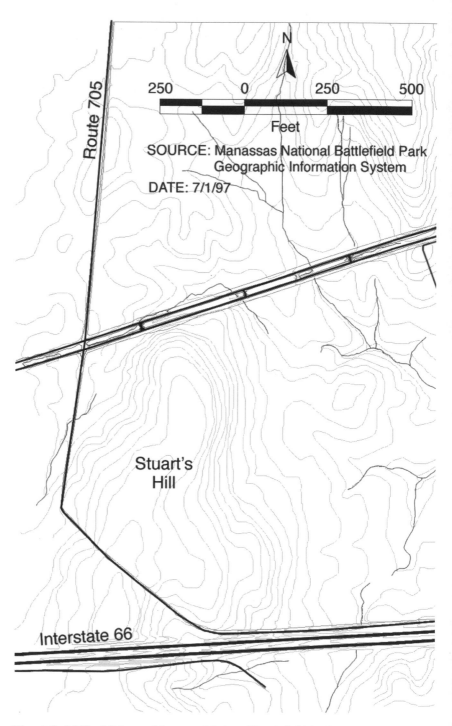

Map A-8. 1988 addition to Manassas National Battlefield Park showing development plans.

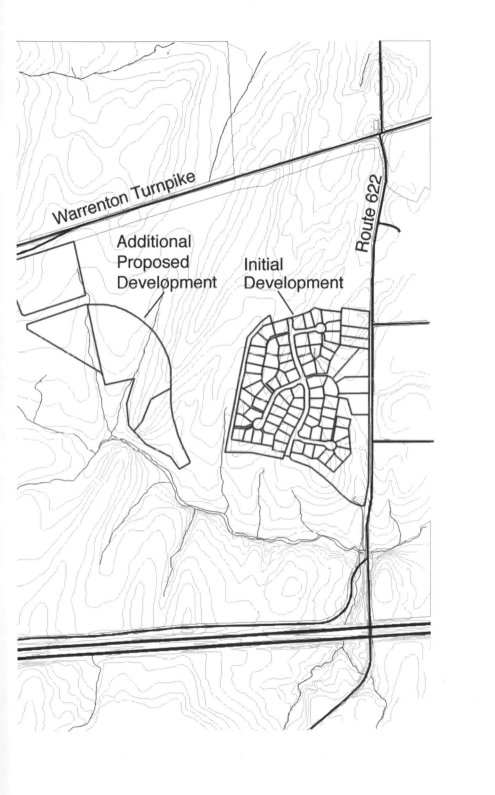

Appendix 6. Land Additions to Manassas National Battlefield Park

Tract[a]	Owner	Acres	Price	Date[b]	Improvements
36	W. S. Hoge and Brothers	171.72	$ 12,000	12 March 1936	none
21	Fannie Lee Henry, W. A. Henry	114.27	$ 6,500	22 May 1936	one dwelling, three outbuildings
2	Cordelia L. Swart et al.	523.74	$ 10,400	30 July 1936	one dwelling
10	William H. Dogan et ux.	30.83	$ 1,440	1 September 1936	none
41	Montgomery J. Peter et ux.	38.97	$ 2,625	1 September 1936	none
12	Samuel A. Moss, Lottie Moss	137.38	$ 7,000	8 September 1936	one dwelling, one outbuilding
11	Lucy A. Senseney, Philip B. Senseney	29.48	$ 1,440	28 May 1937	none
3	George H. Ayers et ux.	52.58	$ 4,000	23 November 1936	none
102	George Golder O'Neil et ux.	10.65	$ 2,500	15 October 1937	none
46	Robert V. Robinson et ux.	30.54	$ 1,375	15 October 1937	none
45	W. K. Caldwell et ux.	6.16	$ 3,500	16 March 1938	one dwelling, four outbuildings
101	Fred H. Collins et ux.	80.55	$ 4,913.25	16 March 1938	one dwelling, one barn
4A	McKinley Robinson et ux.	6.69	$ 2,000	16 March 1938	one dwelling, one barn, two outbuildings
4	Edna May Robinson, John R. Gaskins	242.22	$ 16,120	23 March 1938	none
Henry Farm	Manassas Battlefield Confederate Park, Inc.	0.80	N.A.[c]	8 February 1940	Henry House, two outbuildings

Tract[a]	Owner	Acres	Price	Date[b]	Improvements
Stone House Farm	George H. Ayers Estate	66.055	$ 42,597	1 September 1949	Stone House, two outbuildings
Dogan House	Prince William County Chamber of Commerce	4,914 sq. ft.	N.A.[a]	22 May 1950	Dogan House
Land adjacent to New York Monuments	Charles K. Craver et ux., Beula C. Craver	9.60	$ 24,000	6 July 1953	one dwelling, one outbuilding
Land adjacent to New York Monuments	John H. Parrish et ux., Lucille B. Parrish	3.90	$ 5,100	9 October 1953	none
Land adjacent to New York Monuments	Joseph A. Nycz et ux., Lois M. Nycz	1.0	$ 4,000	12 October 1953	none
Land adjacent to New York Monuments	John T. Hottel et ux., Rose E. Hottel	23.63	$ 12,324.25	2 November 1953	none
Land adjacent to New York Monuments	Joseph W. Patterson et ux., Ruth C. Patterson	10.60	$ 15,000	7 February 1955	one dwelling, one temporary outbuilding
Land adjacent to New York Monuments	Willis G. Early, Elizabeth F. Early	6.90	$ 17,000	19 December 1955	one dwelling, one temporary outbuilding
Land adjacent to New York Monuments	John T. Hottel, Rose E. Hottel	4.66	$ 7,000	13 January 1956	none
Stone House Inn	Frederick A. Miller et ux., Mary F. Miller	2.01	$ 35,000	8 April 1958	Stone House Inn, three cabins, one outbuilding
New York Monument tracts	State of New York	5.80	N.A.[c]	11 June 1958	three granite monuments, each surrounded by an iron fence
56	George O. Sutton, Lois S. Sutton	128.72	$ 94,700	19 May 1960	four dwellings, five dairy buildings, two silos, one outbuilding, pond with earth dam
68	Lis Pendens	40.00	$ 30,200	13 October 1960	one dwelling, one garage

Tract[a]	Owner	Acres	Price	Date[b]	Improvements
36–A Groveton Cemetery	Rowland Reid Adamson	5.00	$ 12,000	7 May 1971	unknown
01–105	Esther D. Terrill et al.	0.90	N.A.[j]	9 October 1973	unknown
01–117	Norine M. Mullikin	189.41	$ 341,000	28 November 1973	unknown
01–135	Commonwealth of Virginia	0.32	$ 1.00	26 August 1974	none
01–108	Adelaide Neily, Francis W. Gittleson	16.94	unknown	12 February 1975	unknown
01–217	Daniel T. Donohoe, executor, et al.	100.50	$ 375,000	20 February 1975	unknown
01–176	McKinley E. Robinson	18.15	$ 23,000	19 April 1976[f]	unknown
01–119	Raymond E. Caton	2.42	$ 45,000	1 May 1980	one dwelling
02–114	Eastern National Park and Monument Association	7.00	$ 73,000	3 July 1984	unknown
02–115	Elmo E. Ball III	10.55	$ 150,000	3 October 1984	one dwelling, two commercial buildings
02–167	Dorothy R. Abbott	46.14	$ 161,500	8 May 1985	none
02–101 (Wheeler Tract)	National Park Foundation	203.66	$ 900,000	12 May 1985	one dwelling, three farm buildings
02–166 (Brawner Farm)	Annie M. Davis	312.50	$ 4,218,750	21 May 1985[f]	one dwelling
02–175	Mr. and Mrs. Frank Entwisle	8.35	$ 101,850	1 July 1985	one commercial building
02–109	Nellie M. Edwards	27.68	$ 196,760	15 November 1985	none
02–170	Solite Corporation	85.50	$ 300,000	2 May 1986	none
01–111	R. H. Downs, heirs	4.00	$ 70,000	21 August 1986	two buildings
02–172[k]	Paul E. Allison et ux.	4.00	$ 4,000	2 December 1986	none

Tract[a]	Owner	Acres	Price	Date[b]	Improvements
02–102	Carol O'Neill trust	59.20	$ 201,000	12 May 1987	none
02–174	B. Oswald Robinson et ux.	8.72	$ 388,500	12 May 1987[l]	one dwelling
Stuart's Hill	Hazel/Peterson Companies et al.	542	$130,000,000	1988[m]	multiple dwellings, access roads
02–110[n]	Cecil Pruitt Jr.	0.72	N.A.	31 May 1989	none
02–164	The Conservation Fund	24.25	N.A.[o]	2 May 1991	unknown
01–119	Raymond E. Caton, Joyce J. Caton	2.42	—	—	one dwelling

[a] The National Park Service assigned an identifying number to each tract of land considered for inclusion in the Manassas National Battlefield Park. These numbers are noted on property maps and were used consistently by the Park Service for land acquisition purposes. In cases where a tract of land was later subdivided and sold by the property owner before inclusion in the battlefield park, the Park Service assigned new numbers to the newly created tracts. By the 1970s, the Park Service assigned new tract numbers to the remaining property. Numbers in this table refer to the tract number used at the time the Park Service acquired the property.

[b] The dates listed are the date the secretary of interior accepted the tract or the date the attorney general gave the final opinion on the settlement.

[c] The Henry Farm was acquired from Manassas Battlefield Confederate Park, Inc., by donation.

[d] The Dogan House was acquired from the Prince William County Chamber of Commerce by donation.

[e] The New York Monuments were acquired from the state of New York by donation.

[f] The Park Service acquired this tract by a declaration of taking.

[g] In exchange for part of tract 52, valued at $15,500, the National Park Service conveyed part of tract 21, valued at $14,000, to William H. Wheeler.

[h] In exchange for the Stone Bridge, the National Park Service conveyed four parcels of land along Route 234, valued at $1,414, to the Commonwealth of Virginia.

[i] The National Park Service placed a scenic easement upon this tract.

[j] The National Park Service acquired this tract by donation from the surviving trustees for Groveton Cemetery for Confederate Soldiers, represented by Esther D. Terrill et al.

[k] In exchange for tract 02–172, the National Park Service conveyed one acre of land near the Sudley Methodist Church to Paul E. Allison et ux., with the payment of $4,000, to be used exclusively for a cemetery.

[l] B. Oswald Robinson retained use of his residence.

[m] The National Park Service acquired this tract by a legislative taking.

[n] The National Park Service acquired tract 02–110 from Cecil Pruitt Jr. in exchange for tract 01–225 and $4,500.

[o] The Conservation Fund donated tract 02–164 to the United States for the Manassas National Battlefield Park by executing a "special warranty deed of gift."

Appendix 7. NPS Regional Oversight of Manassas National Battlefield Park

1940: Region 1, Richmond, Virgina
1962: Region 1 became Southeast Region, Richmond, Virginia
1971: Northeast Region, Philadelphia, Pennsylvania
1973: National Capital Parks, Washington, D.C.
1976: National Capital Parks became National Capital Region

Source: Barry Mackintosh, *National Park Service Administrative History: A Guide* (Washington, D.C.: National Park Service History Division, 1991), 111–14.

Appendix 8. Manassas National Battlefield Park Superintendents and Dates of Service

Raleigh C. Taylor: 21 May 1940 to 15 March 1942
Joseph Mills Hanson: 21 April 1942 to 31 December 1947
James B. Myers: 12 January 1948 to 31 August 1955
Francis F. Wilshin: 1 September 1955 to 19 April 1969
Russell W. Berry Jr.: 29 June 1969 to 20 May 1973
Richard E. Hoffman: 12 July 1973 to 23 April 1977
R. Brien Varnado: 20 May 1977 to 20 April 1980
Rolland R. Swain: 5 September 1980 to 23 April 1988
Kenneth E. Apschnikat: 14 August 1988 to 4 March 1995
Robert K. Sutton: 1 October 1995 to present

NOTES

Introduction

1. Robert Webb, "Storm over Manassas: A Plan to Develop Part of Virginia's Famed Civil War Battlefield Is Provoking the Greatest Preservation Battle in Years," *Historic Preservation* 40 (July/August 1988): 40–45; Jody Powell, "Battling over Manassas," *National Parks* 62 (July/August 1988): 12–13; George F. Will, "Where Men Fought and Fell," *Newsweek*, 18 July 1988, 68; "Hallowed Ground," *The Economist*, 20 August 1988, 25–26.

2. "Civil War Sites Face Grave Threats," *National Parks* 67 (November/December 1993): 11.

3. Civil War Sites Advisory Commission, *Report on the Nation's Civil War Battlefields* (Washington, D.C.: National Park Service, 1993), 3, 28–31.

4. During the Civil War, the officers from the opposing sides sometimes chose different map features to name battles. In the case of Manassas, Federals named the two battles after the nearby Bull Run, while Confederates used Manassas Junction, the rail center that eventually developed into the town of Manassas, for the name.

5. Robert E. L. Krick, "The Civil War's First Monument," *Blue & Gray*, April 1991, 32–33; Ronald F. Lee, *The Origin and Evolution of the National Military Park Idea* (Washington, D.C.: National Park Service, 1973), 16.

6. Lee, *Origin of the Military Park Idea*, 6; Richard West Sellars, "Vigil of Silence: The Civil War Memorials," *History News*, July/August 1986, 19–23.

7. Lee, *Origin of the Military Park Idea*, 6; Edward Tabor Linenthal, *Sacred Ground: Americans and their Battlefields* Urbana: University of Illinois Press, 1991), 94. Michael Kammen notes that beneath the promising signs of reconciliation and nationalism were feelings of hatred and vindictiveness between the North and the South, indicating the need for more healing. See Michael Kammen, *Mystic Chords of Memory: The Transformation of Tradition in American Culture* New York: Alfred A. Knopf, 1991), 106–15.

8. Lee, *Origin of the Military Park Idea*, 6; Linenthal, *Sacred Ground*, 104, 106; Mike O'Donnell, *At Manassas: Reunions, Reenactments, Maneuvers* (Mechanicsville, Va.: Rapidan Press, 1986).

9. Robert M. Utley, "A Preservation Ideal," *Historic Preservation* 28 (April/June 1976); Ary J. Lamme III, *America's Historic Landscapes: Community Power and the Preservation of Four National Historic Sites* (Knoxville: University of Tennessee Press, 1989), 179; Reuben M. Rainey, "The Memory of War: Reflections on Battlefield Preservation," in *The Yearbook of Landscape Architecture: Historic Preservation*, ed. Richard L. Austin et al. (New York: Van Nostrand Reinhold, n.d.), 78; Linenthal, *Sacred Ground*, 115, 216; Georgie Boge and Margie Holder Boge, *Paving Over the Past: A History and Guide to Civil War Battlefield Preservation* (Washington, D.C., 1993), xvii, 7; Thomas A. Lewis, "Fighting for the Past," *Audubon*, September 1989, 58.

10. Jane Brown Gillette, "Fields Forgotten," *Historic Preservation* 45 (July/August 1993): 86.

11. Jerry L. Russell, interview by author, 27 July 1994, transcript, 17–18, NPS.

12. Gillette, "Fields Forgotten," 86.

Chapter 1. Early Preservation Efforts

1. For a concise but detailed discussion of the establishment of the first battlefield parks, see Lee, *Origin of the Military Park Idea.*

2. House, *Protection of Monuments on Battle Field of Bull Run,* 63rd Cong., 2d sess., 1913, H. Doc. 481, 16–19; Frank B. Sarles Jr., "A Short History of Manassas National Battlefield Park," June 1955, 5–7, 10, Library Collection, Manassas National Battlefield Park (MNBP); Krick, "Civil War's First Monument." Measurements of the Bull Run and Groveton monuments provided by the Park Service.

3. Sarles, "Short History," 6–7; Lee, *Origin of the Military Park Idea,* 17–18; Kammen, *Mystic Chords of Memory,* 115–18.

4. Sarles, "Short History," 6–7; "Bull Run Monuments Unveiled by Veterans," 20 October 1906, newspaper article; "Three Monuments Dedicated on Historic Battlefield of Bull Run," 21 October 1906, newspaper article; James B. Meyers, "Report on Lands Surrounding the New York Monuments Near Manassas National Battlefield Park," June-September 1950, last three documents in file Monuments and Markers, N.Y. Monuments and Land Acquisition, Historian's Files, MNBP.

5. "Bull Run Monuments Unveiled"; "Three Monuments Dedicated."

6. Charles F. Walcott, "A Revisit to the Fields of Manassas and Chantilly," in *The Virginia Campaign of 1862 Under General Pope,* ed. Theodore Dwight (Boston: Houghton Mifflin, 1895), 173–77; H. F. Henry, *Souvenir Booklet of the Battlefield of Bull Run Battles of July 21, 1861 and August 28, 29, and 30, 1862* (Manassas, Va.: Manassas Journal Press, 1900), file Battlefield Guides, MNBP; Visitor Register, 1918–40, Museum Collection, MNBP.

7. Lee, *Origin of the Military Park Idea,* 38.

8. George Carr Round, "The Last Signal Message of the War," 1902; "George Carr Round, Father of the Public School System of Prince William County," n.d.; and Rita G. Koman, "George Carr Round 1839–1918," 21 May 1976, all in G. C. Round Papers, GC Round File no. 1, Manassas Museum; Clint Schemmer, "Documents Reveal Background of Illustrious Manassas Leader," *Potomac News* (Woodbridge), 10 August 1988.

9. George Carr Round, "Union Soldier Concerning the Lee Statue," *Confederate Veteran,* November 1910, 529; "George Carr Round, Father of the Public School System"; Koman, "George Carr Round."

10. Ralph K. T. Larson, "The New Battle of Manassas," *Washington Post,* 12 May 1979; House, *Protection of Monuments,* 6; O'Donnell, *At Manassas,* 16; Linenthal, *Sacred Ground,* 94.

11. O'Donnell, *At Manassas,* 16–17; George Carr Round, "The Manassas Jubilee: Aftermath," 7 August 1911, MANA 1250, Museum Collection, MNBP; Koman, "George Carr Round."

12. Round, "Manassas Jubilee"; O'Donnell, *At Manassas,* 16; Linenthal, *Sacred Ground,* 95.

13. House, *Protection of Monuments,* 28–29, 33, 38–39, 40; *A Bill to Protect the Monuments Already Erected on the Battlefields of Bull Run, Virginia,* 56th Cong., 1st sess., 1901, H.R. 277; *Biographical Directory of the United States Congress 1774–1989* (Washington, D.C.: Government Printing Office, 1989), 1722.

14. Lee, *Origin of the Military Park Idea,* 39–40.

15. Ibid., 38–40.

16. H.R. 277; House, *Protection of Monuments,* 33; Lee, *Origin of the Military Park Idea,* 41.

17. House, *Protection of Monuments,* 28–29, 33, 37. Round accompanied General Davis on two occasions in the 1890s when the general surveyed the Manassas battlefields.

18. *A Bill to Establish Battle Park on Bull Run,* 56th Cong., 1st sess., 1900, H.R. 7837; *Biographical Directory of the United States Congress, 1774–1989* (Washington, D.C.: Government Printing Office, 1989), 1597; George Carr Round, "Is the United States Too Poor to Own Its Own Monuments?," 1917, file 1865 Bull Run Monuments, Historian's Files, MNBP; House, *Protection of Monuments,* 28.

19. Lee, *Origin of the Military Park Idea*, 44–45; House, *Protection of Monuments*, 34.

20. House, *Protection of Monuments*, 15.

21. Ibid.; *A Bill to Protect the Monuments Already Erected on the Battlefields of Bull Run, Virginia*, 58th Cong., 1st sess, 1903, H.R. 1964. Round does not divulge why the Department of Pennsylvania first fought the Manassas resolution.

22. House, *Protection of Monuments*, 13–16.

23. *Biographical Directory of Congress*, 743; *A Bill to Protect the Monuments Already Erected on the Battlefields of Bull Run, Virginia, and Other Monuments That May Be There Erected*, 62d Cong., 1st sess., 1912, H.R. 1330.

24. House, *Protection of Monuments*, 30–37.

25. House, *Protection of Monuments*, 1, 32–37. During the 1912 hearings, Round readily disclosed his role as legal representative of the Henry family heirs, which began that year. He also represented Lucinda Dogan. See Round, "Is the United States Too Poor?"

26. House, *Protection of Monuments*, 1–12.

27. House, *Protection of Monuments*, 1–6; Sarles, "Short History," 12.

28. Round, "Is the United States Too Poor?"

Chapter 2. Establishing a Park

1. Michael Kammen describes more fully this American enchantment with history in part 3 of his book, *Mystic Chords of Memory*.

2. Unfortunately, none of the sources reveal Ewing's first name. George Carr Round contributed an article to the *Confederate Veteran* on Manassas park efforts in 1917, which may have influenced Ewing's pursuit of the Confederate park in 1920. E. W. R. Ewing, "The Manassas Battlefield Confederate Park," 1927, 7, MANA 1911, accession (acc.) 52, Museum Collection, MNBP; E. W. R. Ewing, "The Manassas Battlefield Confederate Park Prospectus," rev. ed., 1921, 6, Virginiana Room, Bull Run Library, Manassas, Va.; *Confederate Veteran*, October 1920, 397; Sarles, "Short History," 13.

3. Ewing, "Manassas Park Prospectus," 4–8, 12, 15–16.

4. Ewing, "Manassas Battlefield Confederate Park," 9; Ewing, "Manassas Park Prospectus," 8; J. Roy Price to John Jones, 29 July 1929, 2, file Confederate Park Files, Historian's Files, MNBP.

5. J. Roy Price to John Jones, 29 July 1929, 2; Ewing, "Manassas Battlefield Confederate Park," 8–9.

6. With interest, Virginia eventually appropriated $12,800 toward the Confederate park; see Edmond Wiles to Horace Albright, 23 June 1933, file Correspondence 6/1/33–6/30/37, box 2596A, entry 7, record group (RG) 79, National Archives and Records Administration (NARA). Ewing, "Manassas Battlefield Confederate Park," 9–12; "Manassas Battle Field Confederate Park," *Confederate Veteran*, October 1929, 236; "Manassas Battle Field Memorial," *Confederate Veteran*, May 1923, 197.

7. Ewing, "Manassas Battlefield Confederate Park," 9; Virginia Division, Sons of Confederate Veterans, resolution no. 4, October 1935, Roanoke, Va., 15–17, file Correspondence 6/1/33–6/30/37, box 2596A, entry 7, RG 79, NARA. The Virginia Division of the Sons of Confederate Veterans unanimously adopted resolution no. 4 at their fortieth annual convention. "Funds to Clear Manassas Battle Field," *Confederate Veteran*, July 1929, 277.

8. Sarles, "Short History," 14; Edmond Wiles to Horace Albright, 23 June 1933, Albright to Wiles, 26 June 1933, and Wiles to Albright, 11 July 1933, all in file Correspondence 6/1/33–6/30/37, box 2596A, entry 7, RG 79, NARA.

9. Lee, *Origin of the Military Park Idea*, 47–48.

10. Ibid., 48–49.

11. Ibid., 50, 52; *Study of Battle Fields in the United States for Commemorative Purposes,* 70th Cong., 2d sess., 1928, S. Doc. 187, 3–4; *Study of Battlefields in the United States for Commemorative Purposes,* 72d Cong., 1st sess., 1931, S. Doc. 27, 3, 5–6.

12. Horace M. Albright, *Origins of National Park Service Administration of Historic Sites* (Philadelphia: Eastern National Park and Monument Association, 1971), 18–22. The story of Albright's fortuitous ride with Roosevelt is also recounted in Albright, as told to Robert Cahn, *The Birth of the National Park Service: The Founding Years, 1913–33* (Salt Lake City: Howe Brothers, 1985), 291–97, and in Donald C. Swain, *Wilderness Defender: Horace M. Albright and Conservation* (Chicago: University of Chicago Press, 1970), 224–28.

13. National Park Service, "Administration Manual for Recreational Demonstration Areas," 1938, 3–4, box CCC–2, box code A98, NPS History Collection, Harpers Ferry Center (HFC); National Park Service, *1940 Annual Report of the Secretary of the Interior,* 202, NPS History Collection, HFC; Franklin Delano Roosevelt, *Public Papers and Addresses* (New York: Random House, 1938), 146–47. The Resettlement Administration was an agency under the Department of Agriculture.

14. National Park Service, Resettlement Administration, and Civilian Conservation Corps, *Recreational Demonstration Projects: As Illustrated by Chopawamsic, Virginia,* n.d., 2–3, 6, box CCC–2, box code A98, NPS History Collection, HFC; Roosevelt, *Public Papers,* 146–47.

15. Arno B. Cammerer to Conrad Wirth, 1 March 1935, file Correspondence 6/1/33–6/30/37, box 2596A, entry 7, RG 79, NARA; Howard W. Smith to Wirth, 3 June 1935, 1, attached to "Bull Run Battlefield Recreational Demonstration Project: Summary of Final Project Report" (hereafter cited as "Final Project Report"), 1936, file Park Boundary Study Land Acquisition 1937, Historian's Files, MNBP; Bruce J. Dierenfield, *Keeper of the Rules: Congressman Howard W. Smith of Virginia* (Charlottesville: University Press of Virginia, 1987), 52–54, 74–75. Conrad Wirth wrote Smith in July 1935 saying that the Park Service is "assiduously working to present a Project Plan which can qualify for an allotment of funds under the Emergency Relief Appropriation Act of 1935"—the same act that Smith had opposed. Wirth to Smith, [26?] July 1935, file Correspondence 6/1/33–6/30/37, box 2596A, entry 7, RG 79, NARA.

16. National Park Service, "Administration Manual," 6.

17. The sources do not indicate why the federal government chose "Bull Run" as the name for the recreational demonstration area, but the Northern designation probably seemed more appropriate to the New Yorker Roosevelt and his administration. My discussion of the recreation demonstration area depends on a limited array of planning documents and some correspondence. Unfortunately, the RG 96 field office files, which include case files for land acquisition and the records for resettlement projects for Prince William County, have been destroyed. These documents were under the custodianship of the National Archives and were transferred to the Mid-Atlantic Regional Archives in Philadelphia. "Justification," file 130 Appropriations Estimates, box 130, entry 130, RG 79, NARA; "Final Project Report," 1–2, 6–8, table; Joseph Mills Hanson, "A Report on Proposed Boundaries and Areas for a Manassas National Battlefield Park, Virginia," 10 November 1937, file Manassas Boundary Study, box MANA Retained Info, NPS History Division Archives.

18. National Park Service, *Manassas to Appomattox: National Battlefield Parks Tour in Virginia* (Washington, D.C., 1939), Department of the Interior Library.

19. J. D. Coffman to Director, 4 April 1936; John Shanklin, "Report of the Chief Forester on Bull Run Battlefield," 2 April 1936; Howard W. Smith to Carter Glass, 5 June 1935; Joseph Mills Hanson to Branch Spalding, 14 January 1937, all in file Correspondence 6/1/33–6/30/37, box 2596A, entry 7, RG 79, NARA; Hanson to Verne Chatelain, 3 May 1936, file 101 History Manassas, box 2596A, entry 7, RG 79, NARA; C. P. Grantham to C. F. Clayton, 17 October 1935; John Cross to W. D. Goodale, 29 February 1936, both in file 601–12, box 130, entry 47, RG 79, NARA.

20. Conrad Wirth to Regional Office, Region 1, 2 July 1937, file 201, box 130, entry 47, RG 79, NARA; Joseph Mills Hanson to Branch Spalding, 14 January 1937, and Hanson to Spalding, 3 April 1937, both in file Correspondence 6/1/33–6/30/37, box 2596A, entry 7, RG 79, NARA; Hanson to Branch of Historic Sites and Buildings, 30 August 1937, and Spalding to Lehman Hutchins, 3 November 1937, both in file National Military Parks Corr., box 2596A, entry 7, RG 79, NARA; Joseph Mills Hanson, "Manassas Battlefield Park Markers," 30 January 1937, file Manassas Battlefield Park Markers, box MANA Retained Info, NPS History Division Archives; Hanson, "Proposed Boundaries and Areas"; "National Park Service Marks Manassas Battle Fields," *Manassas Journal,* 6 January 1938; "Final Project Report," 1, 5, 7–8.

21. "Final Project Report," 1936, 2–3 and attached Howard W. Smith to Conrad Wirth, 3 June 1935.

22. "Final Project Report," 2–3. For a discussion of the 1934 National Park Year, see Joan M. Zenzen, "Promoting National Parks: Images of the West in the American Imagination, 1864–1972" (Ph.D. diss., University of Maryland, 1997).

23. "Final Project Report," 8.

24. Arthur Demaray to Acting Secretary, 3 July 1937, file National Military Parks Corr., box 2596A, entry 7, RG 79, NARA; Hanson, "Proposed Boundaries and Areas," 33.

25. Sarles, "Short History," 14; W. L. Hopkins to Wilbur Hall, 8 July 1935, file Correspondence 6/1/33–6/30/37, box 2596A, entry 7, RG 79, NARA.

26. W. L. Hopkins to Arno B. Cammerer, 30 November 1937, file National Military Parks Correspondence, box 2596A, entry 7, RG 79, NARA; TWX, Branch Spalding to Director, 11 June 1936, file Correspondence 6/1/33–6/30/37, box 2596A, entry 7, RG 79, NARA; Spalding to J. Roy Price, 29 July 1937, and Cammerer to Secretary of Interior, 26 April 1940, both in file National Military Parks Corr., box 2596A, entry 7, RG 79, NARA; Sarles, "Short History," 14–16.

27. Park Service personnel exchanged correspondence reflecting varying titles for the proposed battlefield park, using both Bull Run and Manassas as possible names. Spalding supported Manassas National Battlefield Park, while Hanson expressed a preference for Bull Run. See Joseph Mills Hanson to Branch Spalding, 14 January 1937, 2, file Correspondence 6/1/33–6/30/37, box 2596A, entry 7, RG 79, NARA; Sarles, "Short History," 15–16; "Order Designating the Manassas National Battlefield Park, Virginia," 10 May 1940, file National Military Parks Corr., box 2596A, entry 7, RG 79, NARA.

Chapter 3. Settling In

1. Sarles, "Short History," 1, "Statement for Management: Manassas National Battlefield Park," 1989, 7, and Division of Interpretive Planning, Harpers Ferry Center, "A Plan for the Interpretation of Manassas National Battlefield Park, Virginia," draft, 3–4, both in Historian's Files, MNBP.

2. Sarles, "Short History," 1–4.

3. William Thompson Lusk, *War Letters* (New York: privately printed, 1911), 55–59; Susan Leigh Blackford and Charles Minor Blackford, *Letters from Lee's Army or Memories of Life In and Out of the Army in Virginia During the War Between the States,* ed. Charles Minor Blackford III (New York: Charles Scribner's, 1947), 27.

4. O. A. Tomlinson, "Circular for Region Four Field Area," 10 June 1942, file 201–06 Manassas Superintendents and Custodians, box 2596A, entry 7, RG 79, NARA. For a useful guide to the evolution of Park Service regions, see Barry Mackintosh, *National Park Service Administrative History: A Guide* (Washington, D.C.: National Park Service, 1991), 111–14. Raleigh C. Tay-

lor, "Superintendent's Monthly Report for June 1941," 5 July 1941, file 207–02.3 Manassas Superintendent's Monthly Reports, box 2596A, entry 7, RG 79, NARA.

5. "Battle Park Wins Praise," *Manassas Journal,* 25 February 1944; Branch Spalding to Director, 11 May 1939, file Stonewall Jackson Monument, Historian's Files, MNBP.

6. Spalding quoted in Sarles, "Short History," 7–9; "Program, First Battle of Manassas," 21 July 1936, file Correspondence 6/1/33–6/30/37, box 2596A, entry 7, RG 79, NARA; T. Sutton Jett, "'First Manassas' in 1936," *The Commonwealth,* July 1936, 14, box MANA, NPS History Collection, HFC; deed of conveyance between the Manassas Battlefield Confederate Park, Inc., and the United States of America, 19 March 1938, file 01–172 Manassas Battlefield, Inc., MNBP Land Holding Records, Headquarters Files, MNBP.

7. Branch Spalding to Director, 11 May 1939; Virginia Museum of Fine Arts, "Prospectus: The Stonewall Jackson Monument Sculpture Competition and Exhibition," October 1939, both in file Stonewall Jackson Monument, Historian's Files, MNBP. Biographical material on Pollia, A. Snyder Files, MNBP.

8. Publicists would use the term "third battle of Manassas" in referring to each of the controversies relating to land use and acquisition at Manassas. "End of Statue Battle," newspaper clipping, file 501.03 Newspaper Clippings Manassas, box 2596C, entry 7, RG 79, NARA. Michael Kammen points out in *Mystic Chords of Memory* that some of the furor raised by more traditional Southerners towards Pollia's original design was directed against its "modernistic and impressionistic" design (491).

9. The Park Service has since determined that the statue is not on the site where Jackson and his troops held firm. A. J. Ewald to Files, "Report on Conference Regarding Location of Jackson Equestrian Statue," 27 April 1940, file Stonewall Jackson Monument, Historian's Files, MNBP.

10. Freeman quoted in "2,000 See Jackson Statue Unveiled at Manassas Park," *Richmond Times-Dispatch,* 1 September 1940; "Manassas Unveils Statue to Stonewall Jackson Aug. 31," *Times-Herald,* 20 August 1940; and "Jackson Shrine Dedication Focuses Attention on Park," *Sunday Star,* 18 August 1940, all in file 501.03 Newspaper Clippings Manassas, box 2596C, entry 7, RG 79, NARA; Arthur Demaray to Douglas Southall Freeman, 3 September 1940, file Stonewall Jackson Monument, Historian's Files, MNBP; Sarles, "Short History," 17.

11. Deed of conveyance, 19 March 1938, 3.

12. Carl P. Russell to Director, "Master Plan Bull Run Battlefield," 9 November 1937, 6, file National Military Parks Corr., box 2596A, entry 7, RG 79, NARA.

13. Branch Spalding to Regional Director, Region 1, 23 December 1937, "Master Plan"; Spalding to Director, 10 September 1938, "Physical Improvement Project for Manassas"; Spalding to Director, 14 September 1939, "1939 Master Plan," all in file National Military Parks Corr., box 2596A, entry 7, RG 79, NARA; Joseph Mills Hanson, "Preliminary Museum Development Plan, Manassas National Battlefield Park," 1939, 3, box MANA, NPS History Collection, HFC.

14. Deed of conveyance, 19 March 1938. The deed does not stipulate that the museum would serve as a memorial to the soldiers.

15. Thomas Vint to Files, 9 May 1939, file Park Visitor Center, Historian's Files, MNBP; Vint to Regional Director, Region 1, 19 September 1939, file Manassas Correspondence 1939–48, NPS History Division Files; E. M. Lisle to Director, 15 March 1940, file Park Visitor Center, Historian's Files, MNBP; Albert Good to Files, 24 April 1940, "Location of Administration-Museum Building, Bull Run–Manassas Area," file Manassas Correspondence 1939–48, NPS History Division Files; "Work to Start Soon on National Museum for Manassas Field," *Washington Star,* 18 April 1941; Robert E. Smith, "Final Construction Reports, Administration-Museum Building, Manassas National Battlefield Park," 27 August 1942, 1, 6–7, file Park Visitor Center, Historian's Files, MNBP.

16. Oliver G. Taylor, "Notice of Advertisement," 24 March 1941, file Park Visitor Center, Historian's Files, MNBP; "Work to Start Soon"; R. C. Taylor to C. Spano and Son, 9 May 1941, and Acting Regional Director, Region 1, to Director, 30 July 1941, both in file Park Visitor Center, Historian's Files, MNBP; R. C. Taylor, "Superintendent's Monthly Narrative Report for June 1941," 5 July 1941, file 207–02.3 Manassas Superintendent's Monthly Reports, box 2596B, entry 7, RG 79, NARA; E. M. Lisle to Superintendent, Manassas, 25 June 1941; Supervisor of Historic Sites to Coordinating Superintendent, 21 August 1941; Arthur Demaray to Regional Director, Region 1, 9 October 1941, last three documents in file Manassas Correspondence 1939–48, NPS History Division Files; Sarles, "Short History," 20; Floyd B. Taylor, "Report on the Manassas National Battlefield Park Museum and Headquarters Building," June 1942, 1, file Park Visitor Center, Historian's Files, MNBP.

17. Thomas Vint to Files, 9 May 1939; Hanson, "Preliminary Museum Plan," 10.

18. Hanson, "Preliminary Museum Plan," 4–6, 12.

19. Ibid., 6–10.

20. Ibid., 13–26.

21. Evidence that the Park Service expected a largely white audience at Manassas is found in discussions about segregated toilet facilities. One Park Service memorandum noted that "colored toilets" could be incorporated in the service building since they would be "little used." Other memoranda discussed the possibility of building separate facilities for Park Service employees and for white visitors in the museum building, and a third possibility included separate toilets for whites and blacks, without special facilities for park employees. The fact that only one set of facilities was built in the administration-museum building, without mention of complementary facilities for African Americans in another location, implies that the Park Service largely expected white visitors. See memorandum, "Some Suggestions re R. O. Preliminary Plan for Manassas Administration Building," 20 February 1940, and Thomas Vint to Regional Director, Region 1, 19 September 1939, both in file Manassas Correspondence 1939–48, NPS History Division Files; E. M. Lisle to Director, 15 March 1940, file Park Visitor Center, Historian's Files, MNBP. On Hanson's exhibits on the plantations, see Hanson, "Preliminary Museum Plan," 23.

22. Hanson, "Preliminary Museum Plan," 13, 15–17, 22–23.

23. Floyd B. Taylor, "Report on the Manassas Park Museum," 3.

24. Hanson served as acting superintendent from 21 April 1942 to 5 March 1943, acting custodian to 1 December 1945, and finally custodian until his retirement on 31 December 1947. Although his titles changed, his role as chief administrator at the park did not. See Sarles, "Short History," 25. "Battle Park Wins Praise," Manassas Journal, 25 February 1944; Tomlinson, "Circular for Region Four Field Areas"; "Alexandria Rotary Hears Maj. Hanson," Washington Post, 21 March 1945; "Major J. M. Hanson Visiting Briefly in Yankton," Yankton (S.Dak.) Press and Dakotan, 23 October 1947; "J. M. Hanson, Poet and Author, Retires from Park Service," NPS press release, 5 January 1948, file Manassas Correspondence 1939–48, NPS History Division Files; Francis F. Wilshin, interview by S. Herbert Evison, 29 June 1971, transcript, 31, Oral History Collection, NPS History Collection, HFC.

25. R. C. Taylor, "Superintendent's Monthly Narrative Report for June 1941," 5 July 1941, 2, file 207–02.3 Manassas Superintendent's Monthly Reports, box 2596A, entry 7, RG 79, NARA.; Joseph Mills Hanson, "Superintendent's Monthly Narrative Report, May 1942," 2, file 207–02.3 Manassas Superintendent's Monthly Reports, box 2596B, entry 7, RG 79, NARA; "America Is Back on the Road," Manassas Messenger, 16 November 1945; Joseph Mills Hanson, "Annual Report of the Acting Custodian, 1 July 1942–30 June 1943," 3, file 207–01 Manassas Annual Reports, box 2596B, entry 7, RG 79, NARA. Taylor did not have an accurate method for recording the numbers of visitors while he served as superintendent.

26. Hanson, "Annual Report of the Acting Custodian," 1 July 1942–30 June 1943, 3–4, file

207–01 Manassas Annual Reports, box 2596B, entry 7, RG 79, NARA; Hanson, "Superintendent's Monthly Narrative Report," May 1942, 2; February 1943, 2; April 1943, 2; June 1943, 1–2; October 1943, 2, all in file 207–02.3 Manassas Superintendent's Monthly Reports, box 2596B, entry 7, RG 79, NARA.

27. Hanson, "Superintendent's Monthly Narrative Report," June 1944, 1–2; Hanson, "Superintendent's Monthly Report," March 1945, 2–3, both in file 207–02.3 Manassas Superintendent's Monthly Reports, box 2596B, entry 7, RG 79, NARA; Sarles, "Short History," 20.

28. Hanson, "Superintendent's Monthly Narrative Report," March 1945, 3, file 207–02.3 Manassas Superintendent's Monthly Reports, box 2596B, entry 7, RG 79, NARA.

29. Ibid.; Joseph Mills Hanson, "Some Observations on the Manassas National Battlefield Park and Its Problems," 1944, 1–5, file Park History, Historian's Files, MNBP.

Chapter 4. Park Additions

1. Kammen, *Mystic Chords of Memory,* 532–33.

2. Joseph Mills Hanson to Coordinating Superintendent, 9 August 1947, 1; Raleigh C. Taylor to Hiram Duryea, 21 October 1940; Taylor to the Adjutant General State of New York, 1 November 1940, all in file Monuments and Markers N.Y. Monuments and Land Acquisition, Historian's Files, MNBP.

3. Joseph Mills Hanson to Coordinating Superintendent, 28 October 1944, file Monuments and Markers N.Y. Monuments and Land Acquisition, Historian's Files, MNBP.

4. Thomas Allen to Superintendent, Fredericksburg and Spotsylvania County National Military Park, 2 February 1945; Joseph Mills Hanson to E. M. Lisle, 4 October 1945; Hanson to Regional Director, Region 1, 9 December 1946; Hanson to Coordinating Superintendent, 9 August 1947; Hanson to Coordinating Superintendent, 14 August 1947, all in file Monuments and Markers N.Y. Monuments and Land Acquisition, Historian's Files, MNBP. According to the land ownership records at the park, Rush W. Boyer conducted an appraisal in 1946 for the Hottel and individual home tracts. See Land Ownership Records Manassas, MNBP Land Holding Records, Headquarters Files, MNBP.

5. Conrad Wirth to James Evans, 15 February 1950, and Harold L. Peterson, "Draft of Speech for Senator Ives," 1 March 1949, both in file MNBP N.Y. Monuments 1949–1957, NPS History Division Files.

6. Newton Drury to Charles Stevenson, 15 May 1950, file MNBP N.Y. Monuments 1949–1957, NPS History Division Files; Conrad Wirth to Regional Director, Region 1, 18 May 1950, "New York State Monuments and Possible Land Acquisition at Manassas"; James Evans to Arthur McLoughlin, 15 August 1950, both in file Monuments and Markers N.Y. Monuments and Land Acquisition, Historian's Files, MNBP; Sarles, "Short History," 19.

7. Myers originally served as custodian from 12 January 1948 to 21 December 1948 and then received the title of superintendent. See Sarles, "Short History," 25. "Myers Appointed Park Custodian," *Free Lance-Star* (Fredericksburg), 10 January 1948; Conrad Wirth to Regional Director, Region 1, 18 May 1950, "New York State Monuments and Possible Land Acquisition at Manassas"; James Evans to Arthur McLoughlin, 15 August 1950; James B. Myers, "Report on Lands Surrounding the New York Monuments near Manassas National Battlefield Park, June–September 1950"; Evans to Wirth, 8 March 1951, last four documents in file Monuments and Markers N.Y. Monuments and Land Acquisition, Historian's Files, MNBP; Sarles, "Short History," 19.

8. Arthur McLoughlin to Charles Stevenson, 1 June 1951; James B. Myers to Regional Director, Region 1, 30 November 1951; Conrad Wirth to Regional Director, Region 1, 2 June 1952; Wirth to James Evans, 11 August 1952, all in file Monuments and Markers N.Y. Monu-

ments and Land Acquisition, Historian's Files, MNBP. See Myers's breakdown of the priorities for land acquisition in his "Report on Lands Surrounding the New York Monuments near Manassas National Battlefield Park, June-September 1950."

9. Conrad Wirth to James Evans, 5 May 1952; Hillory Tolson to Evans, 6 February 1953, both in file Monuments and Markers N.Y. Monuments and Land Acquisition, Historian's Files, MNBP.

10. Hillory Tolson to James Evans, 6 February 1953, file Monuments and Markers N.Y. Monuments and Land Acquisition, Historian's Files, MNBP.

11. At the time the 1937 report was written, the first priority for land acquisition was the Manassas Battlefield Confederate Park on Henry Hill, then the New York Monument land and then the Dogan House. See Hanson, "Proposed Boundaries and Areas," 35; Joseph Mills Hanson to Coordinating Superintendent, 9 August 1947, 3; Hanson to Coordinating Superintendent, 29 December 1947, 2, file 620 Buildings Dogan House, box 2596C, entry 7, RG 79, NARA; Joseph Mills Hanson and Francis F. Wilshin, "Manassas Museum Prospectus," January 1947, 60, file Park History, Historian's Files, MNBP.

12. Joseph Mills Hanson to Coordinating Superintendent, 29 December 1947, 1–2, 5–6; Hanson to Coordinating Superintendent, 9 August 1947, 3; Sarles, "Short History," 19.

13. James B. Myers to Coordinating Superintendent, 8 March 1948, file Manassas Lands, January 1948–September 1949, box 13, acc. 67A–1022, Washington National Records Center (WNRC); Myers to Coordinating Superintendent, 4 November 1948, file 620 Buildings Dogan House, box 2596C, entry 7, RG 79, NARA; Sarles, "Short History," 17.

14. Joseph Mills Hanson to Coordinating Superintendent, 9 August 1947, 2; Hanson and Wilshin, "Museum Prospectus," 1947, 59–60.

15. Joseph Mills Hanson to Ronald F. Lee, 15 March 1948, file Manassas Correspondence 1939–48, NPS History Division Files; "$17,000 Voted to Purchase Stone House," *Manassas Messenger,* 16 March 1948.

16. Hillory Tolson to Director, 26 September 1947, and Arthur Demaray to Regional Director, Region 1, 17 December 1947, both in file Manassas Correspondence 1939–48, NPS History Division Files

17. Sarles, "Short History," 19; James B. Myers, "Monthly Narrative Report," June 1948, 2, file 207–02.3 Manassas Superintendent's Monthly Report, box 2596B, entry 7, RG 79, NARA; Thomas Allen to Director, 13 July 1948, file Ayres Property Stone House, box 2596C, entry 7, RG 79, NARA; Arthur Demaray to Regional Director, Region 1, 26 July 1948; Director to the Secretary, 23 August 1948; Conrad Wirth to Regional Director, Region 1, 24 August 1948, last three documents in file Manassas Correspondence 1939–48, NPS History Division Files.

18. Michael D. Litterst, "The Stone House: Silent Sentinel at the Crossroads of History," 12, file National Register—MANA, Gary Scott Files, National Capital Region (NCR) Files.

19. Francis F. Wilshin to Superintendent, 25 March 1948, 2, file 620 Buildings Chinn House, box 2596C, entry 7, RG 79, NARA; Wilshin to Regional Director, Southeast Regional Office (SERO), 28 October 1968, file Chinn House, Chinn Family History, Historian's Files, MNBP.

20. Francis F. Wilshin to Superintendent, 25 March 1948, 2; Wilshin to Regional Director, SERO, 28 October 1968, both in file 620 Buildings Chinn House, box 2596C, entry 7, RG 79, NARA.

21. I thank Ray Brown for providing me with a succinct chronology on the Chinn House and an evaluation of its importance to the park's history. Francis F. Wilshin to Superintendent, 25 March 1948, 2; Wilshin to Regional Director, SERO, 28 October 1968, both in file 620 Buildings Chinn House, box 2596C, entry 7, RG 79, NARA.

22. "$14,784 Allocated for National Park Museum," *Manassas Messenger,* 16 August 1946; "National Park Service Officials Inaugurate Expansion Program at Local Battlefield Park," *Manassas Messenger,* 24 January 1947.

23. Hanson and Wilshin, "Museum Prospectus," 1947.

24. Hanson, "Preliminary Museum Plan," 10–11, 21–22. Hanson and Wilshin also drafted a prospectus in 1946 that highlighted their basic ideas on exhibits. See Joseph Mills Hanson, "1946 Prospectus for Museum," file Park Visitor Center, Historian's Files, MNBP.

25. Wilshin, interview, 38–39.

26. O. F. Northington to Regional Director, Region 1, 17 February 1947, with memoranda by Joseph Mills Hanson and Ronald Lee attached, file Park Visitor Center, Historian's Files, MNBP; 1947 Museum Plan, floor layout, Historian's Files, MNBP.

27. Francis F. Wilshin, "Historian's Monthly Report," September 1947, 1–2; Wilshin, "Historian's Monthly Report," October 1947, 2; Wilshin, "Historian's Monthly Report," December 1947, 2–3; Wilshin, "Report of Historian Wilshin," February 1948, 2; Wilshin, "Historian's Monthly Report," August 1948, 1–2, all in file 207–03 Historians Manassas, box 2596B, entry 7, RG 79, NARA; Ralph Lewis, Museum Laboratory, to Chief, History Division, 19 December 1947, 1–2; Charles Porter to Ned Burns, 11 August 1948; Ronald F. Lee to Regional Director, Region 1, 29 October 1948, last three documents in file Manassas Correspondence 1939–48, NPS History Division Files; James B. Myers, "Annual Narrative Report," 1948, 3, file 207–01 Manassas Annual Report, box 2596B, entry 7, RG 79, NARA.

28. James B. Myers, "Monthly Narrative Report," January 1949, 2, and Myers, "Monthly Narrative Report," May 1949, 2–3, both in file 207–02.3 Manassas Superintendent's Monthly Report, box 2596B, entry 7, RG 79, NARA.

29. Photographs of May 1949 museum displays and layout, Museum Collection, MNBP; "Museum Enriched, to Open May 28 at Battlefield," *Manassas Messenger,* 17 May 1949; "Museum to Be Opened on the Site of the First Battle of the Civil War," NPS press release, 23 May 1949, file 501.03 Newspaper Clippings Manassas, box 2596C, entry 7, RG 79, NARA.

30. Arthur Demaray to Regional Director, Region 1, 17 December 1947, file Manassas Correspondence 1939–48, NPS History Division Files.

31. Congressman Howard W. Smith of Virginia introduced H.R. 5911 near the end of the 80th Congress in 1948; there is no evidence of committee action on this bill. Associate Director to the Under Secretary, 1 February 1949, file Monuments and Markers N.Y. Monuments and Land Acquisition, Historian's Collection, MNBP; Secretary of the Interior to Andrew Somers, 17 March 1949, file Manassas Correspondence 1949–57, NPS History Division Files.

32. *A Bill to Authorize the Addition of Certain Lands to Manassas National Battlefield Park,* 80th Cong., 2d sess., 1948, H.R. 5911; *A Bill to Authorize the Addition of Certain Lands to Manassas National Battlefield Park,* 81st Cong., 1st sess., 1949, H.R. 3297; *A Bill to Authorize the Addition of Certain Lands to Manassas National Battlefield Park,* 82d Cong., 1st sess., 1951, H.R. 3041; Assistant Director to Director, 6 March 1953; Hillory Tolson to Wesley D'Ewart, 17 July 1953; Orme Lewis to A. L. Miller, 15 October 1953; D. Otis Beasley to Joseph Dodge, 13 April 1954, last four documents in file Manassas Legislation, NPS History Division Files; *Preserving within Manassas National Battlefield Park, Va., the Most Important Historic Properties Relating to the Battles of Manassas,* 83d Cong., 2d sess., 1954, H. Rpt. 1099; *Preserving Within Manassas National Battlefield Park, Va., the Most Important Historic Properties Relating to the Battles of Manassas,* 83d Cong., 2d sess., 1954, S. Rpt. 1141; Public Law 338, 83d Cong., 2d sess., 17 April 1954, *An Act to Preserve Within Manassas National Battlefield Park, Va., the Most Important Historic Properties Relating to the Battles of Manassas.*

33. P.L. 338.

34. Land ownership records for Hottel tract, 2 November 1953; Patterson tract, 7 February 1955; Early tract, 19 December 1955; Hottel tract, 13 January 1956, all in Land Ownership Records Manassas, MNBP Land Holding Records, Headquarters Files, MNBP.

35. Douglas McKay to Senator Ives, 14 March 1953, file Monuments and Markers N.Y. Monuments and Land Acquisition, Historian's Files, MNBP; land ownership record for New York

Monuments, 11 June 1958, Land Ownership Records Manassas, MNBP Land Holding Records, Headquarters Files, MNBP.

Chapter 5. Reenacting the Past

1. Anne D. Snyder, interview by author, 19 October 1993, transcript, 6–7, NPS.

2. Cary Boshamer, "Former Park Chief Dies," *Journal Messenger* (Manassas), 27 April 1990; Wilshin, interview, 1–5, 29.

3. James B. Myers, "Interpretive Section of the Development Outline for the Master Plan of the Manassas National Battlefield Park," 27 February 1952, 28, 31–38, file Manassas, box 17, acc. 69A–4025, RG 79, WNRC.

4. Ibid., 30, 33.

5. Ibid., 33–35; James B. Myers, "Revision, Proposed Interpretive Tour Plan, Manassas National Battlefield Park," 1954, 1–6, included with Chief Historian to Regional Director, Region 1, 16 March 1954, file Manassas Correspondence 1949–57, NPS History Division Files.

6. Myers, "Interpretive Section of Development Outline," 33–35, and attached December 1953 introduction, 1.

7. Acting Chief Historian to Chief, Design and Construction Division, 19 October 1953, "Introduction Section, Development Outline, Manassas NBP"; Chief Historian to Regional Director, Region 1, 27 October 1953, "Narrative Markers, Battlefield of Second Manassas"; Herbert Kahler to Regional Director, Region 1, 15 March 1954, "Texts for Proposed Narrative Markers, Manassas NBP," and attached marker texts and letter James B. Myers to Regional Director, Region 1, 1 February 1954; Chief Historian to Regional Director, Region 1, 16 March 1954, "Interpretive Tour Plan, Manassas NBP," and attached "Revision, Proposed Interpretive Tour Plan and Self-Guided Tour, Second Manassas," all in file Manassas Correspondence 1949–57, NPS History Division Files.

8. Myers, "Interpretive Section of the Development Outline," 39, and attached 1953 introduction, 3. Handwritten on the approval sheet is the statement "No approval action because of Mission 66."

9. Wilshin, interview, 40; "Statement of Significance and Highlights of Mission 66 Planning for Manassas National Battlefield Park," n.d., file Manassas Correspondence 1958–61, NPS History Division Files; Francis F. Wilshin to Director, 31 January 1957, "Annual Report on Information and Interpretive Services 1956," 1, file K1819 Information and Interpretive Annual Report 1957, box 8, acc. 66A–661, WNRC. L. Van Loan Naisawald, "Supplemental Museum Prospectus for Manassas National Battlefield Park," September 1958, 11–12, 15, file D6215 MANA 1958–66, box 13, acc. 70–A–4388, WNRC. My discussion of the Mission 66 plan is based on Wilshin's correspondence, memoranda, and other planning documents. I have searched NPS history files and National Archives and Federal Records Center files for the 1956 Mission 66 Prospectus that Wilshin prepared, but I have not located it.

10. Francis F. Wilshin to Regional Director, Region 1, 20 November 1957, "On-Site Study," 2, file D18 Manassas 1957, box 1, acc. 68A–2955, WNRC; Public Law 338, 83d Cong., 2d sess., 17 April 1954, *An Act to Preserve Within Manassas National Battlefield Park, Va., the Most Important Historic Properties Relating to the Battles of Manassas.*

11. Although the term "visitor center" may have been used infrequently earlier in the Park Service, Mission 66 formalized its use. Correspondence from the Manassas National Battlefield Park uses the phrase "museum-administration building" until the Mission 66 period, at which points it adopts the newer term. "Statement of Significance and Highlights of Mission 66"; Naisawald, "Supplemental Museum Prospectus," 12–13, 25.

42. Wilshin, "Advance Plan of Proposed Reenactment"; Committee for First Manassas, "First Manassas (A Prospectus)"; J. Leonard Volz to Regional Director, Region 1, n.d., 2–3.

43. "Cooperative Agreement Between Director, National Park Service, and First Manassas Corporation, Incorporated, relating to the Staging of a Re-enactment of the First Battle of Manassas at Manassas National Battlefield Park," draft, May 1961; J. Leonard Volz to Regional Director, Region 1, n.d., 2, both in Museum Collection, MNBP.

44. "Cooperative Agreement," draft, 2–3.

45. The Park Service also attempted to complete restoration of the Stone Bridge before the reenactment but later postponed this work until 1962 so the general public could use the bridge during the centennial. See Orville W. Carroll, "Historic Structures Report, Part 3, on Stabilization of the Stone Bridge," February 1963, i, 1–2, Library Collection, MNBP. For information on the Dogan and Stone houses, see Orville W. Carroll, "Historic Structures Report, Architectural Data, Part 1, Rehabilitation and Restoration of the Dogan House," April 1960, ii–iii; Orville W. Carroll, "Historic Structures Report, Part 3, on Dogan House," June 1962, 3–5, 12; and Orville W. Carroll, "Historic Structures Report Architectural Data, Part 1, Preparatory to the Restoration of the Stone House," November 1960, 26, all in Library Collection, MNBP.

46. Ralph Lewis to Francis F. Wilshin, 14 June 1960, "Exhibit Plan, Manassas NBP," and attached correspondence and plan, Museum Collection, MNBP; Francis F. Wilshin, "The Stone House, Embattled Landmark of Bull Run, Part 1, Narrative and Appendix," 21 March 1961, introduction, Library Collection, MNBP; Edwin C. Bearss, interview by author, 5 April 1994, transcript, 7, NPS.

47. "Certificate of Sponsorship, 100th Anniversary," 2; J. Walter Coleman to Chief Historian, "Conference on Manassas Re-enactment," 17 May 1961, and Conrad Wirth to Virgil Jones, 21 April 1961, both in file Manassas Correspondence 1958–61, NPS History Division Files; Francis F. Wilshin to Director, "Annual Report of Interpretive Services," 31 January 1961, 10, file K1819 Interpretive Activities Annual Report 1960 Narrative, box 8, acc. 66A–661, WNRC; Wilshin, interview, 65, 71.

48. J. Leonard Volz to Regional Director, Region 1, n.d, 3–4; James Fry to Francis F. Wilshin, 8 September 1961, "Summary of Costs of Reenactment," file A8227 Manassas, box 11, acc. 68–A–3048, WNRC.

49. J. Leonard Volz to Regional Director, Region 1, n.d., 4–5; Regional Director to Francis F. Wilshin, 19 May 1961, "Assistance During Final Planning Stage—Reenactment of First Manassas," Museum Collection, MNBP; Volz to Regional Director, Region 1, 11 August 1961, "Suggested Guidelines for Large-Scale Special Events," 2, Museum Collection, MNBP.

50. J. Leonard Volz to Regional Director, 19 June 1961, "Progress Report, Reenactment of the Battle of First Manassas," Museum Collection, MNBP; Volz to Regional Director, Region 1, 11 August 1961; Volz to Regional Director, Region 1, n.d., 7–8; Roger Rogers, Regional Publications Officer, to Regional Director, "Report on Press Relations for Reenactment of First Manassas, July 22 and 23," 25 July 1961, file A8227 Manassas, box 11, acc. 68–A–3048, WNRC; Naisawald, interview, 10.

51. Naisawald, interview, 9–10; Bearss, interview, 7–8.

52. J. Leonard Volz to Regional Director, Region 1, 12 June 1961, "Narration of Reenactment," Museum Collection, MNBP; Naisawald, interview, 11; Francis F. Wilshin and David Thompson, "Script for the Reenactment of the Battle of First Manassas," file Reenactment, Museum Collection, MNBP.

53. Fritz S. Updike, "Bull Run Re-Enactment Shows Spirit America Needs Today," newspaper clipping, file Reenactment, Museum Collection, MNBP.

54. Wilshin, interview, 68, 71; Raymond J. Crowley, "Blistering Sun Again Burns Manassas as Blue and Gray Re-Enact Battle," newspaper clipping, file Reenactment, Museum Collection, MNBP.

55. "Grand Reenactment: The Battle of First Manassas (Bull Run), July 21–23, 1961," promotional pamphlet, file Reenactment, Museum Collection, MNBP; Wilshin, interview, 68.

56. John Howard to Sir, n.d., file Reenactment, Museum Collection, MNBP; Updike, "Bull Run Re-Enactment Shows Spirit"; Crowley, "Blistering Sun Again Burns Manassas"; J. Leonard Volz to Regional Director, Region 1, n.d., 11.

57. "Remarks by Conrad L. Wirth, Director, National Park Service, at the Re-Enactment of the First Battle of Manassas at Manassas National Battlefield Park, Virginia, July 22, 1961," Department of the Interior press release, 22 July 1961, box MANA, NPS History Collection, HFC; Conrad Wirth to Regional Director, Region 1, 14 August 1961, "Re-enactment of Civil War and Other Battles," file Manassas Correspondence 1958–61, NPS History Division Files; Bodnar, *Remaking America*, 214–15.

58. "An Appomattox at Manassas," *Richmond News Leader,* 25 July 1961, file A8227 Manassas, box 11, acc. 68–A–3048, WNRC. The Berryman editorial cartoon in the *Washington Star* dubbed the traffic jam as the third battle of Manassas, file Reenactment, Museum Collection, MNBP; J. Leonard Volz to Regional Director, 11 August 1961, 1; Volz to Regional Director, Region 1, n.d., 11; Kammen, *Mystic Chords of Memory,* 593, 595–96, 605–06.

59. Conrad Wirth to Regional Director, Region 1, 14 August 1961; J. Leonard Volz to Regional Director, Region 1, n.d., 11; Bearss, interview, 8; J. Walter Coleman to R. U. Darby, 4 December 1961, file Manassas Correspondence 1958–61, NPS History Division Files.

Chapter 6. Changing of the Guard

1. W. Mikell to Director, 11 February 1965, "Museum Exhibits—Manassas," and attached memo from Wilshin, Exhibit File Manassas, NPS Historic Photographic Collection.

2. Ralph Lewis to Francis F. Wilshin, 14 June 1960, "Exhibit Plan, Manassas NBP," and attached exhibit plan, especially exhibit numbers 1, 5, 8, 14, 20, 21, Museum Collection, MNBP.

3. Raymond Mulvaney to Director, 9 March 1964, "Exhibit Construction Costs, Visitor Center, Horseshoe Bend"; W. E. O'Neil to Regional Programs Officer, SERO, 17 September 1964, "Museum Exhibits"; Cross-reference sheet, Castillo de San Marcos, 6 November 1964; W. Mikell to Director, 11 February 1965, "Museum Exhibits, Manassas" and attached memorandum Wilshin to Regional Director, SERO, 8 February 1965, "Installation of New Museum Exhibits," all in Exhibit File Manassas, NPS Historic Photographic Collection.

4. "Master Plan of Manassas National Battlefield Park," July 1965, chap. 3, file Park History, Historian's Files, MNBP; Howard Baker to William Hauser, 13 March 1964, and attached letter from Hauser to Stewart L. Udall, 28 February 1964, and William Everhart to Chief, Eastern Museum Laboratory, 11 May 1965, "Manassas Planning Meeting," both in Exhibit File Manassas, NPS Historic Photographic Collection.

5. Bearss, interview, 6; Naisawald, interview, 8–9. Russell Berry, who succeeded Wilshin as superintendent in 1969, confirmed that Wilshin focused on the historical work, leaving administrative duties to Mildred Gay. See Russell W. Berry Jr., interview by author, 10 February 1994, transcript, 32–38, NPS.

6. Bearss, interview, 5, 10; Naisawald, interview, 5, 7.

7. Bearss, interview, 4, 5, 9.

8. In 1960, after Naisawald resigned as park historian and Mrs. Frances Dogan, one of the last residents of the Dogan House, retired as tour leader, Wilshin obtained permission to convert the tour leader position into another park historian job. In this way, Wilshin obtained two park historians. Wilshin also had a seasonal ranger who provided interpretive help during spring and summer. Francis F. Wilshin to Director, 31 January 1961, "Annual Report of Inter-

pretive Services," 1–2, 5–6, 14, file K1819 Interpretive Activities Annual Report 1960 Narrative, box 8, acc. 66A–661, WNRC.

9. Jackson Price to Chief, Division of Museums, 19 August 1968, "Manassas Visitor Center Exhibit Plan," and attached memorandum from Francis F. Wilshin to Regional Director, SERO, 16 August 1968, Exhibit File Manassas, NPS Historic Photographic Collection; "Manassas National Battlefield Park Visitor Center," final draft, August 1968, Museum Collection, MNBP; "Excerpt from Monthly Report Museum Support Group at Harpers Ferry," August 1968, Exhibit File Manassas, NPS Historic Photographic Collection; "Interpretive Prospectus, Manassas National Battlefield Park," 1971, 12, file K1817 (two of three), Headquarters Files, MNBP.

10. "Park Visitor Center," exhibit 18; Hendrickson, Chief, Division of Museums, to Regional Director, SERO, 23 July 1969, "Review and Approval, Manassas Projection Map Script," Exhibit File Manassas, NPS Historic Photographic Collection. The 1971 interpretive prospectus for the park indicates that the battlefield map was being installed in the map room, the second and smaller room of the museum. "Interpretive Prospectus," 2, 8.

11. "Park Visitor Center," esp. exhibits 3, 7–14.

12. Francis F. Wilshin to Regional Director, SERO, 24 July 1968, "Opening of the Stone House," Exhibit File Manassas, NPS Historic Photographic Collection. Naisawald lived in the Stone House when he first came to the park. The building had been renovated to serve as a living quarters when it first transferred to the Park Service, but its heating had deteriorated by the time Naisawald moved in. See Naisawald, interview, 2. The Stone House did not open when Wilshin planned. The 1971 interpretive prospectus suggests that Berry, Wilshin's successor, was in the process of setting up the field hospital exhibit in the early 1970s. Richard Hoffman, superintendent of Manassas during the mid-1970s, remembered later that he oversaw the final installation of the field hospital exhibit at Stone House, replacing an antebellum plantation display that had been on exhibit during Berry's superintendency. I have not found supporting documentation regarding the antebellum plantation display. Richard Hoffman, interview by author, 31 March 1994, transcript, 31, NPS.

13. "Opposition Grows to Park Cemetery," 20 February 1969, *Journal Messenger* (Manassas).

14. Ironically, Snyder and LeKander, both longtime Republicans, had worked hard to get Scott into Congress. "Opposition Grows to Park Cemetery"; George Hartzog to Secretary of the Interior, 13 February 1969, "Proposal of Congressman Scott, Manassas National Battlefield Park," and Francis F. Wilshin to Regional Director, SERO, 17 March 1969, "Friends of the Park Meeting, Prince William County Court House, March 14, 1969," both in file Cemetery, National Cemetery Controversy 1969–70, Historian's Files, MNBP.

15. George Hartzog to the Secretary of the Interior, 13 February 1969; House Committee on Veterans' Affairs, *Proposed Establishment of a National Cemetery Adjacent to Manassas National Battlefield Park: Hearing Before the Subcommittee on Hospitals on H.R. 8818 and Related Bills*, 91st Cong., 1st sess., 23 September 1969, 2457.

16. Russell Train to Olin Teague, Chairman of the Committee on Veterans' Affairs, 22 September 1969, box MANA, NPS History Collection, HFC.

17. Robert Utley to Director, 5 March 1969, and attached memorandum, Edwin C. Bearss to Chief Historian, 28 February 1969, file Manassas Correspondence 1962–72, NPS History Division Files; Bearss, interview, 9.

18. Wilshin, interview, 74–75; Francis F. Wilshin to Regional Director, SERO, 17 March 1969, 1–4.

19. Francis F. Wilshin to Regional Director, SERO, 17 March 1969, 1. An example of the point-by-point rebuttal format used by the Friends of the Park to argue against the national cemetery can be seen in Anne Snyder to Robert Bridges, 9 March 1969, A. Snyder Files, MNBP. Wilshin more than likely provided some of this information; he was working with Snyder's

group in the strategy meetings. An indication of Wilshin's devotion to the battlefield park and his opposition to the national cemetery proposal is a poem he wrote at this time: "This Manassas, this hallowed battleground, fear ye ghostly legions of Bull Run who here 200,000 strong, twice fought with such desperate gallantry for liberty and principle. We pledge you our honor, we shall not falter, we shall not fail, to keep faith in our tryst with the past. We shall not be diverted by the false cry of dual use, nor the callous claim of economic expediency. To the thousands of you whose blood stains these fields—to the hundreds of you who yet silently sleep in unmarked graves—we solemnly swear that time will not dim the luster of your deathless deeds, nor will perverted interest impair your heroic images. Sleep on undisturbed, a grateful nation will find other means to provide your gallant sons honored burial" (Wilshin, interview, 76–77).

20. Charles Carothers to William L. Scott, 28 April 1969, file Cemetery, National Cemetery Controversy 1969–70, Historian's Files, MNBP; Francis F. Wilshin to Regional Director, SERO, 17 March 1969, 2–6; Bearss, interview, 9.

21. Charles Carothers to William L. Scott, 28 April 1969, 1.

22. Barry Mackintosh, conversation with author, Washington, D.C., 3 October 1994.

23. House Committee, *Proposed Establishment of a National Cemetery,* table of contents, 2514–17, 2570–73.

24. Statement of Anne D. Snyder, House Committee, *Proposed Establishment of a National Cemetery,* 2524–27.

25. Snyder, interview, 18–19; *A Bill to Provide for the Establishment of an Additional National Cemetery to Supplement Arlington National Cemetery,* 91st Cong., 1st sess., 1969, H.R. 8921. Representative Bow did not need LeKander to convince him of the value of preserving the park; Bow's grandfather had fought at one of the Manassas battles.

26. Snyder, interview, 18–19.

27. Ibid., 19–20, 23, 24, 26–30.

28. Ibid., 11.

29. I thank Barry Mackintosh for providing background information about NPS management training during the 1960s.

30. Berry, interview, 1–3. Barry Mackintosh clarified for me that the orientation program took eleven weeks and included a history of the Park Service as well as practical skill building in fighting forest fires, rappelling cliff faces, and other ranger activities. Interpretive skill building was also included. Berry's two different administrative titles at Manassas did not reflect a change in duties. The National Park Service had established a group park arrangement with two satellite parks—Manassas and the George Washington Birthplace National Monument—coming under the general supervision of the superintendent at the Fredericksburg and Spotsylvania County Battlefields Memorial National Military Park. During his four years at Manassas, Berry set the overall policy and kept the general superintendent informed, a relationship similar to that between park superintendents and the regional director. See Berry, interview, 3–4.

31. Berry, interview, 34, 37. Ed Bearss tells the story of how Berry convinced Wilshin to move out of the superintendent's house. See Bearss, interview, 12. Mildred Gay, who still lives near the park, declined the author's requests for an interview.

32. Berry, interview, 5, 7, 12–13, 16–17. Naisawald also encountered fox hunting on the battlegrounds while he was serving as the Manassas park historian. See Naisawald, interview, 25–27.

33. Berry, interview, 4–7; map, 1966 PWC telephone directory, Virginiana Room, Bull Run Library, Manassas, Va.; David Hobson, executive director, Northern Virginia Regional Park Authority, telephone conversation with Jacelee DeWaard, 9 May 1995.

34. Francis F. Wilshin to Regional Director, SERO, 17 March 1969, 2, 5–6.

35. The signs restricting recreational use to the picnic area went up and down three times

during Berry's tenure in response to political pressures. Nonetheless, Berry's zoning remains today. Berry, interview, 5, 12–13, 18–19, 38, 41–42; Carl Hanson, interview by author, 19 August 1994, transcript, 16–18, NPS.

36. Berry, interview, 21–22, 25–26, 38. The park's Mission 66 plan had included a Second Manassas driving tour, but Wilshin did not implement the tour.

37. Berry, interview, 28–30; Chief, Division of Museums, to Regional Director, SERO, 23 July 1969, Exhibit File Manassas, NPS Historic Photographic Collection.

38. Berry, interview, 22–25. Berry recalled the man also donated his great grandfather's uniform. Museum records for this donation, however, indicate no uniform items.

39. Ibid., 39.

Chapter 7. Great America in Manassas

1. "Hearing Will Examine Effect on Battlefield," and Kevin Murphy, "Congress Delegation Visits Manassas Battlefield Park," both in *Journal Messenger* (Manassas), 30 March 1973; House Committee on Interior and Insular Affairs, *General and Oversight Briefing Relating to Developments Near Manassas National Battlefield Park: Hearing Before the Subcommittee on National Parks and Recreation*, 93d Cong., 1st sess., 3 April 1973, 2–3.

2. House Committee, *General and Oversight Briefing*, 2–3, 8–9.

3. Ibid., 3.

4. Ron Shaffer, " 'America' Buildings Approved," *Washington Post*, 9 March 1973; Herbert H. Denton and Ron Shaffer, "Pr. William Planners Back Marriott Park," *Washington Post*, 4 April 1973; Prince William County Planning Commission, Staff Report, Rezoning Case #73–18, "Marriott's Great America and Industrial Park," 16 March 1973, 55–59, A. Snyder Files, MNBP.

5. House Committee, *General and Oversight Briefing*, 3, 8; Berry, interview, 42–47; Ron Shaffer, "Amusement Park Site Set at Manassas," *Washington Post*, 15 February 1973.

6. "Prince William Promises Sewage Capacity by 1975 for $35 Million Marriott Park," *Prince William County, Virginia Newsletter*, 17 February 1973, 1, Virginiana Room, Bull Run Library, Manassas, Va.; House Committee, *General and Oversight Briefing*, 39–40.

7. House Committee, *General and Oversight Briefing*, 91.

8. Ibid., 103, 106; Snyder, interview, 37.

9. House Committee, *General and Oversight Briefing*, 100–106; Snyder, interview, 37.

10. Harlan D. Unrau, *Administrative History: Gettysburg National Military Park and Gettysburg National Cemetery, Pennsylvania* (Washington, D.C.: National Park Service, July 1991), 316. The Gettysburg Tower became a subject of discussion during the 3 April 1973 congressional hearing. See House Committee, *General and Oversight Briefing*, 24, 50–51. For Porter's concerns, see House Committee, *General and Oversight Briefing*, 100–103.

11. Berry, interview, 43, 46; House Committee, *General and Oversight Briefing*, 48, 59–60.

12. *Prince William County, Virginia Newsletter*, Virginiana Room, Bull Run Library, Manassas, Va.; Don Wilson, PWC Public Library System, conversation with author, 15 December 1993; Bennie Scarton Jr., "Marriott Official Turns Aside 'Parade of Horrors,' " *Journal Messenger* (Manassas), 4 April 1973; Berry, interview, 46.

13. Francis F. Wilshin, "Historical Evaluation of the Proposed Marriott Tract upon Manassas National Battlefield Park," 28 March 1973, file Marriott/Battlefield, A. Snyder Files, MNBP.

14. House Committee on Interior and Insular Affairs, *National Outdoor Recreation Programs and Policies: Hearings Before the Subcommittee on National Parks and Recreation*, 93d Cong., 1st sess., March 1973, 338; House Committee, *General and Oversight Briefing*, 61, 69; Hanson, "Report on Proposed Boundaries and Areas," 27–28, 34, 38.

15. *An Act to Authorize the Addition of Certain Lands to Manassas National Battlefield Park, Virginia, and for Other Purposes* (81st Cong., 1st sess., 1949, H.R. 3297), introduced by Rep. How-

ard W. Smith, included lands within a two-mile radius of the 29–211 and 234 intersection in the middle of the battlefield park. Stuart's Hill lies about 2.5 miles from this intersection. House Committee on Interior and Insular Affairs, *Providing for Increases in Appropriation Ceilings and Boundary Changes in Certain Units of the National Park System, and for Other Purposes,* 92d Cong., 1st sess., 1971, S. Rpt. 92–452; John G. Parsons, interview by author, 14 June 1994, transcript, 5–6, NPS.

16. Berry, interview, 46.

17. "It's Official," *Journal Messenger* (Manassas), 16 February 1973; Hoffman, interview, 8.

18. On the Hetch Hetchy debate, see Alfred Runte, *National Parks: The American Experience,* 2d ed., rev. (Lincoln: University of Nebraska Press, 1987), 78–81. Throughout his book, Runte also provides examples of the role politics has played in shaping park policies. For another focused treatment on park politics, see Michael Frome, *Regreening the National Parks* (Tucson: University of Arizona Press, 1992).

19. House Committee, *National Outdoor Recreation Programs,* 334.

20. Ibid., 349–50.

21. Ibid., 1–2.

22. Ibid., 2–47, 69–85, 94, 103–14.

23. Ibid., 59–61, 113.

24. Berry, interview, 47–49.

25. Hoffman, interview, 1–4, 7–8, 20; Charles Shedd to Richard Hoffman, 14 August 1973, "Reports on Recent Visits and Marriott Meeting," Marriott Tract binder, MNBP.

26. *Prince William County, Virginia, Newsletter,* 2 March 1973, 1–3.

27. Prince William County Planning Commission, "Marriott's Great America"; "'Positive Attitude Is Warranted,'" *Journal Messenger* (Manassas), 16 March 1973; Denton and Shaffer, "Pr. William Planners Back Marriott Park"; *Prince William County, Virginia, Newsletter,* 6 April 1973, 1–2.

28. Denton and Shaffer, "Pr. William Planners Back Marriott Park"; House Committee, *General and Oversight Briefing,* 13.

29. *Prince William County, Virginia, Newsletter,* 6 April 1973, 1–2.

30. *Prince William County, Virginia, Newsletter,* 6 April 1973, 1. Echoing the concern about social changes in the county, Supervisor A. J. Ferlazzo commented in the 5 April board meeting that "maybe I won't have these thirteen-year old girls in my office, pregnant and with VD" if Marriott provided a recreational alternative.

31. *Prince William County, Virginia, Newsletter,* 6 April 1973, 2; Randi Deiotte, "Board Invites Marriott to Refile," *Journal Messenger* (Manassas), 17 January 1974

32. Deiotte, "Board Invites Marriott to Refile." In April 1977 Prince William Circuit Court Judge Arthur Sinclair ruled in favor of the lawsuit filed by the Prince William League for the Protection of Natural Resources and found that the county had failed to advertise the Marriott rezoning request meeting for the required number of days. This ruling came after Marriott had all but abandoned the Prince William site. See Prince William League for the Protection of Natural Resources, *Newsletter,* May 1977, A. Snyder Files, MNBP.

33. Lee Flor, "Marriott Park Delayed to 1978," *Washington Star-News,* 7 October 1974; Ann Holiday and Marilyn Finley, "Marriott's Great Park," *Potomac News* (Woodbridge), 9 October 1974; "Authority to Review Marriott," *Journal Messenger* (Manassas), 4 November 1974; Joan Mower, "Marriott Plans Hit Snag," *Journal Messenger,* 16 December 1974; "Industrial Interchange Is Planned," *Journal Messenger,* 5 June 1974; "Access Road Studied," *Potomac News,* 28 June 1974; Randi Deiotte, "No One Remains to Pay for Marriott's Ramps," *Journal Messenger,* 20 November 1974; "I–66 Interchange Okayed Without State Funding," *Potomac News,* 20 November 1974; Randi Deiotte, "Marriott's Theme Park on Back Burner," *Manassas Messenger,* 13 May 1976.

34. Flor, "Marriott Park Delayed to 1978"; Deiotte, "Theme Park on Back Burner."

Chapter 8. Expanding the Boundaries

1. Bruce Catton to Roy Taylor, 31 March 1973, 1, file Catton Letter, A. Snyder Files, MNBP.

2. Francis F. Wilshin, Edwin C. Bearss, and Michael Tennent, all Park Service historians, argued for the historical significance of the Marriott tract during the 1970s. See Wilshin, "Historical Evaluation of the Proposed Marriott Tract upon Manassas National Battlefield Park," 28 March 1973, and Tennent, "A Brief Summary of the Historical Significance of the Marriott Property," 10 December 1976, both in file Marriott/Battlefield, A. Snyder Files, MNBP; Bearss, "Manassas NBP and the Proposed Marriott Park," 28 March 1973, file Manassas Correspondence 1962–72, 73–74, NPS History Division Files.

3. Richard Leigh, "County Denies Barring 1980 Marriott Expansion," *Journal Messenger* (Manassas), 28 July 1988; Senate Committee on Energy and Natural Resources, *Manassas Battlefield and Historic Sites: Hearing Before the Subcommittee on Parks and Recreation,* 95th Cong., 1st sess., 28 June 1977, 197–99.

4. Hoffman, interview, 39–43.

5. Ibid., 8–9.

6. Ibid., 9–10; House Committee on Veterans' Affairs, *Proposed Establishment of a National Cemetery Adjacent to Manassas Battlefield, Virginia: Hearing Before the House Subcommittee on Hospitals on H.R. 8818 and Related Bills,* 91st Cong., 1st sess., 23 September 1969, 2525–26.

7. Hoffman, interview, 10; Snyder, interview, 52–53.

8. Senate Committee on Interior and Insular Affairs, *Providing for Increases in Appropriation Ceilings and Boundary Changes in Certain Units of the National Park System, and for Other Purposes,* 92d cong., 1st sess., 1971, S. Rpt. 452, 1; Parsons, interview, 5–6.

9. Parsons, interview, 6–7.

10. Ibid., 8; *Congressional Record,* 92d Cong., 2d sess., 1972, 118, pt. 10:12404; Bearss, "Manassas NBP and Marriott Park," 1.

11. Snyder, interview, 53.

12. *Biographical Directory of Congress;* Herbert E. Harris III, interview by author, 16 June 1994, transcript, 1–3, NPS.

13. Snyder, interview, 53–54; Harris, interview, 4.

14. "Rep. Harris Proposes Expanding Battlefield," *Potomac News* (Woodbridge), 25 June 1975; Harris, interview, 9–10.

15. Harris, interview, 16.

16. Ibid., 12; Senate Committee, *Manassas Battlefield and Historic Sites,* 183–84.

17. House Committee on Veterans' Affairs, *National Cemetery Site Selection, Pennsylvania, and the Vicinity of the District of Columbia: Hearing Before the Subcommittee on Cemeteries and Burial Benefits,* 94th Cong., 1st sess., 17 November 1975, 1146–49.

18. W. W. Lyons to Richard Roudebush, [September 1975?], file Cemetery at MNBP, A. Snyder Files, MNBP.

19. House Committee, *National Cemetery Site Selection,* 1149; House Committee on Veterans' Affairs, *Bills Related to the National Cemetery System and to Burial Benefits: Hearings Before the Subcommittee on Cemeteries and Burial Benefits,* 94th Cong., 1st sess., December 1975, January and February 1976, 1274.

20. Gilbert LeKander to Herb Harris, 4 April 1975, file Battlefield/Marriott, A. Snyder Files, MNBP; Harris, interview, 4–5; House Committee, *Bills Related to the National Cemetery System,* 1233–34.

21. House Committee, *Bills Related to the National Cemetery System,* 1229–41.

22. Harris, interview, 17–21.

23. Hoffman, interview, 37; Betty Curran, "Varnado's Future Reveres Past," *Journal Messenger* (Manassas), 18 November 1977, 5. Varnado declined the author's requests for an interview.

24. Senate Committee, *Manassas Battlefield and Historic Sites,* 184, 186, 188.

25. Ibid., 184.

26. Hoffman, interview, 28–29; Senate Committee, *Manassas Battlefield and Historic Sites,* 23, 184, 198, 211–14.

27. Senate Committee, *Manassas Battlefield and Historic Sites,* 206–9.

28. Ibid., 3, 23, 186, 198, 206, 209.

29. Ibid., 23, 185, 211–12.

30. Ibid., 22, 222, 227, 234.

31. Ibid., 21, 198, 203, 239, 249.

32. Senate Committee, *Manassas Battlefield and Historic Sites,* 228, 234; Alice Humphries to Paul Trible, 18 May 1977, attached to 10 May 1977 Prince William Board of County Supervisors voting result on "Expansion—Manassas Battlefield Park," file Expansion Bill, A. Snyder Files, MNBP; Tennent, "Historical Significance of the Marriott Property." Prince William County supervisors correctly gauged the National Park Service's unwillingness to give up the Marriott tract, as proven by the 1988 publication of NPS director-designate William Whalen's 23 June 1977 internal memo, which urged that Harris's bill incorporate the Marriott tract. See Leigh, "County Denies Barring 1980 Marriott Expansion."

33. Harris, interview, 12–14.

34. Harris stated in the 3 September 1980 Senate hearing that his bills had not passed the Senate before because "we didn't have a man with the leadership of Senator Warner" (56). Harris, interview, 14–15; Senate Committee on Energy and Natural Resources, *Manassas National Battlefield Park, Virginia; and Miscellaneous Hawaii Park Proposals: Hearing Before the Subcommittee on Parks, Recreation, and Renewable Resources,* 96th Cong., 2d sess., 3 September 1980, 50, 52.

35. Senate Committee, *Manassas National Battlefield Park, Virginia,* 52, 61–68, 75; John T. Hazel, interview by author, 17 November 1994, transcript, 3, NPS; Kathleen K. Seefeldt, interview by author, 21 November 1994, transcript, 3, NPS.

36. Public Law 96–442, 96th Cong., 2d sess., 13 October 1980, *An Act to Amend the Act Entitled "An Act to Preserve Within Manassas National Battlefield Park, Virginia, the Most Important Historic Properties Relating to the Battle of Manassas, and for Other Purposes," approved April 17, 1954;* Regional Director, National Capital Region, to Superintendent, Manassas Battlefield Park, 9 January 1981, "Activation of Public Law 96–442 Expanding Manassas Battlefield Park," 4, file Land Acquisition Plan—MANA, NCR Land Use Files; Senate Committee, *Manassas National Battlefield Park, Virginia,* 52–53, 70.

37. Rolland R. Swain, interview by author, 6 April 1994, transcript, 1–3, NPS; Rolland R. Swain, "Superintendent's Annual Report," 1980, 1, box MANA, NPS History Collection, HFC.

38. Dean Owen, "Government Shelves Manassas Battlefield Park Expansion Plans," *Potomac News* (Woodbridge), 21 May 1981; Swain, interview, 14–16.

39. National Park Service, "General Management Plan, Manassas National Battlefield Park," September 1983, 26–27, Historian's Files, MNBP.

40. "Emergency Land Acquisition, Tract 02–166, Manassas National Battlefield Park," 27 July 1984, file Davis, Walker, Headquarters Files, MNBP.

41. "Emergency Land Acquisition"; Swain, interview, 28. There are no known battle trenches or military earthworks on the Brawner Farm tract.

42. "Emergency Land Acquisition"; Richard Robbins to Edwin Meese, 16 May 1985; Robbins to Regional Director, National Capital Region, 10 April 1986; Gale Norton to Assistant Secretary for Fish and Wildlife, 25 June 1986; and Robbins to Herbert Rothenberg, 7 April 1987, last four documents in file Davis, Walker, Headquarters Files, MNBP; Mary Ellen Colandene, "Manassas Battlefield Park Acquires 312.5-Acre Tract," *Journal Messenger* (Manassas), 22 May 1985; Philip Hanyok, "Park Service Takes Title of Civil War Battle Site," *Potomac News* (Woodbridge), 22 May 1985; Robert Kurek, "Family Wins Decision in Brawner Farm Case,"

Journal Messenger, 3 March 1987; Rocky Hopchas, "Court Rules Family Must Wait," *Journal Messenger,* 24 June 1987; Senate Committee, *Manassas Battlefield and Historic Sites,* 21.

Chapter 9. Seeking Partnerships

1. "Remarks by William Penn Mott Jr., National Park Service, for 125th Anniversary of First Battle of Manassas, July 19, 1986," 5, Jerry Rogers Files, NPS History Division Files.

2. Swain, "Superintendent's Annual Report," 1980, 1–2; Swain, interview, 19–20.

3. Swain, "Superintendent's Annual Report," 1980, 2; Swain, interview, 20–21. Financial benefits from the rehabilitated display area remain evident today. Gross sales for 1994 topped $250,000.

4. Swain, interview, 20; Swain, "Superintendent's Annual Report," 1980, 2.

5. Swain, "Superintendent's Annual Report" 1980, 2.

6. Rolland R. Swain, "Superintendent's Annual Report," 1982, 2, box MANA, NPS History Collection, HFC; Joseph Mitchell to Russell Dickenson, 16 September 1982, file Manassas Battlefield, Bruce Craig Files, National Parks and Conservation Association (NPCA).

7. Alan Kent to Manager, Harpers Ferry Center, 30 August 1982, "Trip Report—Manassas (August 26)," unlabeled folder, NPS History Division Files.

8. Alan Kent to Manager, Harpers Ferry Center, 30 August 1982; Edwin C. Bearss to Audiovisual Production Officer, Division of Audiovisual Arts, Harpers Ferry Center, 7 September 1983, "Review of Henry Hill Tour Scripts, Manassas National Battlefield Park," and attached script, unlabeled folder, NPS History Division Files.

9. Jerry Rogers to Regional Director, National Capital Region, 7 January 1985, 1, unlabeled folder, NPS History Division Files; Bearss, interview, 17.

10. Jerry Rogers to Regional Director, National Capital Region, 7 January 1985, 1; [Rolland R. Swain], "Superintendent's Annual Report," 1985, 2, box MANA, NPS History Collection, HFC; Swain, interview, 19; Andrus to Paerce, 12 March 1984, unlabeled folder, NPS History Division Files.

11. Edwin C. Bearss to Associate Director, Cultural Resources, 12 October 1983, "Field Trip to Manassas National Battlefield Park," 3, unlabeled folder, NPS History Division Files; Swain, interview, 19; [Rolland R. Swain], "Superintendent's Annual Report," 1986, 4, Reading File 1987, MNBP.

12. Susan Moore, interview by author, 10 May 1994, transcript, 36, NPS; [Swain], "Superintendent's Annual Report," 1985; [Swain], "Superintendent's Annual Report," 1986; [Edmund Raus], "Superintendent's Annual Report," 1988, 5, box MANA, NPS History Collection, HFC; Edmund Raus, letter to author, 14 March 1995.

13. Rolland Swain to Regional Director, National Capital Region, 2 September 1987, 2, Reading File 1987, MNBP; [Swain], "Superintendent's Annual Report," 1986, 3; American Civil War Commemorative Committee, "The Battle of Manassas," 125th Anniversary Re-Enactment brochure, 1986; Friends of Virginia Civil War Parks, Inc., "Official Program for the Commemoration of the 125th Anniversary First Battle of Manassas (Bull Run)," 1986; Edmund Raus to Staff, 27 July 1987, "125th Anniversary of Second Manassas," last three documents in file Park Special Events, Historian's Files, MNBP. Hennessy went on to publish narrative studies of both Manassas battles.

14. "Remarks by William Penn Mott Jr.," 1–3.

15. Ibid., 3–5.

16. Joel Garreau, "Solving the Equation for Success," *Washington Post,* 20 June 1988.

17. National Capital Planning Commission, "William Center, Gainesville Magisterial District, Route 29, Pageland Lane, I–66 and Groveton Road, Prince William County, Virginia,

Application for Rezoning from A–1, Agricultural, to PMD, Planned Mixed-Use District (application no. 86–61), Executive Director's Recommendation," 25 September 1986, 1, file Manassas Battlefield, Bruce Craig Files, NPCA; Garreau, *Edge City,* 376.

18. Garreau, *Edge City,* 375–77.

19. Seefeldt, interview, 14; Rolland Swain to Deputy Regional Director, National Capital Region, 19 November 1986, "Summary of Park Actions on Rezoning Application #86–61 for William Center," Reading File 1986, MNBP.

20. Seefeldt, interview, 14–15; Rolland Swain to Deputy Regional Director, National Capital Region, 19 November 1986; Lee Hockstader, "Hazel Proposes Prince William Project," *Washington Post,* 10 May 1986; William Penn Mott to Alan Cranston, 8 October 1987, 2, Congressionals Binder (2), MNBP.

21. Hockstader, "Hazel Proposes."

22. Ibid.

23. Swain, interview, 24, 33; Rolland Swain to William Stark, 13 January 1987, 1, and Rolland Swain to Jerry Russell, 21 January 1987, both in Reading File 1987, MNBP.

24. Swain, interview, 24–26.

25. Ibid.; Rolland Swain to Regional Director, National Capital Region, 22 April 1986, "'Weekly' Report, 3/7/86 to 4/22/86," 2, Reading File 1986, MNBP.

26. Swain, interview, 33; Hazel, interview, 3, 5; Dale Bumpers, interview by author, 7 December 1994, transcript, 4, NPS; William Penn Mott to Alan Cranston, 8 October 1987, 2; Rolland Swain to Jerry Russell, 21 January 1987.

27. Rolland Swain to Edwin King, 12 November 1986, Jerry Rogers Files, NPS History Division Files; Rolland Swain to Deputy Regional Director, National Capital Region, 19 November 1986; Swain, interview, 33.

28. Rolland Swain to Edwin King, 12 November 1986; Rolland Swain to Deputy Regional Director, National Capital Region, 19 November 1986.

29. Richard H. Hefter, "Swain Did the Best He Could," *Journal Messenger* (Manassas), 27 May 1987; "Proffer, William Center," revised 2 September 1986, Rezoning File no. 86–61, and "Proffer, William Center," revised 4 November 1986, Rezoning File no. 86–61, both in file Manassas Battlefield, Bruce Craig Files, NPCA; Snyder, interview, 44.

30. Rolland Swain to Deputy Regional Director, National Capital Region, 19 November 1986, 2; Rolland Swain to Regional Director, National Capital Region, 20 March 1988, 2, Jerry Rogers Files, NPS History Division Files; Swain, interview, 34; Seefeldt, interview, 17; Swain to Jerry Russell, 21 January 1987; Anne D. Snyder, address at public rally, 5 February 1988, 2, A. Snyder Files, MNBP.

31. "CWRT Associates Membership Memo," November 1986, 14, Historian's Files, MNBP; Russell, interview, 3, 10; Bruce Craig, interview by author, 16 May 1994, transcript, 35–37, NPS; Rolland Swain to William Stark, 13 January 1987.

32. Moore, interview, 15–16; Bearss, interview, 26; William Penn Mott to Alan Cranston, 8 October 1987; Edwin C. Bearss to Jerry Russell, 31 December 1986, file H42: Manassas, NCR Land Use Files. One resident sent a letter to the local paper also defending Swain's commitment to preservation. See Hefter, "Swain Did the Best He Could."

33. Bearss, interview, 26; Moore, interview, 3–4; Russell, interview, 14–15.

34. Mike Radigan, "Battlefield Park Used for Dump," *Journal Messenger* (Manassas), 4 June 1986; Hanson, interview, 26–28. After the dumping incident, it was suggested that the depressions on the side of Henry Hill may have been man-made, dating to the Civil War.

35. Rolland Swain to Regional Director, National Capital Region, 20 November 1986, 1, Reading File 1986, MNBP.

36. Swain, interview, 30; Jack Fish to William Warner, 12 November 1987, file MANA: Rt. 29/234 Intersection, NCR Land Use Files; Rolland Swain to David Ogle, 5 May 1987, and Swain to Regional Director, National Capital Region, 7 May 1987, both in Reading File 1987, MNBP.

Chapter 10. Stonewalling the Mall

1. Senate Committee on Energy and Natural Resources, *Manassas National Battlefield Park Amendments of 1988: Hearing Before the Senate Subcommittee on Public Lands, National Parks and Forests on H.R. 4526,* 100th Cong., 2d sess., 8 September 1988, 49.

2. Moore, interview, 11, 15; Swain, interview, 35.

3. Cornelius F. Foote Jr. and John F. Harris, "Huge Mall Planned at Manassas," *Washington Post,* 29 January 1988; Edward T. Hearn, "Reaction Mixed to New Mall," *Suburban Virginia Times Manassas,* 3 February 1988; GA/Partners Incorporated, "Summary: The William Center Non-Residential Program: Benefits to Prince William County," January 1988, Apschnikat Office Files, MNBP.

4. Foote and Harris, "Huge Mall Planned"; Hearn, "Reaction Mixed."

5. Swain, interview, 36; Planned Mixed-Use District regulations, approved by the Board of County Supervisors on 15 April 1986, 3, file Manassas Battlefield, Bruce Craig Files, NPCA; Hazel, interview, 4; Anne D. Snyder, Save the Battlefield Committee promotional letter, 8 February 1988, A. Snyder Files, MNBP; Craig, interview, 39; William Penn Mott to Kathleen K. Seefeldt, 5 February 1988, Congressionals Binder (2), MNBP.

6. [Rolland R. Swain], "Briefing Statement," 19 February 1988; and Jerry L. Rogers, untitled and undated statement on the William Center mall proposal, [1988], both in Jerry Rogers Files, NPS History Division Files; Senate Committee, *Manassas National Battlefield Park Amendments of 1988,* 209; Hazel, interview, 9.

7. Foote and Harris, "Huge Mall Planned"; John Owens, "Resident Offers Suggestion," letter to the editor, *Journal Messenger* (Manassas), 27 February 1988.

8. William Penn Mott to Kathleen K. Seefeldt, 5 February 1988.

9. Kathleen K. Seefeldt to William Penn Mott, 19 February 1988, file Manassas Battlefield, Bruce Craig Files, NPCA.

10. Seefeldt, interview, 6, 8.

11. Kathleen K. Seefeldt to William Penn Mott, 19 February 1988, 2; Snyder, address at public rally, 5 February 1988; Anne D. Snyder, letter to the editor, *Journal Messenger* (Manassas), 5 February 1988; Seefeldt, interview, 6.

12. Snyder, interview, 43; Anne Snyder to Judy Summers, 12 February 1988, A. Snyder Files, MNBP; Snyder, address at public rally, 5 February 1988; Swain, interview, 36.

13. Snyder, interview, 9–10, 15, 19, 28–30; Anne Snyder to Judy Summers, 12 February 1988; Russell, interview, 11.

14. Save the Battlefield Coalition, Minutes, 13 February 1988, A. Snyder Files, MNBP; Harold Himmelman to Charles Williams, 17 June 1988, "Manassas National Battlefield Park," and attachments, and Shea & Gardner to Donald Hodel, 4 April 1988, both in file Manassas Battlefield, Bruce Craig Files, NPCA; Craig, interview, 12.

15. Philomena Hefter to Destry Jarvis, 30 January 1988, 2; Bruce Craig, "Issue Paper, Issue: Proposed William Center Mall on Lands Adjacent to Manassas National Battlefield Park," 29 February 1988; Tersh Boasberg to Anne Snyder, 25 February 1988, all in file Manassas Battlefield, Bruce Craig Files, NPCA; Craig, interview, 2, 8–10; Save the Battlefield Coalition, Minutes, 13 February 1988; National Heritage Coalition, "Statement of Purpose," and attachments, 19 May 1988, Jerry Rogers Files, NPS History Division Files; Swain, interview, 36.

16. Anne Snyder to Jody Powell, 20 February 1988, A. Snyder Files, MNBP; Jody Powell, interview by author, 18 October 1994, transcript, 2–5, NPS.

17. Snyder, interview, 22; Swain, interview, 36–37.

18. See Chapters 5 and 6 for a discussion of the historical significance of Stuart's Hill and the National Park Service's attempts to acquire the land for the battlefield park. James A. Schaefer, *William Center: Second Manassas* (Hazel/Peterson Companies, August 1987). Hazel/Peter-

son proffered to have both a historical and an archaeological study on Stuart's Hill completed. Dr. Thomas W. Ray completed a historical land survey and Karell Archaeological Services conducted the archaeological work; these studies reinforced Schaefer's original findings. "Proffer, William Center," revised 4 November 1986, Rezoning File no. 86–61, 9, file Manassas Battlefield, Bruce Craig Files, NPCA; Anne D. Snyder, letter to the editor, draft, 1 April 1988, A. Snyder Files, MNBP; John J. Hennessy, *Return to Bull Run: The Campaign and Battle of Second Manassas* (New York: Simon & Schuster, 1993).

19. Lee Hockstader, "Annie Gets Her Gun for Prince William," *Washington Post*, 24 October 1984; Snyder, interview, 13.

20. Hockstader, "Annie Gets Her Gun"; Snyder, interview, 13.

21. National Park Service, "Manassas Battlefield William Center Shopping Mall Action Plan," 4 April 1988; Donald Hodel to Kathleen K. Seefeldt, 4 April 1988; Hodel to James Burnley, 4 April 1988; Hodel to Gerald Baliles, 4 April 1988; William Penn Mott to Hodel, 18 April 1988, "Manassas Battlefield and the William Center Rezoning," all in Jerry Rogers Files, NPS History Division Files; [Susan Moore], "The 'Third' Battle of Manassas: A Case Study on External Threats to Park," n.d., 7–8, Historian's Files, MNBP; Parsons, interview, 10–11; Bearss, interview, 20.

22. National Park Service, "Shopping Mall Action Plan"; Donald Hodel to Kathleen K. Seefeldt, 4 April 1988; Hodel to James Burnley, 4 April 1988; Hodel to Gerald Baliles, 4 April 1988; William Penn Mott to Hodel, 18 April 1988; [Moore], "Case Study," 7–8; Parsons, interview, 10–11.

23. National Park Service press conference, 28 April 1988, video, Historian's Files, MNBP; [Moore], "Case Study," 7–8; Richard Leigh, "Pact Would Close Va. 234, US 29," *Journal Messenger* (Manassas), 29 April 1988; John F. Harris, "Compromise Offered on William Mall," *Washington Post*, 30 April 1988.

24. [Moore], "Case Study," 8–9; Leigh, "Pact Would Close"; Hazel, interview, 7; Parsons, interview, 11; Swain, interview, 44.

25. [Moore], "Case Study," 8; Save the Battlefield Coalition press conference, 19 May 1988, video, Historian's Files, MNBP.

26. [Moore], "Case Study," 9; Harris, "Compromise Offered"; Save the Battlefield Coalition press conference, 19 May 1988.

27. Michael Andrews, interview by author, 1 November 1994, transcript, 2–3, NPS; Kathy Kiely, "Houston Congressman Fights to Save Civil War Battlefield," *Houston Post*, 30 May 1988.

28. Andrews, interview, 4–6; Kiely, "Houston Congressman Fights."

29. [Moore], "Case Study," 10; Kiely, "Houston Congressman Fights"; Tim Wendel, "DeBartolo Mall Plan Battles Civil War Site," *San Francisco Examiner*, 1 May 1988; "Mrazek Amendment Seeks Halt of Manassas Mall," congressional office press release, 28 April 1988, file Manassas Battlefield, Bruce Craig Files, NPCA.

30. House Committee on Interior and Insular Affairs, *Providing for the Addition of Approximately 600 Acres to the Manassas National Battlefield Park*, 100th Cong., 2d sess., 1988, H. Rpt. 100–809, pts. 1, 5; [Moore], "Case Study," 10–11; Andrews, interview, 10–11.

31. [Moore], "Case Study," 10.

32. Craig, interview, 16; [Moore], "Case Study," 10–11; Senate Committee, *Manassas National Battlefield Park Amendments of 1988*, 22; Fitz to Denny, 6 September 1988, "Manassas Questions and Answers," 4, Jerry Rogers Files, NPS History Division Files.

33. Don Hodel, "A Political Battle over Bull Run," *Houston Chronicle*, 27 May 1988; editorial, "Battlefield Is the Issue, Not Partisan Politics," *Spokane Chronicle*, 11 July 1988; John F. Harris, "Hodel Turns Celebrity Columnist, Offering Opinion on Manassas Mall," *Washington Post*, 14 July 1988; Don Hodel, "'Playing Politics' with a Civil War Landmark," *Newsday*, 9 June 1988.

34. Hazel, interview, 11, 13; Hodel, "Political Battle over Bull Run."

35. Hodel, "Political Battle over Bull Run."

36. "Celebrate America's Heritage Rally, July 16, 1988, Calendar of Events," file Manassas Battlefield, Bruce Craig Files, NPCA; editorial, "Paying Tribute to the Forgotten," *Journal Messenger* (Manassas), 21 July 1988; Jared D. Cohen, "The Third Battle of Manassas (Bull Run): The Grass Roots Civil War That Safeguarded America's Heritage" (master's thesis, American University, August 1991), 47–48.

37. Cohen, "Grass Roots Civil War," 39; editorial, "Paying Tribute"; Anne D. Snyder, "Radio Release," May 1988, A. Snyder Files, MNBP; "Celebrate America's Heritage Rally, Calendar of Events," 3.

38. Senate Committee, *Manassas National Battlefield Park Amendments of 1988*, 17–20; Richard Leigh, "Warner and Trible Split on Battlefield Measure," *Journal Messenger* (Manassas), 9 September 1988; Richard Leigh, "Senate Panel OKs Mall Bill," *Journal Messenger,* 16 September 1988; Cohen, "Grass Roots Civil War," 47.

39. Cohen, "Grass Roots Civil War," 47; [Moore], "Case Study," 11.

40. Senate Committee, *Manassas National Battlefield Park Amendments of 1988,* 4–10.

41. Bumpers, interview, 8, 15–16; Senate Committee, *Manassas National Battlefield Park Amendments of 1988,* 4–10.

42. Senate Committee, *Manassas National Battlefield Park Amendments of 1988,* 60–63.

43. Ibid., 116–19, 204–11.

44. Ibid., 166–69.

45. Ibid., 148, 155.

46. Ibid., 159–61; ibid., 2–3; Leigh, "Senate Panel OKs Mall Bill."

47. Bumpers, interview, 8–11; Craig, interview, 33; Garreau, *Edge City,* 416–17.

48. Garreau, *Edge City,* 417–19.

49. Ibid., 419–20; Andrews, interview, 12; [Moore], "Case Study," 12; Public Law 100–647, 100th Cong., 2d sess., 10 November 1988, *An Act to Make Technical Corrections Relating to the Tax Reform Act of 1986, and for Other Purposes.*

50. Powell, interview, 3–4. Wolf's proposal to use a legislative taking proved crucial for giving the government a vehicle for taking immediate control of the land. Also, as the local Republican representative, Wolf blunted the idea that Democrats were acting hastily. Vento, as chairman of the House subcommittee on national parks, held the necessary hearings and moved the issue quickly to the House floor.

51. Craig, interview, 46; Garreau, *Edge City,* 421–22.

52. Moore, interview, 29; Craig, interview, 28.

53. [Moore], "Case Study," 12–13; Moore, interview, 26–27; Parsons, interview, 17.

54. [Moore], "Case Study," 13–14.

55. Ibid., 14; Moore, interview, 26; Craig, interview, 32; Andrews, interview, 18–19.

56. Hazel, interview, 19; Duley, interview, 27; Swain, interview, 38.

57. Craig, interview, 29–30; Powell, interview, 10; Bumpers, interview, 9–10. Because a legislative taking was used to acquire the William Center tract, the Department of Justice had to determine the value of the land, based on the improvements made by Hazel/Peterson and the other involved parties. The money paid came from the Department of Justice's Claims and Judgment Fund, not the Land and Water Conservation Fund.

58. Seefeldt, interview, 8.

59. Powell, interview, 7; Swain, interview, 36.

60. Craig, interview, 26–27.

61. Brian Pohanka and Donald Pfanz organized the initial meeting that led to the creation of the APCWS. I thank the anonymous reviewer of this manuscript for clarification of this meeting's origins. A. Wilson Greene, interview by author, 2 August 1994, transcript, 2–8, NPS.

62. Ibid., 6–8.

63. Kevin Carmody, "Battlefields to Receive Protection," *Potomac News* (Woodbridge), 16 July

1990; "Interior Secretary Lujan Names Five Members to Civil War Sites Advisory Commission," Department of Interior press release, 14 June 1991, Historian's Files, MNBP; Deborah Fitts, "Interior Dept. Plans National Fundraising for CW Battlefields," *Civil War News,* January/February 1991; Civil War Sites Advisory Commission, "Report on the Nation's Civil War Battlefields" (Washington, D.C.: National Park Service, 1993), summary, 55.

64. Powell, interview, 10; Hazel, interview, 17–19.

Chapter 11. More Battles

1. C. Van Woodward, *New Republic,* 20 June 1994, as quoted in the *Chronicle of Higher Education,* 14 September 1994, B1; Larry Van Dyne, "Hit the Road, Mick," *Washingtonian,* January 1995, 58–63, 114–27.

2. Berry, interview, 18–20.

3. Hanson, interview, 4–5.

4. Hanson, interview, 35–37.

5. Kenneth E. Apschnikat, interview by author, 10 August 1994, transcript, 12, NPS; William Penn Mott to John Hennessy, 18 December 1987, 3, file Manassas Horse facility, Bruce Craig Files, NPCA; Denis Ayres to Regional Director, National Capital Region, 10 November 1986, "Wheeler Barn Renovation"; Mott to Marion Wheeler, 19 February 1987; National Park Service, "Request for Technical Proposals, Horse Remount Facility at Manassas National Battlefield Park," July 1987, 1, last three documents in file Horse Program, Historian's Files, MNBP.

6. Hennessy's comments on Mott letter, attached to William Penn Mott to John Hennessy, 18 December 1987.

7. John Hennessy to Anne Snyder, 10 January 1988, attached to letter from Jack Fish to D. French Slaughter, 17 March 1988, Congressional Binder, MNBP.

8. Edwin C. Bearss to Director, n.d [after 11 March 1988], "Proposed Remount Facility at Manassas National Battlefield Park," 3, file Manassas National Battlefield Park, NPS History Division Files; Assistant Secretary for Fish and Wildlife and Parks to Director, National Park Service, 9 March 1988, "Wheeler Tract Remount Facility, Manassas National Battlefield Park," Jerry Rogers Files, NPS History Division Files; Jack Fish to D. French Slaughter, 17 March 1988; Bearss, interview, 31–32; Edwin C. Bearss, conversation with author, 1 May 1995.

9. Edward T. Hearn, "Park Plan Stalled," *Journal Messenger* (Manassas), 2 February 1988; Apschnikat, interview, 13–14.

10. "Quayles Take Flak for Riding Horses at Underfunded Bull Run Battlefield," *New Haven Register,* 7 August 1989; Kevin Carmody, "Plan for New Stable at Battlefield Moves Ahead," *Potomac News* (Woodbridge), 27 September 1990; Maralee Schwartz, "Quayle Pastime Puts Bur Under Historian's Saddle," *Washington Post,* n.d.; Joseph Petro to James Ridenour, 8 June 1990, Historian's Files, MNBP; "Saddle Sore," *Potomac News,* 12 October 1990; "Interior Secretary Lujan Says Horses Play Vital Role at Manassas Battlefield Park," Department of the Interior press release, 3 May 1991, Historian's Files, MNBP; "Stables for Quayle Planned at Manassas," *National Parks* 65 (March/April 1991): 11; "Quayles to Get Stables at Manassas Battlefield," *Prince William Journal,* March 1991, 27–28; United States Secret Service to Ridenour, 8 June 1990, file Horse Program, Historian's Files, MNBP.

11. "Stables Expansion at Manassas Defeated," *National Parks* 65 (September/October 1991): 14; Pamela Gould, "Battlefield Stable Construction Races On," *Potomac News* (Woodbridge), 8 January 1993; Jaan Vanvalkenburgh, "Death of Stable Expansion Pleases Local Park Official," *Journal Messenger* (Manassas), 10 February 1993; Carlos Sanchez, "Interior Chief Reins in Officials' Perks at Manassas Park," *Washington Post,* 10 February 1993; Roger Kennedy to Dale Bumpers, 1 March 1995, file Horse Program, Historian's Files, MNBP.

12. Peter Rummell, interview by author, 9 May 1996, transcript, 3–5, NPS.

13. Rummell, interview, 3–4, 11.

14. Michelle Singletary, "Disney Sees Daily Draw of 30,000," *Washington Post,* 11 November 1993; John Pulley, "Disney Seeks Making Civil War 'Important,'" *Journal Messenger* (Manassas), 12 November 1993; Michelle Singletary and Spencer S. Hsu, "Disney Says Va. Park Will Be Serious Fun," *Washington Post,* 12 November 1993. Rummell, interview, 9.

15. Singletary, "Disney Sees Daily Draw"; Pulley, "Disney Seeks"; Singletary and Hsu, "Disney Says."

16. Chris Fordney, "Embattled Ground," *National Parks* 68 (November/December 1994): 27, 29; Singletary and Hsu, "Disney Says;" Walt Disney Company, executive summary of rezoning application for Disney's America, January 1994, 14–15, file Disney's America Project, Historian's Files, MNBP; Marcia G. Synnott, "Disney's America: Whose Patrimony, Whose Profits, Whose Past?" *Public Historian* 17 (fall 1995): 45. Rummell, interview, 6–7.

17. Spencer S. Hsu, "Disney Project Runs into Concern About Traffic, Pollution," *Washington Post,* 12 November 1993; Disney, executive summary, 14.

18. Leigh Anne Larance, "Virginia's New Frontier," *Virginia Business,* February 1994, 17–19; John Pulley, "PW: 'Magic Kingdom,'" *Journal Messenger* (Manassas), 12 November 1993.

19. Stephen C. Fehr, "A Cinderella Story—or a Bad Dream?" *Washington Post,* 11 November 1993; Jaan Vanvalkenburgh, "Disney Sizes Up 'Wonderful World of Prince William,'" *Potomac News,* 11 November 1993; Spencer S. Hsu and Maria E. Odum, "Disney Sees Challenge in Honest and Entertaining Past: Residents Fear Park Will Overwhelm Rural Area," *Washington Post,* 13 November 1993; Van Dyne, "Hit the Road, Mick," 59, 114–15; Deborah Fitts, "The Disney Park Looms," *Civil War* 45 (June 1994), 20–21.

20. Singletary and Hsu, "Disney Says;" Courtland Milloy, "Slavery Is Not Amusing," *Washington Post,* 14 November 1993; Fitts, "Disney Park Looms," 19. Rummell, interview, 7–8.

21. Apschnikat, interview, 24, 26–27; Powell, interview, 14; John Pulley, "Disney to Put Limit on Traffic," *Journal Messenger,* 20 July 1994.

22. George Frampton and Roger Kennedy to Gregory Gorgone, 8 September 1994, Rezoning Application no. 94–0011, Disney's America, Prince William County, Virginia; Superintendent, MANA to Park Staff, MANA, 1 June 1994, Disney's America Project, both in Disney's America, Historian's Files, MNBP. The ultimate success of a historic overlay district, placing scenic easements on property, remains uncertain. See Laura McKinley, *An Unbroken Historical Record: Ebey's Island National Historical Reserve, Administrative History* (Seattle: National Park Service, Pacific Northwest Region, 1993) for a discussion of the pros and cons of this designation at this national park site.

23. Apschnikat, interview, 47; Powell, interview, 13–14. Rummell, interview, 13.

24. Apschnikat, interview, 23–24; Singletary and Hsu, "Disney Says"; Roger Kennedy to Regional Director, National Capital Region, and Regional Director, Mid-Atlantic Region, [23 May 1994], file Disney's America Project, Historian's Files, MNBP.

25. Van Dyne, "Hit the Road, Mick," 116, 120; Synnott, "Disney's America," 44; Desda Moss, "Opponents Use History as Weapon," *USA Today,* 2 June 1994.

26. Richard Moe, "Downside to 'Disney's America,'" *Washington Post,* 21 December 1993; Richard Moe, interview with author, 17 November 1995, 10, NPS. The National Trust regularly reported on its fights against sprawl in its newsletter *Preservation News,* which was recently incorporated into its magazine *Historic Preservation* (now simply named *Preservation*). In 1993 the Trust spotlighted the immediate threat of sprawl by naming the entire state of Vermont to its Eleven Most Endangered List. For a recent article outlining the effects of sprawl on communities, see Arnold Berke, "Striking Back at Sprawl," *Historic Preservation* 47 (September/October 1995), 54–63, 108–10, 116.

27. Moe, interview, 7. Van Dyne, "Hit the Road, Mick," 121; Moe, "Downside to 'Disney's America.'"

28. Van Dyne, "Hit the Road, Mick," 121; Moe, "Downside to 'Disney's America;'" Spencer S. Hsu, "Historians, Writers Organize Against Disney Theme Park," *Washington Post,* 11 May 1994.

29. Mike Fuchs, "Disney Park Faces a Mouse That Roared," *Potomac News,* 3 June 1994; Stephen C. Fehr and Michael D. Shear, "For Disney, Fight Takes a New Twist," *Washington Post,* 17 June 1994; George Will, "Disney Should Beat a Retreat on Theme Park," *Chicago Sun-Times,* 17 July 1994; Synnott, "Disney's America," 46–47; Van Dyne, "Hit the Road, Mick," 123–24; Bumpers, interview, 13; Peter Baker and Spencer S. Hsu, "Disney Gives Up on Haymarket Theme Park, Vows to Seek Less Controversial Site," *Washington Post,* 29 September 1994.

30. Seefeldt, interview, 13.

31. Otis L. Graham Jr., "Editor's Corner: Who Owns American History?" *Public Historian* 17 (Spring 1995): 8–11. For a detailed discussion of the *Enola Gay* controversy and other recent debates over the presentation of history, see Edward T. Linenthal and Tom Engelhardt, eds., *History Wars: The Enola Gay and Other Battles for the American Past* (New York: Metropolitan Books/Henry Holt, 1996).

32. Susan Currell examines the response of academics to Disney and Disney's America in "Transitions in the Cultural Interpretation of Disney as an American Icon" (master's thesis, University of Maryland, 1995). Singletary and Hsu, "Disney Says"; Fitts, "Disney Park Looms," 19.

33. James Oliver Horton, "A House Divided: Historians Confront Disney's America," *OAH Newsletter* 22 (August 1994), 8. Historians debated the Disney proposal and the aftermath of the controversy in several historical venues. See, in addition to the essays in the *OAH Newsletter,* Viewpoints Forum, "Public History and Disney's America," *AHA Perspectives,* 33 (March 1995), 1, 3–11; and "Symposium: Disney and the Historians—Where Do We Go from Here?" *Public Historian* 17 (Fall 1995): 43–89.

34. James Oliver Horton, interview with author, 24 August 1996, 5, 6, 8–10, 17.

35. Rummell, interview, 15–16, 18–19.

36. Rummell, interview, 23–24. Michael D. Shear and Martha Hamilton, "Business Leaders Fear Cost of Preservationists' Victory;" Peter Baker and Spencer S. Hsu, "Disney Abandons Prince William County Site, Plans to Find Another Va. Location for Park," both in *Washington Post,* 29 September 1994; Liz Spayd and Paul Fahri, "Eisner Ended Disney Plan," *Washington Post,* 30 September 1994; Synnott, "Disney's America," 48–49; Van Dyne, "Hit the Road, Mick," 124–25.

37. Baker and Hsu, "Disney Gives Up." Rummell, interview, 24.

38. Baker and Hsu, "Disney Gives Up"; Seefeldt, interview, 13–14; Spencer S. Hsu, "Disney Task Force Report Appears Slated for Obscurity," *Washington Post,* 8 December 1994; D'Vera Cohn, "Pr. William Official Says Development Inevitable on Former Disney Tract," *Washington Post,* 30 September 1994.

BIBLIOGRAPHY

Primary Sources

National Park Service Repositories

Manassas National Battlefield Park, Manassas, Va. (MNBP)
- Historian's Files include general management plans, interpretive plans, legislative records, and other documents saved sporadically over the years. The park also holds a series of cultural resources files that contain vertical files for select subjects relating to the park's history, cultural resources, and historic structures. A separate section of the vertical files includes information about individual Civil War units.
  - Library Collection has published materials relating to the Civil War battles, copies of the Sons of Confederate Veterans newsletter, park historic structure reports, and a few secondary sources on Civil War battlefield preservation and topics pertaining to northern Virginia.
- Museum Collection, in addition to its vast artifact collection, includes some documentary materials relating to George Carr Round, early park preservation efforts, visitor center exhibit plans, and the 1961 First Manassas reenactment.
- Newspaper Clippings Files begin in 1973 with the Marriott theme park proposal and continue in chronological order to the present.
- Land Holding Records contain individual files on each tract of land acquired since the 1936 establishment of the Bull Run Recreational Demonstration Area. There is also a useful compilation of land acquisitions from 1936 to 1966.
- Anne D. Snyder Files include personal correspondence, newspaper clippings, federal and local government reports, and other materials related to the many preservation battles Snyder participated in over the years. Snyder donated her files to the Manassas National Battlefield Park.

National Park Service History Division Files and Archives, Washington, D.C.
- NPS History Division Files have correspondence dating from the 1930s through the 1980s between the Manassas National Battlefield Park and other Park Service representatives and various internal reports relating to such topics as land acquisition, historic structures, interpretation, the 1961 First Manassas reenactment, the national cemetery proposal, Interstate Highway 66, and the William Center tract. I also consulted the William Center tract files of former cultural resources manager Jerry Rogers.
- NPS History Division Archives has additional internal reports relating to the park.

National Capital Region Files, Washington, D.C.
• Land-Use Files contain maps for the park's boundary changes and associated correspondence and internal reports.
• Gary Scott Files are the regional historian's office files and contain materials relating to the park's historic structures and interpretive program.

National Park Service History Collection, Harpers Ferry Center, Harpers Ferry, W.Va. (HFC)
• Park Historic Reference Files are organized by individual park and contain park brochures, annual reports, newsclippings, interpretive program reports, management reports, master plans, and other related materials.
• Civilian Conservation Corps Files include background materials on the recreational demonstration area program.
• Oral History Collection has the tapes and transcripts of interviews with Park Service officials; Francis Wilshin's oral history transcript is available here.

National Park Service Historic Photographic Collection, Charles Town, W.Va.
An extensive collection of photographs related to the history of the National Park Service and records relating to museum exhibit production from Mission 66 through the 1970s. Photographs illustrating the Manassas National Battlefield Park and its structures were found in files labeled Civil War, 1861–65, Bull Run; Manassas; Manassas National Battlefield Park; NPS History—Architecture; and Eastern Office of Design and Construction (EODC) files. Exhibit files for Manassas yielded 1960s visitor center plans.

Non–National Park Service Repositories

National Archives and Records Administration, Archives II, College Park, Md. (NARA)
Strong on documents relating to the Manassas National Battlefield Park dating from the 1930s and 1940s.

• Record Group 79 National Park Service is divided by entry. Records pertinent to this history were found in entry 7, Central Classified File, and entry 47, Recreational Demonstration Area Program files.
• Record Group 48 Secretary of the Interior, Central Classified Files, contains a few documents on the Bull Run Recreational Demonstration Area. Copies of many of the documents in RG 48 are also found in RG 79.

Washington National Records Center, Suitland, Md. (WNRC)
Records that remain under the custody and control of the originating agencies. Researchers must obtain permission from the National Park Service's National Capital Region office to review records relating to the Manassas National Battlefield Park. Useful materials ranging in date from the 1940s through the 1980s include Mission 66 planning documents, land acquisition reports, 1961 First Manassas reenactment prospectus, annual reports, monthly reports, museum exhibit reports, and related correspondence.

Prince William County Archives, Manassas, Va.
Minutes of the Board of County Supervisors meetings.

Bull Run Library, Virginiana Room, Manassas, Va.
An array of materials ranging from the 1920s Manassas Battlefield Confederate Park
    to 1980s Prince William County budgets and planning documents. The 1970s
    Prince William County newsletters following the Marriott proposal are also
    located here.

Manassas Museum, Manassas, Va.
Documents and photographs related to George Carr Round.

National Parks and Conservation Association, Washington, D.C. (NPCA)
Bruce Craig Files on the William Center and horse controversies contain correspon-
    dence, planning documents, newspaper clippings, government reports, and
    other associated materials.

Department of the Interior Natural Resources Library, Washington, D.C.
A few Department of the Interior reports and legislative history records related to
    the Manassas National Battlefield Park.

Papers of Howard Worth Smith, Special Collections Department, University of
    Virginia, Charlottesville.
Contain a copy of the 1949 boundary expansion bill that Smith introduced and
    information about Smith's role as honorary chairman of the First Manassas
    Corporation.

Secondary Sources

Albright, Horace M. *Origins of National Park Service Administration of Historic Sites.* Phil-
    adelphia: Eastern National Park and Monument Association, 1971.
Albright, Horace M., as told to Robert Cahn. *The Birth of the National Park Service: The
    Founding Years, 1913–33.* Salt Lake City: Howe Brothers, 1985.
Blackford, Susan Leigh, and Charles Minor Blackford. *Letters from Lee's Army or Memo-
    ries of Life In and Out of the Army in Virginia During the War Between the States.*
    Ed. Charles Minor Blackford III. New York: Charles Scribner's Sons, 1947.
Bodnar, John. *Remaking America: Public Memory, Commemoration, and Patriotism in the
    Twentieth Century.* Princeton: Princeton University Press, 1992.
Boge, Georgie, and Margie Holder Boge. *Paving over the Past: A History and Guide to
    Civil War Battlefield Preservation.* Washington, D.C.: Island Press, 1993.
Civil War Sites Advisory Commission. *Report on the Nation's Civil War Battlefields.* Wash-
    ington, D.C.: National Park Service, 1993.
"Civil War Sites Face Grave Threats." *National Parks* 67 (November/December 1993):
    10–11.
Dierenfield, Bruce J. *Keeper of the Rules: Congressman Howard W. Smith of Virginia.* Char-
    lottesville: University Press of Virginia, 1987.

Dwight, Theodore, ed. *The Virginia Campaign of 1862 Under General Pope.* Boston: Houghton Mifflin, 1895.

Fitts, Deborah. "Interior Dept. Plans National Fundraising for CW Battlefields." *Civil War News,* January/February 1991, 1, 32.

Fordney, Chris. "Embattled Ground." *National Parks* 68 (November/December 1994): 27–31.

Foresta, Ronald A. *America's National Parks and Their Keepers.* Washington, D.C.: Resources for the Future, 1984.

Frome, Michael. *Regreening the National Parks.* Tucson: University of Arizona Press, 1992.

Garreau, Joel. *Edge City: Life on the New Frontier.* New York: Doubleday, 1991.

Gillette, Jane Brown. "Fields Forgotten." *Historic Preservation* 45 (July/August 1993) 34–39, 86.

"Hallowed Ground." *The Economist,* 20 August 1988, 25–26.

Hennessy, John J. *Return to Bull Run: The Campaign and Battle of Second Manassas.* New York: Simon & Schuster, 1993.

Kammen, Michael. *Mystic Chords of Memory: The Transformation of Tradition in American Culture.* New York: Alfred A. Knopf, 1991.

Krick, Robert E. L. "The Civil War's First Monument." *Blue & Gray,* April 1991, 32–34.

Lamme, Ary J. III. *America's Historic Landscapes: Community Power and the Preservation of Four National Historic Sites.* Knoxville: University of Tennessee Press, 1989.

Lee, Ronald F. *The Origin and Evolution of the National Military Park Idea.* Washington, D.C.: National Park Service, 1973.

Lewis, Thomas A. "Fighting for the Past." *Audubon,* September 1989, 58–72.

Linenthal, Edward Tabor. *Sacred Ground: Americans and Their Battlefields.* Urbana: University of Illinois Press, 1991.

Linenthal, Edward Tabor, and Tom Engelhardt, eds. *History Wars: The Enola Gay and Other Battles for the American Past.* New York: Metropolitan Books/Henry Holt, 1996.

Lusk, William Thompson. *War Letters.* New York: privately printed, 1911.

Mackintosh, Barry. *The National Parks: Shaping the System.* Washington, D.C.: U.S. Department of the Interior, 1984.

———. *National Park Service Administrative History: A Guide.* Washington, D.C.: National Park Service, 1991.

———. "The National Park Service Moves into Historical Interpretation." *Public Historian* 9 (spring 1987): 51–63.

O'Donnell, Mike. *At Manassas: Reunions, Reenactments, Maneuvers.* Mechanicsville, Va.: Rapidan Press, 1986.

Powell, Jody. "Battling over Manassas." *National Parks* 62 (July/August 1988): 12–13.

Rainey, Reuben M. "The Memory of War: Reflections on Battlefield Preservation." In *The Yearbook of Landscape Architecture: Historic Preservation,* ed. Richard L. Austin, et al. New York: Van Nostrand Reinhold, n.d., 69–89.

Roosevelt, Franklin Delano. *Public Papers and Addresses.* New York: Random House, 1938.

Runte, Alfred. *National Parks: The American Experience.* 2d ed., rev. Lincoln: University of Nebraska Press, 1987.

Sellars, Richard West. "Vigil of Silence: The Civil War Memorials." *History News,* July/August 1986, 19–23.

"Stables Expansion at Manassas Defeated." *National Parks* 65 (September/October 1991): 14.

"Stables for Quayle Planned at Manassas." *National Parks* 65 (March/April 1991): 11.

Swain, Donald C. *Wilderness Defender: Horace M. Albright and Conservation.* Chicago: University of Chicago Press, 1970.

Unrau, Harlan D. *Administrative History: Gettysburg National Military Park and Gettysburg National Cemetery, Pennsylvania.* Washington, D.C.: National Park Service, July 1991.

Unrau, Harlan D., and G. Frank Williss. "To Preserve the Nation's Past: The Growth of Historic Preservation in the National Park Service During the 1930s." *Public Historian* 9 (spring 1987): 19–49.

U.S. Congress. House. Committee on Interior and Insular Affairs. *General and Oversight Briefing Relating to Developments Near Manassas National Battlefield Park: Hearing Before the Subcommittee on National Parks and Recreation.* 93d Cong., 1st sess., 3 April 1973.

————. *National Outdoor Recreation Programs and Policies: Hearings Before the Subcommittee on National Parks and Recreation.* 93d Cong., 1st sess., March 1973.

U.S. Congress. House. Committee on Veterans' Affairs. *Bills Related to the National Cemetery System and to Burial Benefits: Hearings Before the Subcommittee on Cemeteries and Burial Benefits.* 94th Cong. 1st sess., December 1975, January and February 1976.

————. *National Cemetery Site Selection, Pennsylvania, and the Vicinity of the District of Columbia: Hearing Before the Subcommittee on Cemeteries and Burial Benefits.* 94th Cong., 1st sess., 17 November 1975.

————. *Proposed Establishment of a National Cemetery Adjacent to Manassas National Battlefield Park: Hearing Before the Subcommittee on Hospitals on H.R. 8818 and Related Bills.* 91st Cong., 1st sess., 23 September 1969.

U.S. Congress. Senate. Committee on Energy and Natural Resources. *Manassas Battlefield and Historic Sites: Hearing Before the Subcommittee on Parks and Recreation.* 95th Cong., 1st sess., 28 June 1977.

————. *Manassas National Battlefield Park, Virginia; and Miscellaneous Hawaii Park Proposals. Hearing Before the Subcommittee on Parks, Recreation, and Renewable Resources.* 96th Cong., 2d sess., 3 September 1980.

————. *Manassas National Battlefield Park Amendments of 1988: Hearing Before the Subcommittee on Public Lands, National Parks and Forests on H.R. 4526.* 100th Cong., 2d sess., 8 September 1988.

U.S. Congress. Senate. Committee on Interior and Insular Affairs. *Providing for Increases in Appropriation Ceilings and Boundary Changes in Certain Units of the National Park System, and for Other Purposes.* 92d Cong., 1st sess. 1971, S. Rept. 452.

Utley, Robert M. "A Preservation Ideal." *Historic Preservation* 28 (April/June 1976).

Van Dyne, Larry. "Hit the Road, Mick." *Washingtonian,* January 1995, 58–63, 114–27.

Webb, Robert. "Storm over Manassas: A Plan to Develop Part of Virginia's Famed Civil War Battlefield Is Provoking the Greatest Preservation Battle in Years." *Historic Preservation* 40 (July/August 1988): 40–45.

Will, George F. "Where Men Fought and Fell." *Newsweek,* 18 July 1988, 68.

Personal Interviews

In conjunction with the researching and writing of this history, the author conducted twenty-three interviews with people prominent in the history of the
park. These interviews, in addition to one with Francis Wilshin conducted by
S. Herbert Evison in 1971, are listed below. All interviews have been tran-
scribed. The National Park Service retains custody of the audio cassettes and
transcripts. The Wilshin interview is held at Harpers Ferry Center; the interviews conducted by the author are held at Manassas National Battlefield Park.

Michael Andrews, U.S. House of Representatives (D-Tex.), 1983–95. 1 November 1994

Kenneth E. Apschnikat, MNBP superintendent, 1988–95. 10 August 1994

Edwin C. Bearss, NPS chief historian, 1981–94. 5 April 1994.

Russell W. Berry Jr., MNBP superintendent, 1969–73. 10 February 1994.

Dale Bumpers, U.S. Senate (D-Ark.), 1974–present. 7 December 1994.

Bruce Craig, cultural resources program coordinator, National Parks and Conservation Association. 16 June 1994

Betty Duley, local activist. 14 July 1994.

A. Wilson Greene, president, Association for the Preservation of Civil War Sites.
2 August 1994.

Carl Hanson, MNBP park ranger, law enforcement, visitor protection, 1970–present.
19 August 1994.

Herb Harris, U.S. House of Representatives (D-Va.), 1975–81. 16 June 1994.

John T. ("Til") Hazel, president, Hazel/Peterson Companies. 7 November 1994.

Richard E. Hoffman, MNBP superintendent, 1973–77. 31 March 1994.

James Oliver Horton, historical advisor to the Walt Disney Company. 24 August 1996.

Richard Moe, president, National Trust for Historic Preservation. 17 November
1995.

Susan K. Moore, MNBP management assistant, 1986–88. 10 May 1994.

L. Van Loan Naisawald, MNBP park historian, 1957–60. 2 February 1994.

John Parsons, National Capital Region, associate regional director, land-use coordinator, 1977–96. 14 June 1994.

Jody Powell, public relations, Ogilvy-Mather, 1988. 18 October 1994.

Peter Rummell, president, Disney Design and Development. 9 May 1996.

Jerry L. Russell, national chairman, Civil War Round Table Associates, 27 July 1994.

Kathleen K. Seefeldt, chairman, Prince William County Board of Supervisors, 1976–
present. 21 November 1994.

Anne D. Snyder, local activist. 19 October 1993.

Rolland R. Swain, MNBP superintendent, 1980–88. 6 April 1994.

Francis F. Wilshin, MNBP superintendent, 1955–69. 29 June 1971.

INDEX